Land Development

Ninth Edition

D. Linda Kone

Home Builder Press®
National Association of Home Builders
1201 15th Street, NW
Washington, DC 20005-2800
(800) 223-2665
www.builderbooks.com

This publication is designed to provide accurate and authoritative information in regard to the subject matter covered. It is sold with the understanding that the publisher is not engaged in rendering legal, accounting, or other professional service. If legal advice or other expert assistance is required, the services of a competent professional person should be sought.

—From a Declaration of Principles jointly adopted by a Committee of the American Bar Association and a Committee of Publishers and Associations.

Land Development
ISBN 0-86718-500-7

Cover design by David Rhodes, Art Director, Home Builder Press

Cover photo by Alex S. MacLean/Landslides

Printed in the United States of America

Library of Congress Cataloging-in-Publication Data

Kone, D. Linda 1949-
    Land Development / D. Linda Kone -- 9th ed.
      p. cm.
    Includes index.
    ISBN 0-86718-500-7
    1. Housing development. 2. Land subdivision. I. Title.

HD259 .K66 1999
711'.4--dc21

                                                  99-052273

For further information, please contact:
        Home Builder Press®
        National Association of Home Builders
        1201 15th Street, NW
        Washington, DC 20005-2800
        (800) 223-2665
        www.builderbooks.com

12/99 Harlowe/P.A. Hutchison 4000

Contents

Figures

Chapter 5. Major Environmental Regulations Affecting Development

Chapter 6. Developing a Master Plan Concept

Chapter 7. Site Engineering and Stormwater Management

About the Author

Author D. Linda Kone received her master's degree in architecture from the University of Texas and worked as a project planner and manager in the design-build industry for 7 years. She was an associate professor of Building Construction in the University of Florida's College of Architecture from 1987 to 1993. During that time she maintained a consulting practice specializing in environmental impacts of construction and residential construction and development. She now divides her time between her private practice and writing about land development issues.

Acknowledgments

The author wishes to thank Kurt Lindblom, Acquisitions Editor, for his insightful management of the progress of the book. Special thanks go to Joseph Molinaro, Director of Land Development Services, and Debbie Bassert. Former Director of Publications Rosanne O'Connor deserves a special recognition for her hard work on the 8th edition of *Land Development*, the precursor to the 9th edition. Finally, this book bears the mark of the experienced hand of Developmental Editor Michelle Robbins, whose advice and help was indispensable.

In addition, the author and Home Builder Press wish to thank the many other people from NAHB and around the country listed below who reviewed the outline and/or part or all of the manuscript. Their knowledgeable comments also provided excellent assistance in improving the manuscript.

Susan Asmus, NAHB, Director, Water and Wetlands Policy; Debra Bassert, NAHB, Senior Land Use Planner; Michelle Desiderio, NAHB, Analyst, Environmental Policy; Chuck Ellison, Legend Properties, La Plata, MD; Paul Handler, Handler Corporation, Wilmington, DE; Bob Kaufman, Michael T. Rose Company, Laurel, MD; David Kent, Department of Business, Plymouth State College; Larry Lawhon, Department of Regional and Community Planning, Kansas State University; David Ledford, NAHB, Staff Vice President, Mortgage Finance Department; Joe Molinaro, NAHB, Director, Land Development Services; Jerry Novak, JBS Development Services, Colorado Springs, CO; Creigh Rahenkamp, Creigh Rahenkamp & Associates, Palmyra, NJ; Darrel Seibert, Seibert Development Corporation, Hudson, OH; Marc Smith, University of Florida, Gainesville, FL; Richard Steiner, Steiner, Inc; Bethel, CT; Mary Stinson, Land Use Consulting, Mendocino, CA; and Jan Wells, Bloustein School of Planning and Public Policy, Rutgers University.

The author and Home Builder Press also wish to thank the following people whose assistance with previous editions of *Land Development* helped to make the book a success: Peter M. Allen; Farhad Atash; Brian D. Autio; Charlotte Bahin; Russell James Berry; Frank M. Bosworth; Parsons Bromfield; Brian A. Ciochetti; John Crosland, Jr.; Rhonda Daniels; Vernon P. Deines; Mary DiCrescenzo; Thomas Dorsey; William H. Ethier; Patricia R.B. Francis; Stephen S. Fuller; Roger Gatewood; Saundra Harris; David Kent; William H. Kreager; Nathan D. Maier; Michael P. Maxwell; Mort L. Mazrahi; Tim Mrozowski; Vincent Napolitano; Tim R. Newell; Manual E. Nunes; James V. O'Conner; Lisa Quinn; Richard M. Redniss; Michael L. Robbins; Marc Smith; Kerry D. Vandell; Nino Pedrelli; Matt R. Wall; Mark Weaver; and Scott Weinberg.

Book Preparation

Land Development was produced under the general direction of Tom Downs, NAHB Executive Vice President and CEO, in association with NAHB staff members Bob Brown, Staff Vice President for Knowledge Management; Adrienne Ash, Assistant Staff Vice President, Publishing Services; Charlotte McKamy, Publisher; Kurt Lindblom, Acquisitions Editor and Project Manager; David Rhodes, Art Director; Elisa Subin, Production Editor; and Michelle Robbins, copyeditor and proofreader.

Disclaimer

The methods described in this book for land development are based on the development philosophy and experience of the author, D. Linda Kone. While the book acknowledges some of the exciting new development concepts being used in the industry today, it does not purport to cover every possible technique used nationwide for land development. In addition, while regional differences are mentioned throughout the book, those described are by no means exhaustive of the many development standards and practices currently in use throughout the country. The publication of this book does not constitute an explicit or implicit endorsement by the National Association of Home Builders or Home Builder Press of any specific development technique. Furthermore, neither NAHB nor Home Builder Press makes any representation as to the effectiveness of any of the development techniques discussed in this book. Finally, NAHB hereby disclaims any and all liability that may arise from the use of this book or its contents.

Introduction

Land development is both an art and a science comprising an astonishing number of interrelated parts. The timely application of each part to the whole project produces an efficient process from start to finish. The most important aspect of this process is its holistic nature and the way each separate part informs the others to produce an elegant solution.

Perhaps the most significant change in the process of land development within the last 10 years is the rapid rate of change in the characteristics of the marketplace. An unprecedented shift in demographics is largely responsible. By the year 2005, baby boomers will constitute both the majority of the so-called mature market and the largest age group—the first time this has ever happened. Therefore, this market will show a variety of important new characteristics. Also, the almost daily changes in technological advances will continue to greatly influence the marketplace. Computer-connected work, services, and recreation already have made a permanent impact.

The process of land development usually begins with a good idea for the creation of a new community; one that will serve the needs of its inhabitants and take its place as a good neighbor within the local urban or suburban area. The new development must acknowledge its relationship to adjacent communities, create minimal negative impacts, and prove economically viable for both its inhabitants and the developer. To formulate a successful idea, the developer should begin with a good understanding of the local marketplace and what the targeted buyer needs and wants in a new community.

Good timing, instincts, and planning play important roles in the process of creating a new community. Knowledge and experience foster good instincts. Good timing and planning are greatly improved when the developer becomes aware of the nature of the process of land development and the impact of each of the various components involved.

The Process

The process described in this book begins with formulating the concept. As Figure I.1 shows, to accomplish this, three major categories of investigation must work together to create a master plan or program for a new community on a selected site. Researching existing conditions begins the process. Analyzing the conditions for project constraints and opportunities moves the process forward. Finally, synthesizing the results into a coherent, functional plan that supports the original idea for the new community produces the desired outcome.

This is not a linear process. At many points, steps must be retraced with the discovery of new information and its subsequent effect on previous decisions. This synthesis of information, the discarding of unworkable ideas, and the moving back and forth to reach new conclusions, defines the hallmark of the process. The appropriate modification of original impressions and decisions at various stages along the way will result in a successful effort.

Since the process may be approached from several different standpoints, where it begins influences the order of the process itself. If a parcel of land has already been acquired, the search begins with determining the most marketable use for the site. Another approach might begin with a search for a suitable site to support a previously determined marketable idea. The process can also begin by determining the best marketable idea for a given local area, followed by the search for the best site to accommodate that idea—the approach taken by this

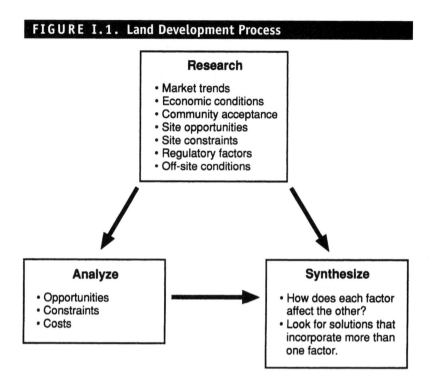

FIGURE I.1. Land Development Process

Research

- Market trends
- Economic conditions
- Community acceptance
- Site opportunities
- Site constraints
- Regulatory factors
- Off-site conditions

Analyze

- Opportunities
- Constraints
- Costs

Synthesize

- How does each factor affect the other?
- Look for solutions that incorporate more than one factor.

book. However, once the site and the idea are placed together for serious consideration, the process of researching, analyzing, and synthesizing data to produce the final master plan remains virtually the same for each approach.

Key Elements of Land Development

As shown in Figure I.2, the key elements of the land development process are: market research, site selection and analysis, project design, site engineering, project cost, and financial feasibility. Each plays a unique role. Market research involves determining which type of buyers are best to capture; understanding their buying power, lifestyle characteristics, and product demands; matching housing types and master plan concepts with those characteristics; and advertising and selling the product to them.

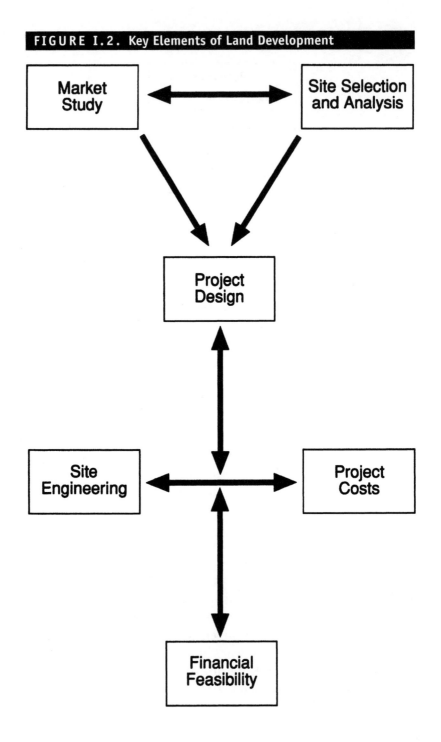

FIGURE I.2. Key Elements of Land Development

Site Selection and Analysis involves developing a list of desirable site characteristics for which to search; discovering all the physical, regulatory, geotechnical, and social characteristics of a particular site; and analyzing them for their contribution to the project's viability. Project Design matches marketing information concerning buyer preferences with the site's innate characteristics to produce a master plan with housing types that best satisfy these requirements. Site Engineering deals with the physical manipulation of the topography and the installation of the infrastructure necessary to support the master plan concept. Project Cost determines the soft costs (fees, marketing, investigation) and the hard costs of each item of work (labor and materials) together with the schedule to complete each task and produce an accurate project cash flow. Financial Feasibility determines the profitability of the project from sales forecasting and project costs.

Increasing Constraints of Land Development

Land development remains an important part of the economies of both the United States and local areas through the provision of housing and jobs for growing populations. But despite its necessary role, land development becomes ever more complicated. Compared to the past, there are more project constraints than ever before in the form of regulations and in the characteristics of the land remaining to be developed. The realities developers must confront include the increased costs of site work and construction; shrinking municipal budgets for providing community services, security, schools, and other infrastructure; and the public's growing concern about increasing density and decreasing environmental quality.

To compound these problems, more evidence exists that heightened public scrutiny is being manifested in more organized attempts to influence the way land is developed. In general, the good land has already been developed and the remaining land contains many restrictive qualities that caused it to be passed by in the first place. When the residential development boom first began, developers naturally chose sites that were optimally located and most easily developed, bypassing sites that had engineering problems or no available utilities. This means that developers today face problems that were relatively scarce in the 1950s and 1960s; yet, a great deal of this remaining land exists in prime marketable locations and is worth developing, if done correctly. All these factors point to the increased necessity of discovering, analyzing, and synthesizing all the critical marketing, financial, geophysical, regulatory, and social information to determine project success.

The Project Team

The multidisciplined nature of land development requires input from a variety of sources of expertise. Assembling the right mix of professionals and consultants to provide the specialized knowledge required for the various aspects of creating a viable project will launch you on the path to project viability. The developer assembles and directs the project team, which then determines the factors each project must investigate and analyze. Proper coordination of data and information from consultants by the developer can mean both project success and reduced costs.

Primary members of the project team include the person(s) in charge of marketing and financial analysis, the project planner, and the members of the design team (see Figure I.3). Marketing and financial analysis may be done by two separate team members or handled by the same person or firm. Marketing information may be purchased or produced with in-house capabilities. In a similar fashion, the financial analysis may be performed by an outside consultant or by in-house staff. The marketing team member handles directing the efforts to determine the appropriate buyer, discovering buyer preferences, and planning the advertising and selling of the project. The financial planner determines the feasibility of the project under various sales rate projections when all project costs are considered.

The project planner, or director of the project, might be a professional urban planner, an architect, or a landscape archi-

FIGURE I.3. Project Team

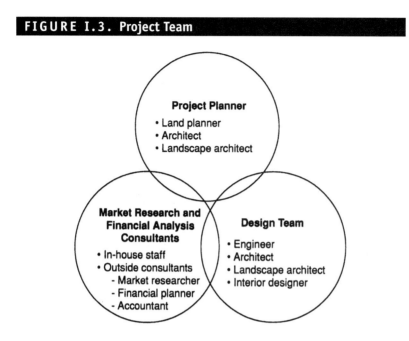

tect. Although one of these professionals might be in charge, each would require some input from the other disciplines. The project planner oversees the development of the conceptual master plan from the information about buyer preferences and costs provided by marketing and financial planning as well as appropriate design concepts from other design team members. The civil engineer, another member of the design team, might be responsible for determining all geotechnical conditions and their corresponding infrastructure requirements. The most successful master plans result from the architect, landscape architect, and engineer working together to produce a vision for the new community conceived by the developer.

At times, it proves necessary to call in auxiliary project consultants to help the primary members in their decisions about the master plan. These might include hydrologists, geologists, soil scientists, environmental experts, construction managers, and attorneys. The size of the project, as well as the location of the site, will help determine the kinds of consultants needed. The project planner should determine the need for additional consultants, advise the developer about their respective roles, and coordinate the distribution of all information among the design team.

The goals of the team should be clearly defined by the developer to prevent duplication of work, the gathering of unnecessary information, and increased predesign/preconstruction costs. The coordination of information among team members should be carefully monitored through regular meetings. Effective methods of communication, which include how the information will be shared and the scheduling of deadlines, should be described and communicated to all team members by the developer. The developer's leadership must drive the team to stay focused upon those aspects of the project that are critical to success.

Although the expense of a good project team must be borne up front, it can actually help to hold down the rising costs associated with proving project success and complying with a more complex regulatory climate. New project constraints are created by the increased regulation of social and environmental impacts and usually cannot be avoided. A good team, however, can help the developer look for the ways to turn measures required to deal with project constraints into opportunities for new designs with increased market appeal. Buyers today are more sophisticated about the issues involved in land development. Quality in the form of environmental and community sensitivity sells. Marketing your development by emphasizing the measures taken to preserve the natural features of the land and the integrity of the community can provide the foundation for a quality-based approach with a great deal of buyer appeal.

Because of the swift rate of change in demographics, social conditions, technology, and law, it's important to keep flexibility in mind. A little flexibility can be especially helpful in determining site plan design, target market, and housing product. As the process of determining a market and choosing a site moves forward, keep alternative uses and choices on reserve should sudden unforeseen changes occur. Basically this means avoiding a site suitable for only one purpose unless there is a high level of confidence in the target market availability.

In spite of growing constraints, it's an exciting time for land development. New target markets, virtually unheard of 10 years ago, are making viable inroads into the list of reliable markets. The addition of new technology companies can make a previously sleepy location highly desirable overnight. And new trends in social interactions, types of jobs, and commuting preferences serve to create a steady supply of new markets.

1

The Market Study

B y the end of the 1990s, the market study had become entrenched as a critical part of the land development process for two reasons: minimizing project risks and obtaining financing. The market study attempts to justify the need for a proposed residential development in a chosen area. It allows you to evaluate buyer characteristics, location, and site attributes to produce a strategy for targeting specific kinds of potential buyers. With a good market plan you can provide them with the best product possible.

Consider the market study essential if you want to understand the nature of acquisition capital and development loans, increased competition, government regulations, and changing population characteristics. Knowing the market means you can offer the intended buyers the type of community and home with the most appeal.

Why Do a Market Study?

Historically, developers relied primarily on intuition, mimicking their own and others' past successes to determine the type and location of new projects. In the late 1940s, the largest target market—returning GI's—was so lucrative that most developments and housing types focused solely on it. For almost 15 years this favored market changed only slightly in its characteristics. Inexact approaches to defining the group's needs usually did not produce negative results because demand was so high. A growing economy and money supply, along with ample available land, only increased overall confidence, resulting in a much smaller budget and schedule for marketing.

Early residential market studies frequently took the form of a buyer preference survey that determined what buyers thought desirable or undesirable about their newly purchased homes. The responses were used in making decisions about new developments.

Another early market study consisted of basic questions forecasting housing supply and demand in a future year. The result usually did not move much beyond determining a forecasted number of units in a given price range for a certain year in order to decide how many units to offer in a new project. The decision was based on predicting the number of households within a given income that would require housing (estimating demand).

Now the shift seems to be from studying what has been successful in the past to predicting what will be successful in the future. You must study the unique and changing characteristics of a particular kind of buyer to better tailor a product to that buyer's specific needs. The pinnacle of success in this endeavor occurs when you provide a particular kind of buyer (the target market) with a development and housing type that contains not only desired attributes but also unexpected ones. The idea is that once presented, these new concepts become attributes the buyer cannot do without.

Changing Target Markets

Twenty years ago no one could have predicted the variety of target market groups that exist among potential buyers today. The rise in single-parent households, young urban professionals, and couples waiting longer to start families has created a number of these new markets. Another set of target groups centers on demographic trends such as people living longer after retirement or retiring early. Longer work hours, more job stress, and telecommuting have also created mini-target market groups among preretirement groups. Increased government regulations, decreasing availability of land, and the sometimes poor condition of that land add to the need for a good market study.

To identify a good market research firm, ask lenders or other developers who they like. Cities and towns have pretty good data associated with their master (comprehensive) plans. Most state universities have research centers that collect economic and demographic data.

Both lenders and investors use the market study as a tool to justify a large capital allocation to a specific project. Initial project feasibility can only be proven by thoroughly documenting the market itself, the land's development capacity, the cost of compliance, and projected sales and cash flows.

Types of Market Studies

Market studies come in many forms and sizes, from large and comprehensive to small and select. Small projects sometimes require answers to only a few questions if you are experienced and working in a familiar area. Conversely, the questions are numerous and complicated when large projects are developed in phases over a long period of time and offered to several target markets.

Some broad-based goals of market studies are:

1. to understand housing supply, demand, and absorption rate in a given geographical area (Absorption rate is the rate at which residential units are sold or leased within a given period of time. The term can apply to the housing supply and demand of a given geographical area or to a particular project's rate of sales. It can also refer to rental property.)
2. to determine both a chosen target market and the type of development and home to provide (The target market is a distinct segment of all potential buyers who share the same demographic characteristics such as age, race, gender, marital status, number of children, income, education, and profession.)

3. to acquire specialized knowledge of the market, for example, regional preferences and other lifestyle characteristics of targeted buyers
4. to provide information that helps sell the project to lenders, investors, and other builders
5. to demonstrate to planning authorities that a housing demand exists in the area

Most market studies can be grouped into four basic types of studies: general, site-specific, highest-and-best-use, and target market profile studies. (See Figure 1.1.)

General Studies

You can conduct general studies in a large geographical area such as a state, county, or city to determine a location for a known type of development. These studies are usually performed by larger development companies that have both experience and success in building specific types of development in other locations. The study could include information about demographic characteristics of buyers, economic conditions of the area, and future conditions based on such elements as new

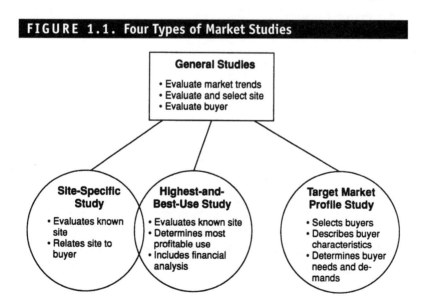

FIGURE 1.1. Four Types of Market Studies

General Studies
- Evaluate market trends
- Evaluate and select site
- Evaluate buyer

Site-Specific Study
- Evaluates known site
- Relates site to buyer

Highest-and-Best-Use Study
- Evaluates known site
- Determines most profitable use
- Includes financial analysis

Target Market Profile Study
- Selects buyers
- Describes buyer characteristics
- Determines buyer needs and demands

major employers. General studies can also include questions about the nature of the marketplace, the competition, the possibility of new target markets, and economic influences on a buyer's ability to purchase a home.

Site-Specific Studies

If you already own a parcel of land or hold a purchase option, you can conduct a site-specific study. This evaluates site characteristics in terms of location, capacity for number of units, and overall density per acre. Use it to discover and analyze prominent site features such as mountains, hills, or waterfront, as well as regulatory considerations. Once collected and analyzed, this information reveals what marketing information you need to determine the best development for the site. It also helps reveal which type of buyer to target.

Highest-and-Best-Use Studies

If you already own land or a developed parcel in need of revamping, you need a highest-and-best-use study. The goal is to determine the most profitable use of the site permissible by site constraints and regulations. You conduct this type of study under the same circumstances as the site-specific study, with the same general objectives. It also includes a financial feasibility analysis.

Target Market Profile Studies

Target market profile studies determine the type and number of different socioeconomic groups in a given area. It further defines the outstanding demographic and lifestyle characteristics of specific groups of buyers with similar socioeconomic backgrounds.

This study also works for a single target market group. For example, target market profiling can uncover the driving forces behind such current trends as greater requirements for privacy and security, increased need for office space at home, or desires for high-tech maintenance features within a traditional setting. Your knowledge of these trends can inform design decisions.

Through this study, you may also uncover a potential target "market window" (a group whose needs are not being met with existing product offerings). The study helps define the specific market niche (narrowly defined segment of the homebuying public). Your goal is to discover the particular demands and desires of this group and provide the most marketable product possible, thereby increasing project success.

What Kind of Study Do You Need?

No matter what type of study you conduct, begin by clearly defining your goals. If you employ a marketing consultant, that person should work with you to set the goals and explain alternative approaches for achieving them. This includes the most appropriate type of study to use as well as the type of information needed to realize your goals, how this information will be gathered, the relative cost of each approach, and what you can expect in the final product you are purchasing.

Each of the four types of market studies must offer answers to a broad range of questions. These studies are usually conducted at the beginning of a project—before site selection and purchase. However, if you already own your site and wish to find the best use for it, a comprehensive market study (a combination of the full range of issues covered by the other three types of market studies) might also be in order. As an alternative, if you are familiar with an area and are contemplating a smaller development, you might forgo a comprehensive effort and limit a market study simply to the investigation of one or more specific questions.

The comprehensive study can address four basic issues:

1. What will be the size of the total market in your local area at a future time and what proportion can your project capture?
2. What are the demographic and psychographic (lifestyle) characteristics of your chosen target market within a certain household income range?
3. What lifestyle preferences such as types of developments, location, amenities, and services does your target

group demand? (This question should account for the difference between demand and desire for a product. If demands are not met, the buyer will reject the product. If the project goes beyond meeting demands to also meet some of the desires, this enhances the product in the buyer's eyes. This question also addresses any specialized information pertinent to the target market.)

4. Given the nature of the target market, the local area, the competition, and the economic factors affecting the target market's buying power, what is your project's anticipated absorption rate within a given period? What are your cash flow requirements and anticipated rate of return?

A comprehensive study might also include a variety of other information relevant to the project, such as the desirability of the site's location or an in-depth study of the competition's offerings to the target market.

An example of the type of broad questions a comprehensive study might answer is, How many households in a certain area are within a particular income range or what percentage of households in a particular income range are married with children? A more specific question might be, How many households in the $200,000 income range are professional, double-income families with no children? Finally, an example of a narrowly focused question is: How many in the range prefer playing golf as their predominant leisure activity?

You may also sometimes need to reexamine the market to adapt to sudden changes. For example, suppose a site was purchased to develop single-family homes for first-time buyers. When the site was purchased, interest rates were 8 percent. By the time the project is ready to be offered to the public, interest rates have risen 3 points and the original target market can no longer afford the product designed for the purchased site. In this case, you may need a quick study to find a new target market for the original product and assess what changes, if any, may be required.

Housing Supply and Demand

One of the first decisions you must make for your new venture is the number of housing units to supply to the market in a given period. As a first step, define the macromarket area from which the project will draw potential buyers. The macromarket area is a chosen geographical region from which the data that support the demand for housing will be gathered. That area could be everything within the city limits or a portion of a highly populated city. For smaller cities and towns, the macromarket area might be the entire county.

Once you've determined the macromarket area, study the housing supply and demand there within a specific time frame. From this, you can forecast demand for a future period. Housing supply consists of all the existing housing stock (homes) on the market, including stock currently under construction. When you look at a previous year, the houses sold represents the demand for that year.

Consequently, if supply and demand are quantified yearly, you can determine the absorption rate (supply divided by demand). Study the absorption rate over a period such as five years, and you begin to form a picture of the health of the housing market that includes both sales and vacancy rates. Given the cost of construction financing, evaluating the absorption rate helps you project both the number of houses you might reasonably offer and your anticipated sales rate.

The key factor when determining housing supply and demand is the number of houses in a given price range that can be sold the year the project comes online (in other words, when the units are ready for sale). Once you know that number, you can determine how many of those your project can capture. Begin your study by gathering the following information: housing mix, population projections, household size and configuration, destroyed or razed housing, age of householder and income, and current unsold inventory.

Housing Mix

From data found in the local building permit department, you can find the percentage of all housing provided during the year within the categories of single-family, multifamily, and mobile homes. These percentages are known as the housing mix. If these data are gathered for at least five years, you can predict the percentage of each category you might offer at sales time. Your prediction will be based on whether the percentages of the past will continue. Whether they continue, increase, or decrease depends on the amount of unsold units in each category, the general health of the economy, and any potentially significant change in the local economy, such as zoning changes or the gain or loss of a major employer.

Projecting Demand

Future demand is based on population growth, the increase or decrease in household size due to social change (household formation), the number of destroyed or razed housing units, and the over or under supply of existing housing. To project future demand, you must first forecast the population increase into the macromarket area. You can obtain this data from several public sources, including chambers of commerce, the local government's economic development office, or various state research bureaus.

Once you have determined the increase in population influx into the area, examine the trend in changing household size due to social change. Since the average household size changes from year to year, you must predict its size based on the trend for that future year. For example, over the last 20 years, the trend shows the average household size steadily decreasing.

After you know the population increase for the macromarket area, determine the average household size. First examine the household size for five or more previous years. Note the amount of decrease for each year, then predict the average household size for the year your project will begin sales. Many public sources such as census data, state and local agencies, and published marketing reports provide current and predicted household size. Once you have projected the average household size for the chosen year, divide the projected population increase by the projected average household size. This will give you the number of housing units needed to supply an increase in population in the macromarket area. Figure 1.2 illustrates this technique for projecting housing demand.

Adjusting the Projection

At this point, you are predicting demand based only on increases in population in the macromarket area. Keep in mind this number is associated only with growth. You have not yet accounted for existing households that want to purchase first-time or move-up homes or that are experiencing a lifestyle change such as divorce or retirement. They can also generate additional demand for new housing. However, predicting this type of demand requires more speculation because it cannot be easily quantified and is based on shifting trends.

If you want to include these potential home buyers in your estimate of total demand, make an educated guess by studying the number of housing starts and reviewing building permit activity over the last five years. Local real estate associations sometimes have breakdowns in the number of people purchasing starter homes, moving up in each price range from existing homes in the area, as well as how many purchases were made by people moving into the area. This number can be added to the number of total of housing units predicted from demand derived only from incoming populations.

Lifestyle and Other Trends. To adjust the number of units predicted from incoming population demand, account for changes in household size due to lifestyle changes. Figure 1-3

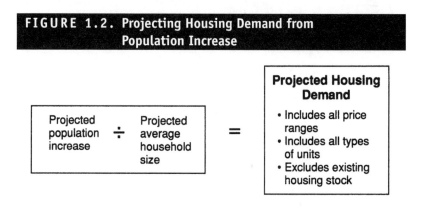

FIGURE 1.2. Projecting Housing Demand from Population Increase

$$\text{Projected population increase} \div \text{Projected average household size} = \text{Projected Housing Demand}$$

Projected Housing Demand
- Includes all price ranges
- Includes all types of units
- Excludes existing housing stock

shows one method for calculating this. Subtract the projected average household size from the existing household size, then multiply by the total number of existing dwelling units. Dividing the new total by the projected average household size will give you the projected housing demand from lifestyle changes.

Razed Housing. You can further adjust the projected housing demand by adding the projected number of razed housing units for the chosen year. Reviewing the average number of razed houses over the five-year period can help you project this number. Of course, if a catastrophic event such as a hurricane or earthquake has occurred, the average number over time will be irrelevant.

From this new total, subtract existing unsold housing stock to get the adjusted housing demand. At this point the total number of projected units still includes all housing types. Since you are interested only in the type of housing you plan to offer, multiply the total number of projected housing units by the percentage of the projected housing mix that applies to your project. This last total is the final adjusted housing demand for your particular housing type. Figure 1.4 shows the full

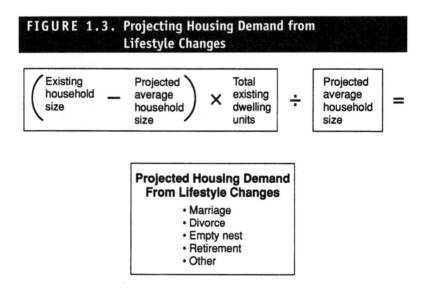

FIGURE 1.3. Projecting Housing Demand from Lifestyle Changes

$$\left(\begin{array}{c} \text{Existing} \\ \text{household} \\ \text{size} \end{array} - \begin{array}{c} \text{Projected} \\ \text{average} \\ \text{household} \\ \text{size} \end{array} \right) \times \begin{array}{c} \text{Total} \\ \text{existing} \\ \text{dwelling} \\ \text{units} \end{array} \div \begin{array}{c} \text{Projected} \\ \text{average} \\ \text{household} \\ \text{size} \end{array} =$$

Projected Housing Demand From Lifestyle Changes

- Marriage
- Divorce
- Empty nest
- Retirement
- Other

FIGURE 1.4. Adjusted Housing Demand

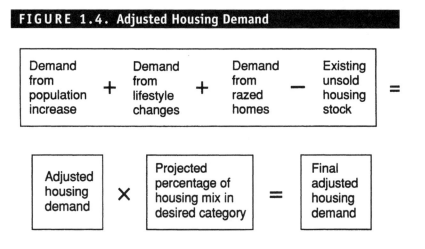

process of adjusting the projection for housing demand in a given year.

Income Profile. At this point, you have predicted the total number of units in a unique category (single-family, multi-family) for all price ranges in a future year. You can further fine-tune this number by selecting out the units to offer in a particular price range. To do this, study the percentage of area households in each income bracket. Both national and local trends can affect this mix.

If conditions in the local area are relatively stable, income trends for households coming into the area will probably remain similar to those of the past. But if a major change has occurred, the number of those households in each income category might vary. For instance, a major employer moving into an area can draw a significant number of people in a particular income bracket, thereby shifting the previous distribution of the area's income profile. The income profile can give you an idea of what to expect from incoming households if conditions remain stable, while presenting a picture of the current makeup locally.

To create an income profile for a chosen macromarket area, use the population, household size, and income data from census information or other sources such as the business research bureau associated with your state's major university. Produce a graph depicting the number of households in each income group. Plot number of households as a percentage of the population on one axis and annual incomes on the other (see Figure 1.5).

The income profile for the area will show how many households are found within certain income ranges. You can then correlate the household incomes with the price range of houses that those households can afford. This gives you an idea of what percentage of units might be needed in each price range. Each income range represents the broad boundary of a potential target market that you can later divide into groups with similar socioeconomic characteristics.

You can use the income profile in several ways. If you are interested in building housing in a certain price range, the income profile will show how many households in the area will find your homes affordable. It will also show which income ranges have the largest number of households. If you believe incoming households will continue to reflect the existing local income percentages, you can use those percentages to determine the number of incoming households within a certain income range.

In deciding the price range for your units, consider price ranges with which your company has experience or that presently sell well in the area or will sell well in the future. After choosing an income range to target, decrease the number of units in the projected housing demand by the percentage of households in the target income range. Remember this assumes that the number of households that will move into an area will have approximately the same mix of income ranges as in the past. If this is not the case, adjust the total number of units by the expected number of households in the desired income range.

Demographic Data. At this stage, you know the number of households in a given income range desiring a certain category of housing in a future year. However, you have not yet consid-

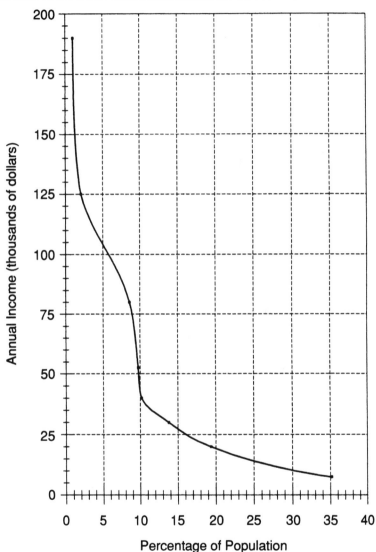

FIGURE 1.5. Income Profile

ered the demographic characteristics of these households. Each household income range contains many groups with different demographic characteristics. For example, consider a single- or double-income household with a yearly income between $120,000 and $150,000. The household could have two married adults with or without children or its members could be retired. The income earners could be between the ages of 35 and 45 or 65 and 75.

Within a given price range you will find a variety of housing needs, so you should narrow the chosen household income range to target a particular demographic group. Each income range contains a certain number of households. By looking at census data or population studies of the area, you can determine the percentage of particular demographic groups in each income range. The total number of households could include singles and married couples both with and without children. For example, if the income range of $75,000 to $85,000 contains 2,000 households, you can determine what percentage is married with two incomes and no children.

For your chosen category of household income range, adjust the total number by the percentage of households in the particular group you are targeting. If you are investigating a small local area and census data are unavailable, use national data if you believe households in the macromarket area reflect national averages. As with incomes, they will either be the same as the national mix or different because of regional peculiarities such as a high number of retirees. You can then adjust the number of projected units marketed toward a particular income range to target only the chosen broad demographic or target market groups.

Sources of Demographic Data

When investigating the population characteristics for your local area, gather demographic information by purchasing data from private sources or obtaining it from public sources at little or no cost. Raw facts and figures are relatively easy to obtain from both sources. However, interpretive data resulting from the analysis and synthesis of various kinds of information are more elusive and usually must be purchased. Appendix A lists some public and private sources of demographic data.

Census Data

The most common source of almost all demographic information is the U.S. Bureau of the Census, which is part of the U.S. Department of Commerce. The census is taken every 10 years and forms the basis for the population estimates most public and private sources use. Various census publications can provide statistics on the social, demographic, and economic characteristics of population. Household size, individual and household incomes, housing characteristics, types of heads of households, gender and race characteristics, and marital status are among the kinds of information in the census. Most reports will provide statistics on the national and regional level; some also provide information on the state, county, or metropolitan level.

Sources of Census Data. Census statistics are gathered from surveys taken by census tract; the last data year for the 2000 census is 1999. The most attractive aspect of the census is that the general public has easy access to it. The local public library usually has a variety of census reports available. You can also try the nearest state university or college library, which frequently have separate government documents sections and librarians and staff trained in their use. The easiest way for you to access census data is the Internet.

There are three cautionary notes about using census data. The first concerns income accuracy. You must take the household incomes reported in the census data year for 1999 and adjust them for the year your project will be offered to buyers. This means you must index 1999 incomes up to a projected amount for the future year.

Indexing Incomes. Although there are numerous methods for doing this, a simple one is the Consumer Price Index (CPI). The Consumer Price Index is the average change over time in the cost of goods and services reported by the U.S. Bureau of Labor Statistics. By reviewing the change in the Consumer Price Index over a period of 5 or 10 years, you can make a prediction about the CPI in a future year based on the trend.

The next step is to divide the CPI for the chosen year by the CPI for the data year to obtain a multiplier to use in indexing money up for the future year. Use the CPI multiplier to index the incomes upward for the year you will begin selling homes. Figure 1.6 shows one way to apply the Consumer Price Index to obtain projected income for a future year.

Outdated Census Data. The second caution concerns using outdated demographic data. The entire range of population could be 5 to 10 years older than that surveyed, depending on how long ago the data were gathered. If census data is too outdated, get this information from other sources that have taken this into consideration. You can obtain updated data from marketing data vendors or recently published market reports for the local area commissioned by the state, county, or city.

Validity of the Census Data. The third caution concerns the validity of the population statistics themselves. Many groups

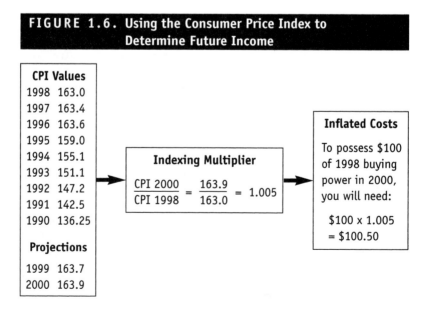

FIGURE 1.6. Using the Consumer Price Index to Determine Future Income

CPI Values

1998	163.0
1997	163.4
1996	163.6
1995	159.0
1994	155.1
1993	151.1
1992	147.2
1991	142.5
1990	136.25

Projections

1999	163.7
2000	163.9

Indexing Multiplier

$$\frac{\text{CPI 2000}}{\text{CPI 1998}} = \frac{163.9}{163.0} = 1.005$$

Inflated Costs

To possess $100 of 1998 buying power in 2000, you will need:

$100 x 1.005 = $100.50

have complained about the accuracy of the census due to the immense social changes in the United States. For the 1990 reports, census takers said data was dramatically more difficult to gather in 1989 than in the past. Many people would not open their doors, others ignored the census, and many moved too many times to be tracked down. Increased security fears and more frequent address changes are continuing trends. Even so, the census remains the most comprehensive demographic data available to most.

Other Sources of Demographic Data

Various agencies and research institutes throughout the country provide another public source of information. Much of this is free to the public and found in various types of libraries. For example, many state universities have a business and economics research institute affiliated with the college or business school. These research bureaus produce and publish data for the express purpose of guiding and evaluating all types of businesses in the state. Some reports are for sale for a minimal fee but the cost is negligible compared to that of purchasing demographic information from private companies.

Using state-affiliated research centers has several advantages. Since these organizations are in the business of producing and evaluating data, they all employ methods for updating population projections to produce the most accurate and current data available. They might use driver's licenses, building permits, voter registration, or some other method to count population on a year-to-year basis in the state or local areas. Therefore, data from these sources is more current than that from the census. These research centers also specialize in data unique to the state or region, helpful when you consider a project located within that area.

Some counties or cities provide these data as part of their comprehensive plans. Local population characteristics are used in making growth planning decisions. Along with general demographic data, these comprehensive plans may include housing and neighborhood studies to project future housing needs for the area. Some reports that describe local conditions contain both general demographic data and analysis and an interpretation of that data.

Capture Ratio

At this point in your study, you have determined that a builder or developer can offer a certain number of units within a given price range and category marketed to a specific target market in a future year. This prediction is based on population and household projections and demographic data for the local area. The final question remains, How many of these units will your project attempt to capture?

The capture ratio describes your portion of the market or market share. In forecasting this ratio, you need to consider capacity. Capacity describes your company's cash position, number and type of personnel, ability to take risks, ability to take a loss, and your own confidence in the marketability of the new development. You should evaluate your own capacity as well as your competition's. Cash position and personnel requirements are relatively easy to determine because they can be quantified. Your company's ability to take risks and the marketability of an idea are more qualitative variables, both of which require a thorough understanding of the target market.

Understanding the Target Market

The homebuying public is not a homogeneous group whose choices are driven only by income, affordability, and family composition (demographics). Home buyers break down into numerous target markets according to both demographic and psychographic (lifestyle) characteristics. Your design decisions must tailor the new community to the target market. More than ever, marketing information must go beyond the basic demographic characteristics of age, race, gender, marital status, and children to include more specific and sometimes more subtle buyer habits and concerns. These are frequently referred to as psychographic characteristics, a term first used in the advertising industry.

Psychographic Data

Essentially, psychographic characteristics are the lifestyle choices of a particular socioeconomic group with similar demographic profiles. The needs and desires that emerge from these characteristics make up the psychographic profile. Generally, the more thoroughly these are understood, the more marketable the resulting product will be.

The trend toward having market studies address these issues comes from American manufacturers and retailers' success in tailoring their products by understanding the increasing number of groups that differ widely in their demographic and psychographic profiles. American society is undergoing dramatic changes as the population ages; lengthening life spans create larger numbers of active retirees, and divorce rates increase. With this change comes a corresponding rise in single-parent households, a prevalence of two-income families, and the counter movement of one parent decreasing or eliminating outside work to stay at home with the children. These changes, in turn, have created a greater polarization of groups with dissimilar psychographic profiles and, therefore, dissimilar demands as home buyers.

Here are some currently recognized target groups whose demographic and psychographic characteristics have been studied:

- double-income professionals, no children
- double-income professionals, school-aged children
- single-income households, 1-3 children
- single-parent households, 1-3 children
- households with one or both incomes derived from home-based business
- young professional singles
- mature professional singles
- empty nesters
- active retirees
- semi-active retirees
- assisted living retirees

Depending upon location, the list could include many more or entirely different categories. For instance, some parts of the country have a disproportionate number of retirees over the age of 65. We no longer consider this group to be a homogeneous target market categorized only by income. Retirees are as diverse as the rest of the population in income, marital status, recreational preferences, health, education—and desired services and amenities.

In areas where retirees represent a disproportionate percentage of the population, it is safe to assume this group will contain larger numbers within each particular target market subset than in areas with fewer retirees. Therefore, the various groups making up the 65 and over population will have a wider range of demands and desires. Consequently, in areas such as these, you may want to offer a greater variety in the types of developments and homes to satisfy the needs of the various subgroups of this target market.

By studying the psychographic characteristics of target groups, you can often translate lifestyle preferences into quite specific design ideas. For example, if one group frequently entertains business acquaintances at home, while another group primarily entertains family and friends, the two groups' requirements for formal and informal entertaining space will be quite different. The group that entertains business acquaintances might demand more space and quality in formal living and dining rooms with preferences for more open plans. The group that entertains family and friends might opt for more space in the informal living and dining areas with the formal dining room de-emphasized or eliminated altogether. Figure 1.7 shows some specific groups, characteristics, and the resulting design equivalencies.

Effective marketing focuses as narrowly as possible on those characteristics and details of developments and homes preferred by the target market. The idea is to capture as many buyers out of the chosen group as possible, not worrying about whether the product will appeal to all. If it appeals to others, so much the better. However, making homes and developments neutral in appeal in hopes of expanding the favorable response and selling more homes usually proves to be a losing strategy.

FIGURE 1.7. Target Market Preferences

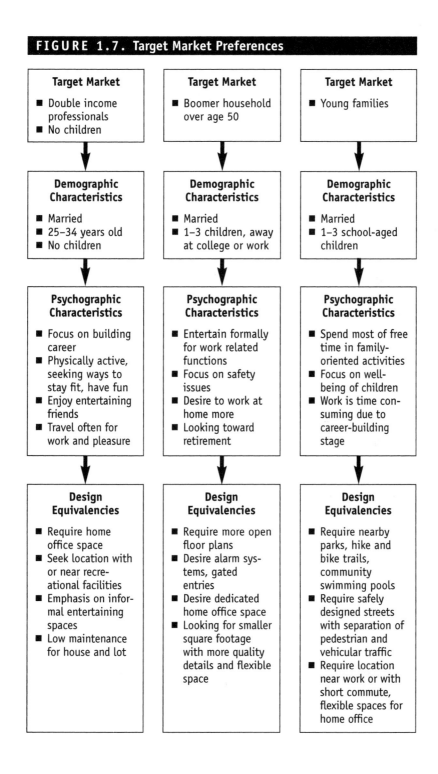

Target Market

■ Double income professionals
■ No children

Target Market

■ Boomer household over age 50

Target Market

■ Young families

Demographic Characteristics

■ Married
■ 25–34 years old
■ No children

Demographic Characteristics

■ Married
■ 1–3 children, away at college or work

Demographic Characteristics

■ Married
■ 1–3 school-aged children

Psychographic Characteristics

■ Focus on building career
■ Physically active, seeking ways to stay fit, have fun
■ Enjoy entertaining friends
■ Travel often for work and pleasure

Psychographic Characteristics

■ Entertain formally for work related functions
■ Focus on safety issues
■ Desire to work at home more
■ Looking toward retirement

Psychographic Characteristics

■ Spend most of free time in family-oriented activities
■ Focus on well-being of children
■ Work is time consuming due to career-building stage

Design Equivalencies

■ Require home office space
■ Seek location with or near recreational facilities
■ Emphasis on informal entertaining spaces
■ Low maintenance for house and lot

Design Equivalencies

■ Require more open floor plans
■ Desire alarm systems, gated entries
■ Desire dedicated home office space
■ Looking for smaller square footage with more quality details and flexible space

Design Equivalencies

■ Require nearby parks, hike and bike trails, community swimming pools
■ Require safely designed streets with separation of pedestrian and vehicular traffic
■ Require location near work or with short commute, flexible spaces for home office

Sources of Psychographic Information

You can find psychographic data in public information sources such as journals, books, and other publications. But frequently you must purchase from marketing data services the most sophisticated information on regional and specific location differences. The more elusive specialized information—for example, a local target group's specific lifestyle characteristics—is almost always purchased. The methods by which this kind of information is gathered can be quite costly because public sources such as census data or other available market information sources cannot easily answer them. (See Appendix A for a list of sources for psychographic information.)

You may be able to obtain marketing information that determines the target market's preferences for location, housing types, density tolerances, image, and master plan style from psychographic studies that are public information. Local governments often commission professional marketing studies to further business development or to evaluate the level of support for new museums, civic buildings, or airports. These studies are invaluable sources of both demographic and psychographic information because they are specific to the local area.

However, in using these sources, note the purposes for which the lifestyle profiles were generated to see if they closely match the purpose of your residential market study. Other sources of psychographic information include professional studies found in public and university libraries, professional marketing and residential homebuilding publications. You can also conduct your own focus group.

Specialized Knowledge

At times you might need to find answers to specific questions about a target market or to know about special characteristics of buyers unique to the area or group. The kind of information you need is vital to project success but unavailable from the typical sources. This type of information goes beyond the normal scope of most public sources, to include any information that must be gathered by survey, requires specialized knowledge to interpret, or pertains only to a specific geographical region. Figure 1.8, Types of Specialized Information, shows some examples of the many questions you might need to investigate to understand what kind of product to provide and how to market it effectively.

When to Use Specialized Information

When considering the use of specialized information, determine whether the success of the project warrants the extra cost. If your project relies heavily on selling a new idea to the target market, the project budget should have provisions for testing that idea. If you are developing in an unfamiliar geographical region, for example, you might need to know any special preferences in materials and style particular to the region.

Sources of Specialized Information

Some of the sources that may have useful specialized demographic information include local real estate boards, home builders associations, chambers of commerce, and utility, telephone, and title companies. Local universities and colleges,

---

FIGURE 1.8. Types of Specialized Information

Types of Information	Specific Question
Financial Characteristics	■ Amount of equity in present home? ■ Average amount of debt? ■ Amount of disposable income?
Psychographic Characteristics	■ Types of leisure activities? ■ Amount of time spent playing golf? ■ Most utilized room in the house? ■ Preferred service amenities? ■ Conduct business at home? ■ Separate playroom for children?
Regional Characteristics	■ Preferred architectural style and materials? ■ Preferred type of outdoor activities? ■ How does weather impact home design?

along with associated research institutes, may have generated data or studies pertaining to the special questions for which you need answers. In addition, you may gather these data from marketing subscription services, surveys, and focus groups.

Surveys. Surveys may be one of the most effective ways to gather both specialized demographic and psychographic information. For example, surveys of buyers and customers are most likely to provide design preferences or financial characteristics of target groups. Survey questions are intended to uncover information that can lead to design and marketing ideas the group would potentially find desirable.

Focus Groups. If you are contemplating untested ideas for a new development and have sufficient resources in the project budget, consider holding a focus group. In a focus group a dozen or more people that represent the target market are brought together to supply responses to ideas and questions about the proposed project. You should select the members from the target market profile. The group is intentionally kept small to facilitate discussion. At the beginning of the discussion, you may decide to show examples of the new community's features and homes. After ideas are presented, the group is asked to respond.

Testing ideas using focus groups is expensive and usually coordinated by marketing professionals. Using the results from the focus group discussion, a skilled group leader can develop a profile of the target buyer's needs, preferences, and motivations. However, the results are sometimes invalid because of group biases. Conducting several focus groups can help validate the responses as a whole, but this becomes even more expensive, although the size of the project and the unique nature of the development sometimes warrant this expense. Finally, note that some types of information not only require surveys or focus groups to gather but also may require specialists to interpret.

Project Viability

A well-crafted market study is sometimes necessary to convince financial supporters of a project's chances for success. Most lenders today require a market study as part of their list of documentation requirements. A good study can always help persuade the lender that you have considered all possible variables. The study can prove helpful if the lender is very familiar with the area and the success of other projects, and your market study accurately reflects the characteristics of the targeted buyer and the location. If your project depends on investors for part or all of its financing, a market study presents the clearest picture to the collection of investors who may or may not understand the market or the development process.

When to Study the Market

You can conduct market studies at several different stages of the project. Although they are most commonly conducted in the beginning stages, you should study the market throughout the project, depending on various situations. A company can even study the market independent of a project to answer more far-reaching questions about trends, economic issues, locations, and the company's capacity for new types of business ventures. Two common points at which to conduct a market study are before the land purchase or, if you already own the site, before you decide on the appropriate type of development. You may also want to study the market during project build-out and sales and after the project is completed.

Before Land Purchase

Before purchasing land, use the market study's primary purpose to establish the feasibility of an idea. The goal: to find appropriate markets to target and new locations in which to develop, understand local economic factors and national economic trends that influence homebuying, match potential locations with target market preferences, and survey the competition. The study can lead to your purchase of the best parcel of land for a given development type or merely answer questions about the feasibility of developing particular parcels of land for new target markets.

Determining Location. A market study can answer questions that help you find new locations favorable for development and reduce your risk when purchasing a parcel of land for a known type of development. If you have already chosen the target market, this study can help you understand which lifestyle preferences will help determine the location and site features that best suit the group. This will narrow your search and provide an invaluable tool for evaluating land purchase.

The following are examples of the many questions a market study can answer to assist you in selecting a site:

- How important is resale? Will this group become move-up buyers in a few years or will they tend to hold onto the home for an extended period of time?
- What commuting distances does this group tolerate?
- Where is undeveloped land that is or can be zoned appropriately for your home type and density?
- What desirable, close-by services, institutions, and amenities would make this site more marketable to this group?
- What services and amenities should you provide in your new community?
- Where are the other developments that target this same group? What are their most desirable characteristics? What are their most detrimental?
- What safety and security requirements does this group have? What parts of the local area meet their minimum requirements?

New Ventures. If your company has the capacity to operate in larger national or statewide geographical regions, a market study can uncover potential locations for new ventures. You can have the study done whether the target group is known or unknown. If you know the target group and its characteristics, the study can provide a list of the most important variables to consider when examining new locations. A study of this sort might evaluate some of these considerations:

- health of the local economy and the factors on which it depends
- types and number of major employers and the possibility of job expansion or decline
- relationship between quality of life issues and employment opportunities
- availability of affordable land that can be zoned appropriately
- impact of taxes, regulations, and political climate on development

After Land Purchase

If you already own the site and are looking for its most appropriate use, you may commission a market study to determine the best type of home buyer to target for that particular site. The study can evaluate the compatibility of a chosen target group with the kinds of lot sizes and configurations, housing density, housing types, and community image best suited for your site. As part of the study you can also have design concepts tested on focus groups before making final design decisions.

During Project Build-Out and Sales

You may also study the market during project build-out and sales to answer questions about why sales might be lagging, to determine the best methods to advertise the project, or to determine what changes, if any, should be made in the next phases of the project. If you know the target market and have answered many of the bulleted questions above, the market study can examine sales and marketing strategy for this group.

This market study can include information about the necessity and role of a model sales center, the type of furnishings needed, the most appropriate type of sales staff, and the way you present the development to potential buyers. For instance, should your sales staff and advertising focus predominately on selling security, prestige, sound investment, or a particular lifestyle? Should the sales staff emphasize the development over the home or the opposite? What type of advertising media and cost might appeal to most of the group? Then decide on the amount and scheduling of advertising required for selling the project and compare it to predicted sales rates for cost-effectiveness.

After Project Completion

After project completion, conduct buyer surveys to evaluate the effectiveness of design and marketing decisions. Analyze sales rates according to predicted project absorption rates as well as the marketability of units to their expected target market. This information can help you to refine decisions in future projects marketed towards the same target market.

When to Purchase Market Information

If you are primarily a small-volume builder or developer, you still must gather many kinds of information and prepare market studies for a contemplated project or find new business opportunities in new types of developments and locations. This is especially true when the questions you ask are specific and verifiable by data or numbers. An example: projecting the demand for housing units in a certain price range and a given local area in a future year. This sort of information is available from a variety of public sources and costs only the time you or your employees spend gathering it. When the questions become more complicated and require you to analyze and interpret many different kinds of information, you need more expertise.

Do Your Homework First

Before you commission a study or produce one in-house, investigate conditions yourself. Talk to key brokers and sales professionals in the area for their opinions about buyer characteristics and locational preferences. Visit all other developments in the area. If you can, talk to other area developers to obtain their opinions about market and land characteristics. Familiarize yourself with the inventory of resales that fit your target market's price range. Also, talk to potential lenders to find out their views on the market. Although these types of inquiries are purely subjective, they can go a long way toward helping you firm up your own ideas of the type of information the market study should provide.

In-House Market Studies

You should consider gathering marketing information in-house under the following circumstances:

1. Questions are specific and rely upon data or numbers easily obtained from public sources.
2. Project size is small, and the product is aimed at a familiar target market.
3. You are confident the market study's goals (questions) are clear and sufficient for the project's needs.
4. Financial supporters and lenders do not require a formal study done by an outside professional before approving your loan or investment.

One of the most important things to consider is whether you can obtain the information needed to answer the study's questions from public sources or inexpensively from private sources. Evaluate the quality of the available information in terms of who produced it, for what purpose, and whether it is up to date. Finally, have sufficient experience to determine whether the study's goals are adequate for achieving project success.

Professional Market Studies

Project size can influence the decision to use a professional marketing consultant. Marketing studies are frequently expensive and higher-volume developers usually have better resources to fund them. However, consider the cost of the studies well worth the expense because they help prevent the mistakes in design decisions and strategic planning that cause projects to fail. For large projects, lenders and investors usually require a formal study as part of the project's preliminary feasibility documentation. Figure 1.9, Reasons for Purchasing Professional Market Studies, contains a list of other reasons to purchase a professional market study.

Why are professional market studies so often associated with larger developments? Larger developments face the same range of problems smaller developments do but their increased size can compound the problems. They often have greater infrastructure requirements and greater offsite impacts on local infrastructure such as heavier traffic and utility loads. Potential environmental and regulatory impacts pose much greater challenges and usually cost more in time and money.

Larger projects have the potential to contain many different products aimed toward a variety of target groups. Consequently, they frequently take the form of a collection of neighborhoods. This raises the question of how to phase the project to build for higher marketability, rate of sales, and appropriate cash flow.

While more crucial for larger projects, professional market studies are imperative for all projects in situations where competition is intense, the market is near capacity, or the developer's financial capacity demands a critical project-absorption rate to assure adequate cash flow and profitability. Consider a professional market study when you propose new housing units or development concepts or when you require highly specialized information.

Evaluating Professional Services. Once you decide you need a professional study or consultant, have a system for evaluating market studies to ensure you are paying for the most helpful information. First hire a reputable company or consultant to do the study. Require that the person who has major responsibility for the study provide credentials and a list of projects on which he or she has worked. Here, as in any service, ask that the references include former clients, and take the time to check them. Also ask to review copies of other stud-

FIGURE 1.9. Reasons for Purchasing Professional Market Studies

- Project size
- Potential project phasing
- Lender and investor requirements
- Study's affordability
- Restrictive regulatory climate
- New concepts and target markets
- Critical sales rate required

ies that the company or consultant has done to check scope, format, and quality. Use your local Building Institute Authority as a resource for finding a good consultant.

Before commissioning the study, you should find out what sources of data the market consultant intends to use; this will affect both quality and cost. Professional studies, which utilize only public information sources, should cost less than those using more definitive techniques such as surveys and reputable demographic information services. If the consultant plans to use only public information sources, you should once again determine if you have the in-house capability to gather and interpret this information yourself.

Clearly define the scope of your study in the initial consultation with the marketing firm. A professional marketing consultant can usually indicate whether the scope of the study can adequately provide the information you need for your project to succeed. If the scope of the study is inadequate or the cost of a full study too high, the consultant should provide some viable alternatives.

After a thorough understanding has been reached about scope and cost, carefully evaluate whether your company or project has enough financial capability to warrant the study. If it does not, you may want to consider conducting the study in-house rather than paying for a professional study limited in scope. However, large projects or those with untested ideas almost always warrant a study. In this case, if your project budget cannot support a market study, you might be undercapitalized.

Before signing the contract, you and the consultant can set firm guidelines for the study's scope and delivery. Then, throughout the research and analysis phase, stay in frequent contact with the consultant to ensure that the study progresses according to the original agreement.

Evaluating Market Studies. Professional market studies are by no means foolproof. The cost of the market study does not ensure that accurate decisions result from the collected data. This is why, after making the decision to purchase information, your primary quality control is carefully hiring reputable consultants. Whether commissioning a study or taking data from a previously generated study, ask the following questions:

- Does the marketing firm or consultant have a solid reputation?
- Did the marketing firm recently conduct the study or collect the information that forms the basis of the study? (The market is volatile, giving market studies a short shelf life.)
- Does the market study address the specifics of your region? (If it does not, it may not be valid for your project.).

Finally, market studies are not foolproof. They are no substitute for your ability to make informed decisions about the market. This is another reason why you should do as much "grass roots" investigating as possible on your own. Talk with professionals in the area and learn about trends through the media so you as the developer may keep current with the latest socioeconomic trends that may affect changing demands in homebuying.

Continue to Market

Once you have completed the market study and identified the target group, you must plan and implement a strategy for marketing and selling the product to that target group based on your market study. This ongoing process must be carried out in some form until the sales are completed. Once sales are underway, monitor traffic, sales rates, buyer responses, and the types of units that are the most popular or unpopular.

The sales staff should be vigilant in monitoring the reactions of potential buyers. One approach for getting feedback is to use a short questionnaire on buyer responses and preferences. If a questionnaire seems too intrusive for potential buyers, simply keep a sign-in sheet. After the potential buyers leave, you can record your own impressions on a separate record. Your notes can include family status, source of income, approximate age and your perception of the driving forces behind their negative or positive responses. You can then hold regular meetings to review and discuss this and any other feedback from the sales staff. This information will allow you to keep your marketing strategies flexible to respond to changing conditions or unforeseen problems.

Advertising and Other Marketing Activities

Advertising should occur regularly and be designed to appeal specifically to the target market. You should also strive to tailor media and sales events to the target market while satisfying the dictates of your marketing budget. Monitor response to advertising in local newspapers and other publications, using sales centers and open house events, and mailing flyers and brochures to potential buyers. You can then update all advertising and marketing data frequently, present them to sales staff, and discuss them in regular meetings to find new strategies and discard unworkable ones.

Selling the Project

The strategy for selling the project depends on whether you will sell to builders only, to home buyers only, or a combination. This is the first decision to be made in designing a sales strategy.

Selling to Builders

Whether you will be the only builder in a community or will allow other builders to buy lots depends on several issues. The advantage of being the only builder is greater control over design and construction standards as well as higher profits if the project is successful. However, carefully weigh this decision against your company's capacity to meet the anticipated project absorption rate. Your company's cash position and ability to take risks, obtain financing, mobilize subcontractors, and increase staff should be considered. If a project's appeal is strong but you do not have the capacity to keep up with the demand, consider selling lots to other builders to maintain momentum while the market is good.

When selling lots to builders solely or in part, decide on the standards to use for prequalifying them. Selected builders should be limited to those who meet these qualifications. Prequalification standards include builder reputation, financial and manpower capacity, safety record, project completion record, and bonding capacity.

Before you begin selling lots to builders, develop a written document outlining the following performance standards:

- design and construction standards
- standards for noise, dust, erosion, and runoff control
- methods for installing temporary utility service and roads
- methods for materials delivery and storage
- safety requirements
- time limits for project completion
- behavior of construction workers
- clean-up standards

Clearly communicate the contents of this document to each builder, who must agree in writing to adhere to the standards.

In the post-development construction period, carefully monitor each builder's compliance with these standards with a warning about fines for builders who fail to adhere to them. Use your prequalifying program and performance standards as a marketing tool to assure potential buyers that the community intends to maintain a high standard of quality throughout sales and construction.

Selling to Home Buyers

If you are selling the project to home buyers, base your sales strategies on techniques that appeal most to the target market. Various groups respond differently to heavily structured, hard-sell tactics as opposed to a more hands-off approach. Some groups, such as first-time buyers, need and want to be educated. More experienced buyers will not respond well to this approach. The way the model center is used and the time when it is open should relate well to the lifestyle characteristics of the target group. Some groups have more time than others and enjoy being catered to with conversation and refreshments. Others just want to get down to business.

One important decision is what the sales staff should sell: the lifestyle offered by the community or the home itself? Another question: whether to answer buyers' fears regarding security, safety, privacy, retained property value or energy efficiency or emphasize the more positive aspects of the development, including recreation, leisure activities, and social interaction with neighbors.

Reducing Risk in Today's Marketplace

In today's competitive marketplace, you as the developer must take greater care to reduce the risks inherent in land development. The first step in reducing the risks associated with a new venture and ensuring success remains a well-prepared market study. The information it provides can give you solid reasoning to back many of the future choices you will be required to make. Use the market study as the driving force behind all decisions concerning project cost and scheduling, type of master plan concept and homes, and project location. The study can also form the basis for developing your marketing and selling strategies.

Remember that the market study can clarify your goals for the new project to lenders and investors. A thorough and well-presented market study provides a convincing piece of evidence that your project has the potential to succeed. As such, it is an important part of the project documentation you present to lenders and investors when seeking financial backing.

Always continue to educate yourself about the market. Home buyers today are more conscious of the choices available in homes and communities because of an unprecedented increase in media coverage which began in the late 1990s and includes everything from publications to television. Attend continuing education classes offered by various organizations and private enterprise as well as professional conferences. Finally, study the Internet. Many developers have websites to showcase their company, new communities, and homes. The public is looking at these same websites; it's also a good way to get to know your competitors.

2

Financing Your Project

The best project ideas in the world amount to nothing more than wishful thinking unless you have the capital in place to finance the project. But finding sources of capital for land acquisition and development can be challenging. Sources may vary according to shifts in prevailing economic conditions or newly enacted regulations. This creates both a fluid list of capital sources you might use to obtain financing and an ever-changing list of documentation requirements and regulations. For example, consider the prevalence of savings and loan institutions (thrifts) funding land development in the 1980s compared to today. When it comes to financing, the rules of the game always seem to be changing.

Federal regulations now require banks and thrifts to have written guidelines for land development, residential construction, and commercial lending. These guidelines include definitive procedures for evaluating loan applications and administering loans. This mandate and many others are contained in the Real Estate Lending Rules, which were issued jointly by agencies that regulate insured banks and thrifts. They went into effect in 1993. One important aspect of the rules is the specific guidance on loan-to-value ratios. Figure 2.1 Loan-to-Value (L-T-V) Limits shows the ratios that banks and thrifts must generally follow for each type of loan category. Note,

FIGURE 2.1. Loan-to-Value (L-T-V) Limits

Loan Type	Maximum L-T-V Ratio[a] (percentage)
Raw land	65
Land development	75
Construction (commercial, multifamily)	80
1- to 4-family residential construction	85
Improved property	85

a. As specified by the 1993 Real Estate Lending Rules.

however, that these rules could be subject to change, so be sure to check with your lender regarding current requirements.

Exceptions to these requirements can be made on a case-by-case basis if the developer can compensate with other relevant attributes. These include overall creditworthiness, strong financial capacity, income from other property, secondary sources of loan repayment, and various forms of additional collateral.

Lenders and investment sources play an important role in land development simply because they supply most of the investment capital for residential as well as commercial projects. That means they also bear a lot of the risks. As a result, lenders minimize their risks by dictating the terms of the loan and even by refusing to finance a project if they perceive the risks as too great. Financing land development presents lenders with unique circumstances that make assessing these risks more difficult than for some other types of commercial loans. While other sources of financing are mentioned, this chapter focuses on obtaining lender financing.

Commercial lending generally bases a loan on the market value of a tangible product such as an automobile. In land development, the loan is based on an idea for a product that does not yet exist and whose value the lender can assess only by predicted sales performance. This prediction makes various assumptions about the future such as the state of the economy, housing needs, lifestyle trends, interest rates, labor and material availability, and general growth patterns. The design for the proposed product (the land development project) comes from these assumptions. If the product proves undesirable in the marketplace, the lender is left with something that may be difficult to liquidate.

After 1989, changes in lending practices resulted in at least one-third of builders and developers having to produce significantly more documentation for lenders. Developers found these increased requirements directly affected projects by increasing the length of time required to get loan approval, the types of outside consultants needed to produce the documentation, and the cost of both to the project.

Therefore, to minimize risks, lenders want to be assured as much as possible that the project you propose will succeed. As one of the first steps you take, talk with other developers in the area if you are unfamiliar with the time required to gather documentation and produce all feasibility studies for a development project. Be prepared to sustain yourself and your company financially during this lengthy time required for loan approval.

Development Financing

The amount of available capital for lending and investing relates directly to the economy. The partial deregulation of lenders, particularly thrifts, combined with a significant migration from economically depressed areas of the country to those with job growth, resulted in a 1980s building boom that saw lenders and investors scrambling to be involved. This gave rise to an unprecedented variety of sources for residential development capital and an increase in lender equity positions. As the economy took a downturn and poor lending practices grew in the thrift industry, many failed residential projects took savings and loan institutions down with them and vice versa.

The federal government's response to the rate of thrift bankruptcies was the sweeping reforms of the Financial Institutions Reform, Recovery, and Enforcement Act of 1989 (FIRREA). These events culminated in 1993 with the issuance of strict regulations on a variety of lending practices. Among other things, the new regulations limited both the percentage of value the borrower could obtain (loan-to-value ratio) and the amount of loans to one borrower. As a result of the savings and loan crisis, bank examiners began to scrutinize loan structures more carefully. The backing of real capital (money up front) instead of paper equity (anticipated fees and profit) became mandatory for all land development projects. Loan-to-value ratios decreased, thereby increasing the equity position demanded from the developer. Builders responded by initiating fewer projects and offering a smaller number of units per phase.

The economy and money supply began improving in the mid-1990s, and builders became accustomed to the increased documentation required by lenders. Population shifts to newly created high-tech job centers continued, helping fill the large vacancy rates. Public confidence in improving job availability and security increased home sales. Housing starts continued to rise during the latter half of the decade, mirroring a healthy climate for building and developing.

Sources of Capital

Before 1989 savings and loan institutions were the major source of capital for land acquisition. Since many thrifts went out of business and tighter regulations restricted the volume of residential lending, commercial banks became the primary source of capital for residential development in the 1990s. Although FIRREA generally did not directly affect commercial banks, many tightened their own requirements in a manner similar to that of the thrifts. Other lending entities increased their requirements for documentation to prove project feasibility. That's resulted in a lending climate characterized by increased requirements for higher equity positions, lower loan-to-value ratios, and increased amounts of financial and feasibility documentation required for acquisition, development, and construction loans.

Increased Documentation Requirements

Documentation comes in two broad categories: proof of the borrower's financial capacity and proof of the project's feasibility. Documentation of personal financial position has remained relatively unchanged over the years. However, talk with your lender in the beginning to understand the types of feasibility documentation required for your project. Requirements tend to change in response to economic conditions. Lending institutions also may vary in their requirements. Finally, your project may require additional documentation due to special circumstances such as environmental or regulatory concerns.

Financial Position. Lenders have always required developers to document their creditworthiness and financial standing, including their personal financial position. One important result of FIRREA—the lowering of loan-to-value ratios— forced developers to provide more money up front. That put developers in a riskier position since the loan-to-value ratio considers the total value of the project, then specifies the proportion of project equity (the developer's money) needed in relation to the amount the lender will finance. Loan-to-value ratios eased up a bit as the 1990s progressed and the overall economy improved. These ratios, which are a key indicator of the health of the building industry, vary constantly and are directly tied to such things as interest rates and the health of the regional and national economy. Both the borrowing company's present financial condition and track record for project success and the owner's personal financial position also affect the loan-to-value ratio.

In the past, the developer might have put up capital for around 20 percent of the project while the lender financed the remaining 80 percent. Although loan-to-value ratios differ across the country, today it is unusual for a developer to obtain an 80 percent loan-to-value ratio. This means you must put more of your own money into the project up front or find investors willing to do so. In addition, your project bears the added burden of time and money spent acquiring investors.

Approval of the remaining amount of money the lender is financing is based upon your personal ability and your company's ability to repay the loan. Your reputation and proof of financial position can demonstrate your worthiness for loan approval. Basic requirements for evaluating financial position have traditionally included personal guarantees, secured collateral, personal and business tax returns, and company financial statements. After you have established a history of project success and business responsibility, a lender may sometimes not require personal guarantees. However, since FIRREA, requirements for personal guarantees have reportedly risen even among those developers who have well-established relationships with their lenders.

Feasibility Study. Chief among the types of increased project documentation required for loan approval is the feasibility study. With it you take into account and document other considerations besides market data and analysis, considerations that include site and financial feasibility. Remember that the market study examines the viability of the project's concept, appropriateness of the target market, and projected absorption rate.

As part of the feasibility study, you might provide the lender with a study that targets site feasibility, including project and site constraints. Once the market analysis is complete, evaluate the site and its compatibility with the information in the market analysis. Carefully analyze the chosen site for constraints that may impact the unit density required for profit, the project's image and appeal to the target market, and anticipated site development and construction costs. Finally, consider the impact community response and regulatory constraints will have on the project.

Additionally, you must produce a financial feasibility study that examines project cash flow and profit to determine its potential for success. The pro forma analysis, discussed later in this chapter, will show cash flow, rate of sales, and construction costs based on site conditions and design. A financial analysis is then presented to the lender based on expected project schedule and costs. As part of the analysis, you place the cash flow of the project, including all expenditures and revenues, on a time line for the duration of the project.

In the beginning, the project is characterized only by expenditures or money flowing out. As sales occur, project revenue begins to flow in and offset expenses. At a particular point in time, the money coming into the project equals the money you have expended, which is known as the break-even point. From the break-even point on, money coming into the project should outpace project expenditures, producing a positive cash flow. You would want this amount to be as great as possible since it represents money you use to pay back the loan and cover unforeseen or new expenditures, with the remainder accumulating as profit. A successful project depends on a positive cash flow throughout.

Lenders want to view your project in terms of the total and periodic cash required and the profit expected under a variety of specific conditions such as rate of sales and interest rates. You must assure them that, once the project is underway, unforeseen political, site, and market conditions will not cause project delays, drive up the cost of site development, or provide insufficient funds to support the project. These unexpected costs and delays can quickly render inadequate your original predictions for project cash flow and profit based on a sales rate. If this happens, the cash disbursed by the lender will be inadequate to keep the project going.

Other Documentation. Depending on the type and location of the project, the lender may require a wide range of additional documentation. Regulatory and environmental clearances are particular areas of concern in today's business climate. Lenders frequently will ask for proof that the project will not encounter zoning roadblocks. For example, if you plan to develop a project on land that requires a zoning change, the lender might require documentation that shows the necessary zoning change will be approved. Some areas direct future zoning by using a comprehensive land use plan, which shows both zoning changes the local government will approve and the intent of those changes. If you are considering a parcel of undeveloped land zoned agricultural, the comprehensive plan will show whether it can be changed to residential zoning. Comprehensive plans and zoning are discussed in greater detail in chapters 3 and 4.

As environmental regulations increase, lenders tend to grow more cautious. They want assurances that a funded project will comply with local, state, and federal environmental regulations and will continue to completion. Depending on location and environmental conditions, lenders may require proof that the project can meet regulatory requirements for development and that the cost of compliance will not adversely affect project cash flow or profit. Examples of the kind of documentation required include environmental impact statements, wetlands reviews, special studies for endangered plants and wildlife, archaeological and historical reviews, and hazardous waste studies.

Loan Application Packages. The loan application package has traditionally contained documentation of various kinds. Check the guidelines provided by the bank to make sure yours is complete, then meet with the lender to confirm your understanding of what is required. The requirements may differ according to the size of the bank, its location, and the type of project. Figure 2.2 Documentation for Development Loans summarizes some of the typical documentation a lender might require. However, requirements can vary; talk with your lender for particulars before you assemble your loan application package.

Types of Loans

As a developer you may require a variety of loans to finance a project. Typical loans include land acquisition, development, and construction loans; interim loans or gap financing; and permanent mortgage loans. Each has unique requirements for repayment periods, interest rates, and disbursement schedules. Land acquisition loans purchase the land. Development and construction loans pay for making the land ready for building and for the construction of the houses themselves.

After the houses are built, the developer takes out another loan that essentially covers each house's permanent mortgage while the house is waiting to be sold. The amount of this loan

FIGURE 2.2. Documentation for Development Loans

Personal and Company Financial Documents
- Current financial statements of all borrowers and investors
- Contract documents for investor partnerships or joint ventures
- Proof and description of personal collateral
- Personal guarantee
- Company income tax statements
- Personal income tax statements

Other Company Documents
- Company history
- Company organizational structure
- List of previous projects
- Personal and business references

Project Documents
- Physical location and legal description of project
- Land appraisal
- Land survey
- Proof of clear title to the land
- Market study
- Project feasibility study
- Pro forma analysis
- Conceptual site plan
- House plans and elevations
- Conceptual estimate of all project costs
- Project approval, land development, and construction schedules
- Proof of required and timely zoning approval
- Proof of approval to use existing infrastructure
- Development agreement outlining the project's contribution of infrastructure to the city or county, length of time for installation, and method of dedicating infrastructure over to the city or county
- Proof of all required environmental clearances and permits
- Description of development and marketing plans

pays off the development and construction loan, leaving the developer with one loan—the permanent mortgage. As houses are sold, the individual purchaser's mortgage buys out a portion of this permanent mortgage. In some cases, interim financing is required to bridge the gap between the paying off of the construction and development loan and the amount of the permanent mortgage.

Even though, in theory, this assembly of loans covers the expenses of each portion of development and construction, you'll need some creative planning in your development and construction schedule as well as in your planned rate and dollar value of sales. The front-end development costs represent a huge financial hurdle because money must be spent on environmental and regulatory clearances, marketing and feasibility studies and land, and on the installation of major infrastructure such as roads and amenities. As you create your project spreadsheet representing expenditures and revenues on a time line, it will be apparent how much money you need to begin the project.

Acquisition Loan

In recent times it has become common for the developer to purchase land through private means such as a small group of investors or from his or her own capital. However, land acquisition loans are still used in land development. The collateral necessary to obtain an acquisition loan usually consists of your personal assets, your company's assets, and the land itself. This type of loan is essentially a short-term first mortgage comprised of the note secured by your assets and the mortgage secured by the value of the land. As part of the loan application process, the lender requests an appraisal that sets the loan-to-value ratio. In addition, the lender may require a good-faith deposit, returnable if the loan application is not approved. The lender will also require a current survey of the site along with proof of clear title to the land and of your ability to obtain title insurance once the title is in your name.

The lender may require other documentation when you apply for an acquisition loan. These items may include proof of your ability to obtain the appropriate zoning, an evaluation of the location and capacity of existing infrastructure, letters from the city or county showing intent to install infrastructure if it is not present, and various environmental approvals such as those mentioned earlier.

Interest rates vary for acquisition loans but are generally set at 1 to 4 points above the prime lending rate. Frequently the lender may require a variable or floating interest rate tied to a certain range of fluctuation in interest rates over time. The duration of the acquisition loan usually averages about two years, but you can sometimes get an option to renew or to stretch the repayment period to as much as five years.

In some cases the land acquisition loan is combined with the development loan and the payment schedule regularly spaced over its duration. Increasingly the structure of a development loan includes a balloon payment toward the end of the payback period. A balloon payment is a lump sum due at the end of the amortization period.

If your acquisition loan is combined with a development loan, payment schedules can differ. The lender may structure the loan as a line of credit with periodic draws taken as needed from the loan amount. Loan repayment begins after the first portion of the site development work is completed, with money included for repaying the land purchase price. You can also use your equity to finance all or part of the land purchase, reducing the total amount of the loan. Whatever the loan amount, when lots are sold the lender receives the release price represented by an amount slightly higher than the loan-to-value ratio of each lot. In this way each permanent mortgage repays a portion of the acquisition loan.

Other Types of Land Purchase Agreements

Lenders are much more cautious now about approving the financing of a land purchase for residential development. Frequently they ask that a portion of the developer's equity position go toward purchasing the land. This is not always desirable because tying up a large portion of equity at the beginning leaves less for protecting short periods of low or negative cash flow throughout the project. As a result, some developers turn to various purchase options or equity partnerships with landowners to finance their land purchases.

Getting landowners to participate as partners in new development lacks the desirability it had for landowners before the federal tax law changes of the 1980s. Those changes limited the real estate tax deduction and made limited partnerships in development projects less lucrative, although some landowners still will participate in a successful project. When looking for a landowner to act as a partner in your project, you have several alternatives.

Purchase Money Mortgage. Purchase money mortgages offer one alternative to having a landowner act as a partner in your project. With this mortgage, the owner can establish a price for the land to which you both agree. Then, upon closing, the landowner takes a second mortgage to the construction lender at a predetermined loan-to-value ratio.

In effect, you are presenting a note to the landowner secured by the mortgage on the property; the landowner then expects to make money by charging an interest rate higher than the lenders. At this point, you may pay interest only for the life of the loan with the balance of the principal repaid in a balloon note at a designated time in the future. Payments can also be amortized over the life of the loan or a combination of the balloon and amortized methods can occur.

Participating in such an arrangement represents a fair amount of risk for the landowner. Do your homework to convince the landowner of the project's viability. Once again, there is no substitute for a good business reputation and the right kind of project feasibility documentation. It's also easier to make this kind of deal if you are already holding some property contiguous to the landowner's or have already built a successful phase of the project.

Options on Land. Options on land are commonly used to secure the right to develop a parcel of land. An option, a fixed fee paid to the owner, gives the developer a certain period of time to perform feasibility work to prove the project will be viable. During this time the owner cannot sell the land to someone else. This is a good choice if you want to ensure that the prospective parcel has good development capability.

If you decide to go forward with the project, the option price frequently applies toward the purchase price. However, if the project proves not viable, you lose the money you spent on the option unless you can sell it to another developer.

Options are short- or long-term in duration with renewal clauses and land purchase price agreements attached. A fixed option, usually short-term, establishes a future price at which the land may be purchased. It can come with a full credit clause allowing you to apply the option price to the land purchase price or a declining credit clause that reduces the amount you can apply to the purchase price over time. Rolling options are most often seen with longer time periods and large tracts of land that are developed in phases. The option rolls forward to each subsequent parcel to be developed. Stepped options are also a choice for either large or small tracts of land. This option features a stepped increase in the purchase price of the land over time.

When building a project in phases, you'll probably want to use some type of option for several reasons. With a successful first phase, you'll want assurance the project can be expanded. However, if the first phase lags in its success, you may prefer to have spent the option price than be left holding an undeveloped parcel with uncertain potential.

Not knowing whether remaining parcels of land will be permitted for your development when you are ready to expand makes the purchasing of all available land risky. If regulatory requirements change before you begin another phase the land might suddenly be unsuitable for the type of development you had in mind. For example, in areas requiring sufficient infrastructure before a project can receive permits, subsequent development around your project may have exceeded road capacity, making the approval of your next phase difficult. An option can hold the land until these types of uncertainties are clarified.

Development Loan

The development loan requires the same type of personal and company collateral as the acquisition loan. As with the land acquisition loan, the lender is offering money for a product that does not yet exist. Here again the documentation required may be extensive. Development loans, also short-term, have about the same interest rates as acquisition loans.

The development loan is disbursed according to a draw schedule set by the lender or by a line of credit. A draw schedule determines when the lender will release portions of the loan and is divided up into percentages of work required to prepare the site for building construction. This work includes the soft costs of fees, permits, and testing along with the hard costs of clearing, installing utilities and roads, and preparing building pads. As each percentage of work is completed, the money required to pay for the work is released.

The lender will usually hold back a small percentage of the total loan amount for each draw. Known as retainage, this ensures the work completed is adequate and the developer has paid all subcontractors. In case of project foreclosure, the retainage makes up the difference when another contractor is hired to finish the work. The amount of money in retainage plus interest returns to the developer at the end of the project.

If you are not using a line of credit, the lender sets the draw schedule and describes the items of work that represent each draw. Once the items of work for the first draw have been completed, you may request an inspection for verification. The inspection is based on a schedule of values, a description of the work completed along with its costs. The architect of record or project engineer usually verifies the schedule of values. The lender then uses an in-house or independent inspector to verify that the submitted schedule of values represents the work finished, and thus the value of the draw. Each subsequent draw is treated in the same manner. Here, too, the lender will usually retain a small portion of the value of work completed until the project is finished.

Whether you use a line of credit or draw schedule for your development, always be aware of the costs incurred with project start-up. The costs of the various consultants' reports for environmental and regulatory clearances, marketing information, and project design will be paid for out of your own assets to produce documentation to take to the bank. After loan approval, some of these costs can be built into the draw schedule as more definitive work is completed on overall permitting and design.

When ready for construction to begin, the developer may sell a site to a builder or transfer it from the company's development division to its building division. A representative portion of the development loan is then repaid. Once the acquisition and development loan are repaid, the lender releases the note so the construction lender can have first lien on the property.

Construction Loan

The construction loan is obtained for building the homes in the development. Interest rates on construction loans average around 4 points above the prime-lending rate. As with acquisition and development loans, FIRREA and the new Real Estate Lending Rules have also affected the loan-to-value ratio associated with construction loans. Loan-to-value ratios for construction loans differ among institutions and locations but generally average around 70 to 75 percent. You as the developer are expected to supply the remainder of the capital for the value of the project if it is needed for cash flow. The lender will require a first mortgage on the property so that if for some reason you cannot repay the loan, the lender will collect the debt ahead of other lien holders.

Again, the lender disburses the construction loan by draw schedules set by the lending institution. These differ widely among lenders as well as individual developers. If you are building only a few houses, the lender sets the draw schedule for each one, representing at each stage a portion of the work completed. Typical draw schedules have four and five draws with the corresponding items of completed work listed for each draw. The lender requests an inspection after the work for each draw is completed, with that cost usually built into the charges to the permanent mortgage holder.

If you are building a large number of units and have favorable credit, the lender may extend you a line of credit. Many builders and developers prefer to work this way because they control the number and timing of draw requests as well as which work items are involved. A specified draw schedule, however, leaves little room for confusion about which items of work constitute what percentage of project completed. With a line of credit you pay interest only on the amount drawn down. You then repay the remaining principal with the permanent mortgage.

Permanent and Interim Financing

Permanent mortgages are long-term loans that essentially pay off the developer's previous development and construction loan. Typically they're obtained on an individual basis by the homebuyer. All the permanent mortgages accumulated should be enough to pay off the development and construction loan and provide profit.

In medium to large developments where a portion of the sales come from speculative homes and lot sales to builders, the lender requires a commitment on permanent financing from another lender before approving the construction loan. Because construction loans are short-term, the construction lender wants assurance that funds are available to repay the amount. This permanent financing commitment is known as a take-out commitment. A loan based on the loan-to-value ratio is an amount less than the total value of the project. You may sometimes obtain interim or gap financing if you cannot come up with the difference. A lender other than the construction or permanent mortgage lender usually provides interim financing, which is difficult to obtain and more common for commercial projects. The high cost poses an additional consideration; interim financing usually runs around 5 points above the prime lending rate.

As lots are sold and houses closed with titles transferred to new owners, a portion of the construction loan is released and repaid by the new owner's permanent mortgage. If you as the developer are carrying lots and finished houses because they have not sold in a timely manner, your own permanent mortgage will take over. The portion of the construction loan represented by those items will then be released and repaid from your permanent mortgage.

Lenders usually use this permanent financing for large projects with many speculative homes or for income-producing property such as multifamily housing and speculative office projects. Permanent mortgages may be required when the project includes financing and building model homes and amenities such as clubhouses and swimming pools. In these circumstances, the lender offers a permanent loan commitment under a set of contingencies that include project completion on a timely basis, clear title to the land, evidence of a secured construction loan within an agreed time, and the lender's right to approve change orders affecting plans previously approved by the permanent mortgage lender.

Alternative Sources of Financing

Developers have used alternative sources of financing for a long time. However, because of the tightening of credit extended to developers and the decline of savings and loans as sources of land development capital, developers in recent years have increasingly turned to alternative means of raising funds. Among the many alternative sources of capital are partnerships, limited partnerships, Real Estate Investment Trusts (REITs), private domestic or foreign investors, joint ventures, pension funds, and creative land purchase agreements with owners.

Partnerships and Investors

A developer may form a general partnership to raise capital to finance the equity and support the cash flow of a new project. Since lenders require more money up front, finding sources of equity can be a major step in financing land development. Partnerships offer one means of raising capital for the required project equity. Partners can actively participate in the project or merely contribute money. Regardless, each is liable for the project's debts. Furthermore, liability can extend to the individual partner's personal finances.

A limited partner only invests money, leaving the management and policy making to the general partner. The general partner assumes all operating liabilities on behalf of the passive investor, the limited partner.

Investors can come into a project as either limited or full (general) partners. Private investors more commonly operate as limited partners, providing capital to fill out the equity position required for the project. They may be individuals, groups of individuals, investment funds and trusts, or foreign investors. A syndication describes a group of individuals, corporations, or trusts formed to invest in entrepreneurial ventures such as a residential development project.

REITs

The Real Estate Investment Trust is essentially a mutual fund for investing in real estate. A trust is technically an entity in which one party holds property for the benefit of others. Shares are sold to raise equity for a project, thereby holding the real property or mortgage in trust for shareholders. This option benefits those wishing to invest in real estate without being subject to personal liability if the project fails. The trust is professionally managed. Investors are paid dividends resulting from profits on the real estate, and if more than 100 investors are involved, the trust itself is not subject to taxes. However, investors receive none of the tax breaks from owning real property.

REITs pose a risk for investors since they operate on the premise that dividends will rise each year. They also tie up investment capital for a long period of time with no interim income or yield. This can make a joint venture between the REIT and you as the developer attractive to both when the REIT agrees to acquire the project upon completion. REITs can be an attractive source of capital for highly marketable products because so many investment structures can be negotiated. In recent years, REITs have played a minimal role in financing land development.

Joint Ventures

Companies formed to complete one project at a particular point in time are called joint ventures. With the structure of a corporation, limited partnership, or general partnership, they have two primary advantages: combined financial assets and combined employee skills. Sometimes a joint venture forms to provide adequate bonding capacity for government or other large-scale projects. Perhaps it's to raise the amount of equity required for a project. Regardless, combining staff from all companies or talents from the various individuals into a team can also provide great benefits.

A major challenge with joint ventures is delineating clearly the distribution of profits, losses, and responsibilities. Ensuring sound project management through effective communication among participants is another. Remember, a joint venture is essentially a new company. Clearly structured agreements on goals and team participation, strong leadership from the developer, clear methods of communication, and effective management of cash flow on the project can keep a joint venture running smoothly.

Pension Funds

A viable source of capital funding, pension funds handle more than 55 percent of the money available in the United States for investment. Developers are increasing their efforts to pursue this possible source of project financing. In the past, pension funds have not played a large role in acquisition, development, and construction financing because the trustees, having great fiduciary responsibilities and at times personal liability, tend to be conservative.

However, with the health of the economy and stock market, pension funds are increasing their investing in larger land development projects, primarily by direct investment in specific projects. This began to shift in the late 1990s into the indirect funding of land development through publicly marketed securities. Direct investment tends to be relegated to areas of high-yield special investment programs. Pension fund managers feel more comfortable having land development substantially secured with holdings spread broadly among pension and mutual funds both nationally and internationally. It remains unclear what the future holds for pension funds as a capital source for land development. If the economy continues to improve and the stock market remains steady, this category of capital sources will bear watching due to the large amount of money available for investing.

If you use a pension fund as a source of capital, be prepared to convince the fund of the planned project's soundness as an investment. Factors that limit pension funds from investing in land development projects are the risks inherent in land development, federal tax provisions that discourage investment in land development, lack of information on the performance of equity investments, and the size of the pension fund itself. Pension funds command a large amount of capital. With $10 trillion in capital available for investment, pension funds could supply residential developers with $1 trillion worth of investment financing, if they invested only 1 percent more in residential development.

Large developers may convince a pension fund to invest in their projects by making a private offering of stock to a local fund. Some developers induce union pension funds to invest in projects that promise to use only union labor. However, to use pension funds as a source of capital, you still must find ways to convince them your project makes a sound investment.

Is Your Project Financially Feasible?

Once you know the costs associated with land acquisition, development, and construction, test a variety of scenarios of sales rates and conditions to determine which ones might produce positive cash flow and a satisfactory return on your investment. The pro forma analysis helps provide a picture of your venture's money requirements. You'll want to perform a pro forma analysis for as many different conditions as possible, an easy task using one or more of the available software spreadsheets. Using computerized software makes it simple to change the variables and conditions of your project (such as higher interest rates, slower rates of sales, etc.). Once you plug in all the numbers, you can get almost instantaneous results.

Pro Forma Analysis

Lenders and investors require a cash flow analysis throughout the duration of the proposed project to determine its expected cash requirements and profit. As part of this documentation, you will be required to submit a pro forma analysis of your project's revenues and disbursements. A pro forma analysis essentially shows an itemized list of the project disbursements and revenues over the life of the project given anticipated sales rates and costs. The cash flow of the project (money coming in and going out) can be determined from the pro forma.

As part of the pro forma analysis, you can use various methods to evaluate yield measures (ratios and standards) for projected profit compared with such variables as the original equity invested. Any project that eventually proves profitable requires adequate positive cash flow to succeed. Analyzing projected cash flow from the pro forma can help prevent situations where periods of negative cash flow could cause loan default.

To show the cash coming in and going out of the project over time, the pro forma usually lists the project's hard and soft costs in a vertical column. Hard costs include the price of all materials and labor necessary to install the physical improvements. Soft costs are all those other than direct labor and material and can include fees associated with design, legal, marketing, and financial services. They also include fees for testing site conditions and for project overhead. Along with the hard and soft costs listed in the vertical column are projected cash inflows represented by sales of lots or units. The horizontal row is divided up into years, quarters, or months for the duration of the project and sell-out period.

Figure 2.3 Pro Forma and Cash Flow Analysis shows a simplified pro forma and cash flow analysis, divided into quarters, for a land development project. The pro forma analysis in Figure 2.3 begins at an arbitrary point in time (namely, after the site work has been completed and the lots are ready for sale) and shows a simplified analysis for illustrative purposes only.

However, the conversion from raw land to improved lots to finished product usually occurs throughout development.

The complex scheduling of land purchasing, management of infrastructure construction, development programming, and marketing makes pro forma and cash flow analysis for land development projects tough to predict. You might schedule in a four-month period to build roads but find construction halted for two to three weeks due to unforeseen severe weather. That severe weather could damage some of the installed infrastructure components, which then must be removed and replaced. Naturally, your original pro forma and cash flow analysis did not include these events. You cannot anticipate

FIGURE 2.3. Pro Forma and Cash Flow Analysis

Project Data

Total number of lots:	60
Lot price:	$25,000
Total lot sales:	$1,500,000
Absorption rate per quarter:	10 lots
Loan-to-value ratio:	70%
Interest rate:	9%
Original loan amount:	$1,050,000
Loan reduction per lot	
(original loan ÷ 60 lots):	$17,500

Project Data

- Amortized payments repay the land development loan at 6% over the sales life of the project.
- Depreciation and appreciation are excluded.
- Cash outflows and inflows are calculated as before-tax cash flows.
- The gross profit margin is assumed to be 10%, 6% of which is a portion of the developer's profit and 4% of which is the cost of land development.
- The pro forma analysis begins after the site work has been completed and the lots are ready for sale. The portion of the developer's profit is counted as an expense, while the site development costs are allocated to the period of time before this pro forma begins.

(Continued)

FIGURE 2.3. Continued

Quarter	1	2	3	4	5
Cash Outflows					
Marketing and closing costs (6% of line 1 below)	$15,000	$15,000	$15,000	$15,000	$15,000
Overhead and misc. soft costs (2% of line 1 below)	5,000	5,000	5,000	5,000	5,000
Tax on lots	2,250	1,875	1,500	1,125	625
Portion of developer's profit (6% of line 1 below)	15,000	15,000	15,000	15,000	15,000
Total Expenses	$37,250	$36,875	$36,500	$36,125	$35,625
Cash Inflows					
1. Lot sales (10 x $25,000)	$250,000	$250,000	$250,000	$250,000	$250,000
2. Total lot sales value	1,500,000	1,250,000	1,000,000	750,000	500,000
3. Net project income (line 1 – total expenses)	212,750	213,125	213,500	213,875	214,375
4. Loan reduction per quarter (10 x $17,500)	175,000	175,000	175,000	175,000	175,000
5. Loan balance, end of quarter (current loan amount – line 4)	875,000	700,000	525,000	350,000	175,000
6. Interest payment per quarter (current loan amount x 0.09 x 0.25, rounded off)	23,625	19,688	15,750	11,813	7,875
7. Cash flow per quarter (line 3 – line 6)	$189,125	$193,437	$197,750	$202,062	$206,500

these or a multitude of other changes that might occur as a result of external forces beyond anyone's control. Your pro forma and cash flow analysis for an actual project continually change as conditions change throughout the project, hence the importance of evaluating as many worst-case scenarios as possible.

Cash Flow Diagram

Plot the revenues and expenditures of the cash flow, and a line will appear representing the cash flow diagram over the life of the project. The first point of the line will be negative and continue to fall as money is spent. Once revenue begins to come in, the line will begin to rise until it reaches the break-even point where revenue and expenditures are equal. The cash flow diagram in Figure 2.4 Cash Flow Diagram shows a typical configuration of cash flow expected from a successful project.

Predict cash flow on a monthly basis for the most accurate assessment of cash requirements. The cash flow diagram reveals important points when cash will be needed and profits realized. This allows you and your lender and investors to plan strategi-

FIGURE 2.4. Cash Flow Diagram

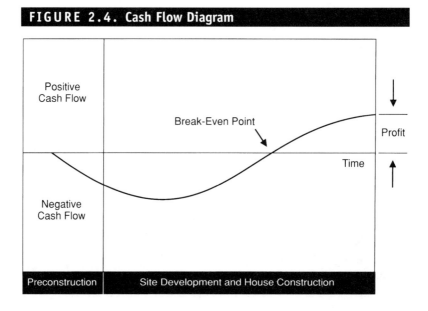

cally and determine the amount and timing of potential investment returns.

Sensitivity Analysis

The pro forma shows specific conditions of costs and sales rates but is accurate only for those conditions. For this reason, a single pro forma and cash flow cannot account for a change in any variable of cost and sales such as the amount of interest charged, a significant increase in material cost, a change in the sales price of the home, or a change in the sales rate. Therefore, you need to vary the conditions of the project under expected ranges to see how those changes affect the project's cash flow.

For instance, the pro forma may show the project heavily financed with the cost of borrowing money at a particular interest rate. If interest rates rise sharply before the project receives approval, this line item cost will be much greater, rendering the original pro forma inaccurate. A jump of 2 points in interest rates can sometimes create an unaccounted-for project cost that results in an inadequate cash flow.

Wherever possible, know beforehand how potential changes in costs and sales rates during the project will affect cash flow. Do this by evaluating all the possible costs and sales rates on separate pro formas. The process of changing the variables of costs and sales rates to evaluate changes in cash flow and profit is called a sensitivity analysis.

With a sensitivity analysis, you can change either one variable or a combination. When pro formas were done by hand, this was a formidable task. Today, however, the format lends itself to a variety of computer spreadsheets. Having the pro forma entered into a spreadsheet makes changing cost variables quick and easy. You can then produce the same pro forma with any number of changes for each line item.

Figures 2.5 and 2.6 show simplified sensitivity analyses, each taking into account a change in only one variable—the interest rate or sales rate. In actuality, you would take a number of variables important to the project and vary them according to a predicted range to determine their effect on one another and their eventual effect on profit and cash flow.

FIGURE 2.5. Sensitivity Analysis: Interest Rates

Assumptions
- Change the interest rate from 9% to 11%.
- All other project data and assumptions are the same as those for Figure 2.3.

Quarter	1	2	3	4	5
Total Expenses (from Figure 2.3)	$37,250	$36,875	$36,500	$36,125	$35,625
Cash Inflows					
1. Lot sales (10 x $25,000)	$250,000	$250,000	$250,000	$250,000	$250,000
2. Total lot sales value	1,500,000	1,250,000	1,000,000	750,000	500,000
3. Net project income (line 1 – total expenses)	212,750	213,125	213,500	213,875	214,375
4. Loan reduction per quarter (10 x $17,500)	175,000	175,000	175,000	175,000	175,000
5. Loan balance, end of quarter (current loan amount – line 4)	875,000	700,000	525,000	350,000	175,000
6. Interest payment per quarter (current loan amount x 0.11 x 0.25, rounded off)	28,875	24,063	19,250	14,438	9,625
7. Cash flow per quarter (line 3 – line 6)	$183,875	$189,062	$194,250	$199,437	$204,750

Profit Analyses

You can also assess risk by methods meant to measure project profit, chiefly ratio analysis and discounted cash flow analysis. The two methods may be used together. Single-period ratio analysis basically assesses cash flow and profits for a single

FIGURE 2.6. Sensitivity Analysis: Sales Rates

Assumptions
- Change the sales rate from 10 to 5 lots per quarter.
- All other project data and assumptions are the same as those for Figure 2.3.

Quarter	1	2	3	4	5
Total Expenses (from Figure 2.3)	$37,250	$36,875	$36,500	$36,125	$35,625
Cash Inflows					
1. Lot sales (5 x $25,000)	$125,000	$125,000	$125,000	$125,000	$125,000
2. Total lot sales value	1,500,000	1,375,000	1,250,000	1,125,000	1,000,000
3. Net project income (line 1 – total expenses)	87,750	88,125	88,500	88,875	89,375
4. Loan reduction per quarter (5 x $17,500)	87,500	87,500	87,500	87,500	87,500
5. Loan balance, end of quarter (current loan amount – line 4)	962,500	875,000	787,500	700,000	612,500
6. Interest payment per quarter (current loan amount x 0.09 x 0.25, rounded off)	23,625	21,656	19,688	17,719	15,750
7. Cash flow per quarter (line 3 – line 6)	$64,125	$66,469	$68,812	$71,156	$73,625

period, while discounted cash flow considers the cash flow and profits of the project over time.

Ratio Analysis. The ratios in ratio analysis are calculated on before-tax cash flows and do not cover such indirect benefits as property appreciation and tax breaks. The ratios also do not reflect the potential volatility of the project over time (what happens when unexpected contingencies occur) but are useful in comparing certain discrete aspects of a land development investment with similar aspects of other types of investments.

The ratios commonly used in ratio analysis include operating, break-even, debt-service, and return-on-equity. Operating ratio describes the percentage of income used to pay operating expenses. Break-even ratio illustrates the amount of vacancy or unsold housing stock the company can tolerate before all cash inflow goes to pay operating expenses and debt service. Debt-service ratio describes how low the net income can fall before the debt-service payment (the cost of borrowing money) cannot be met. Return-on-equity ratio measures the relationship of profit to the original equity position.

For investors, these ratios must fall into certain ranges before the investment is considered worthwhile compared with other investments. For instance, if the return on equity for your project is 6 percent, an investor would be better off putting money in a certificate of deposit for a no risk 5 percent. Industry standards are published for all ratios used to evaluate the profit on any business investment. You can determine the minimum and maximum ranges of profit measures for a residential development from these published data. Your financial officer or consultant can recommend the type of ratio analysis you should use in your pro forma. If you want to perform preliminary calculations yourself before hiring a financial consultant, check with your lender to determine which types of ratio analysis they prefer to see.

Discounted Cash Flow Analysis. The discounted cash flow analysis is one of the preferred methods of estimating a project's value. Use this method to estimate after-tax returns and cash flows. These are more realistic estimates of how money behaves over time for a given project than single-period ratio analysis. You can also use this method to determine the discount rate, which is the same as the rate of return required relative to the risks of the venture. The discounted cash flow analysis can also

reveal bottom-line results or yield measures such as the investment value, the net present worth or value (NPV), and the
internal rate of return on equity for the project.

The investment value describes the investor's value or claim
on income compared to that of the lender's value. This simply
means that, if your development costs are lower than your
investment value, you have a viable project. Net present value
(NPV) results when you convert the future net income of the
project back to the present-day value of the money invested. To
calculate NPV, first convert all expenditures and revenues over
time to the present-day worth of the dollar. The difference
between the present value of cash inflow and outflow represents
the NPV. If the NPV equals zero or greater, the project is a
sound investment. The internal rate of return is the interest rate
at which the NPV equals zero. If your internal rate of return is
equal to or greater than your required rate of return, the investment is also sound.

Your financial expert can calculate these various standard
yield measures for the project and compare them with acceptable ranges for yield measures associated with different types
of investment. Also, most standard spreadsheets can do this
for you now. Once your financial expert has performed these
calculations, he or she can advise you on the soundness of
the venture. Remember, though: These evaluations cannot be
done without a pro forma analysis of costs over the life of the
project for which you consider fluctuating costs and sales
rates.

Accuracy of Methods

The importance of an accurate pro forma cannot be overem-
phasized. It remains the basis both of the lender's and your own
estimates for the value of the project and the determination of
the necessary cash flow needed to sustain it. Remember that the
pro forma is based on a number of assumptions, such as future
material costs, that can only be viewed as educated predictions.
To reduce the potential for errors, consider several factors that
influence the accuracy of the pro forma.

Realistically predicting project absorption rates or monthly sales rates can be perhaps your greatest challenge. This variable has the potential to be unpredictable; study it carefully using a sensitivity analysis that varies the sales rates from a pessimistic to optimistic viewpoint. Basing the pro forma solely on an optimistic rate could mean an inadequate cash flow under slower absorption rates. Consider predicting the worst-case scenario to determine the slowest absorption rate under which the project can survive so you'll have a realistic picture of possible outcomes for the project.

Project costs are based upon design information and the construction schedule. Even though in many cases your project team will not yet have produced the actual construction documents, you must have an accurate conceptual estimate to predict costs. This estimate lists costs produced before the design and construction documents are completed. It is based on understanding the assemblies or components of broad categories of work involved in the project, such as building a road or an entire exterior wall system. In the conceptual estimate, the units that make up the building system are priced and the quantity estimated.

As the developer, you must adjust costs for location and the point at which materials are ordered and labor paid for. The construction schedule evolves from the conceptual estimate, which gives a picture of the type and amount of construction involved. The schedule must take into account the cost of materials at a future time, the timing for ordering the materials, the amount and type of labor and equipment necessary for installation, the costs of each, and the provision for days lost due to bad weather.

From the estimate and schedule you can then estimate the draws necessary to pay subcontractors and suppliers. Having inadequate design and scheduling information can skew the predicted costs of the project and make the pro forma inaccurate. Make sure you hire experienced and reputable construction professionals to produce the kind of information required for an accurate conceptual estimate and schedule.

Future of Development Financing

Trends worth studying include the movement of financing away from direct project or individual financing toward entity-based financing (such as pension funds, mutual funds, or syndicates), the effect of the stock market on REITs, the availability and cost of both public and private REIT stocks, and the rise of commercial mortgage-based securities (CMBS). Banks will continue to originate loans, but increasingly these loans may be pooled for sale to a Wall Street securitization entity. Therefore, banks will write construction loans to convert to permanent mortgages, and those will be written to standards allowing them to be securitized.

This in turn will create more scrutiny of the quality of the loans, along with faster feedback. Should this occur, you as a developer will continue to face more requirements for documentation. These trends point to a permanently lower cost of capital for the land development industry, even though equity positions for developers will remain high. The advanced stages of recovery developers now enjoy create higher values than five years ago, but the overall debt is steady.

Even when the climate seems favorable to business success, you should educate yourself as much as possible on the nature of economic trends and current regulations for investing. The availability of money is cyclical; anticipating a downward trend can save your company. When times favor development, the risk of overbuilding always exists.

Proper Documentation Eliminates Potential Mistakes

Acquiring financial backing for a land development project is always challenging. It has become a more complex endeavor in today's business climate, requiring a complete and thorough loan application package. An awareness of the business arena in which you operate and a carefully studied and prepared approach will go a long way toward allowing your development project to go forward. In the end, the project's ability to attract investors and lenders will depend on the successful integration of market information with the pro forma analysis of the project cash flow and profit.

When considering a new project, remember the importance of accurately estimating the length of time expected for project approval from lenders and regulatory agencies. If you are holding land and paying for the associated costs in taxes or loan payments, recognize that a longer project approval time can affect the point at which the project gets under way and begins realizing revenues and profit. Anticipating this length of time beforehand gives you time to decide what you can afford in obtaining project approval and financing.

For the developer with a sound business reputation and land development proposal, these new trends become extra details to address and added associated costs to consider. Even so, you can save yourself a lot of time and money by going into a project with your eyes open, leaving as little to chance as possible. The market study, project feasibility documentation, and financial analysis all play an important role in gaining approval of and financing for your project. They can also help to prevent costly mistakes once the project is underway. Ultimately, they become stepping-stones to your project's success.

3

Site
Selection

The land you choose for your new development should have attributes that both appeal to buyers and enhance the project's market potential. At the same time, these site characteristics should not pose a significant threat to the development capacity required for profit. Before deciding a particular site suits your planned development, you must determine if the development idea and the site are compatible.

To do this, investigate a variety of physical and regulatory site factors, then use the resulting information to help convince lenders and investors of the potential for project success. Lenders now require more information about project feasibility, in part due to the increasing number of restrictions placed on development; most are related to the site's characteristics. The lender wants to know you've considered all aspects of any site characteristics that might become project constraints. Project constraints—such as poor drainage or environmentally sensitive areas—present special problems for project approval, design, and construction.

Evaluating these constraints allows you to plan adequately for the costs and amount of time necessary to win approval for developing the land. This permission can range from regulatory and environmental approvals to community acceptance. Properly investigating site characteristics also helps you better understand the cash requirements and profit generated by a particular type of development on a chosen site. You can use this knowledge to protect your company's cash flow against possible loan default.

Two Approaches to Site Selection

There is no single approach to successfully matching a site with a development idea. Your approach depends on two factors: whether you have already determined the idea for a new development or development program and whether you already own the site. Think of the possibilities of matching a site with a type of development in the following ways:

- development idea in search of a site
- site in search of a development idea

If you own the site, it makes good business sense to find the most marketable kind of development that's compatible with its characteristics—in this case, the highest and best use of the site. On the other hand, if you start with a certain type of development in mind, you must search for a site whose characteristics support your idea.

Development Idea in Search of Site

After conducting a local market study and deciding the type of development your target buyers want, formalize these ideas into a program or concept for a master plan. The conceptual master plan—the basis of your subsequent final master plan—centers around the type and number of housing units.

The conceptual plan drawing depicts the layout of streets, lots, amenities, and open space based on chosen ideas that appeal to your target group. Use this plan to determine the preferred size, shape, and required slopes in the parcels of land you are considering for your new development. Finding a site that can support a predetermined concept for a new development begins with translating specific target market demands into site characteristics.

Design the final master plan after choosing and thoroughly analyzing the site, including doing all appropriate formal studies. That way you'll avoid the inevitable changes mandated by site conditions particular to your parcel of land. If your development's success depends on specific design factors such as density, type of housing units, or project amenities, make sure the site can support these critical factors. Site analysis and selection contain overlapping processes; the more definitive portions of site analysis are discussed in Chapter 4.

Density of housing units is one important site selection criterion. Every project has a critical range for the number of units needed to realize an adequate return on investment. From the financial feasibility study you already know the minimum number of units in a certain price range required for an acceptable profit. You also know the maximum number of units that the market can bear and you are able to build. These limits form the range for the number of units you want a potential site to support. The site's zoning classification and physical features ultimately dictate its development capacity. These site characteristics therefore become priority items to investigate when you are selecting the site.

For example, suppose you are building a development containing starter homes. Since the profit margin on each unit is smaller than that of a luxury home, you need a specific number of housing units to justify the cost of site engineering and infrastructure. If a previously undetected wetlands area is found on that site, the amount of remaining buildable land might be too small to provide the number of units required for profit.

In addition to project density and housing types, the target market's demands should influence project location, shape and size of lots, site appearance, privacy and safety requirements, and marketable amenities. Understanding these characteristics can help you choose the appropriate selection criteria to investigate for each site under consideration.

Various site conditions sometimes have a mitigating influence on one another. For example, suppose you are looking for a 25-acre site to accommodate the number of units required for your project. You find a larger site with at least 20 percent that's unbuildable. This factor is critical if the land available cannot support the project's required number of units.

However, it is not critical if the land available can support the density requirements and the cost of the land is commensurate with other sites with full development capacity. If the costs of the parcels of land are similar, having 20 percent unbuildable land may even be advantageous if you can convert it into a project amenity such as a natural buffer or nature trail.

Site in Search of Master Plan Concept

If you already own a site with potential as a successful development, you need a marketable idea that complements its characteristics. If you already have one in mind, transform the demands of the target market into site characteristics and compare them with those on your site. If both sets of characteristics do not form a good match when compared, consider a different target market or development idea.

For example, suppose you determined an appropriate demand in the target group of young married professionals with children. This group might have some specific demands about location. They want a safe, secure place not too far from necessary shopping and services—and in a good public school district. Since their life centers around their children, this characteristic becomes a top priority.

Locating in a school district perceived as less than adequate can affect your development's marketability to this group. Other site characteristics, no matter how desirable, probably won't overcome this negative one. But remember, this same location may appeal to other groups. A target market of active retired couples may be attracted to other aspects of the site's location, and for them, the school district may not be an issue.

If you own a site but have not determined the type of development that best suits it, you can follow a similar procedure to that mentioned above. The site's size, shape, location, and appearance can start you thinking of target markets to investigate as potential buyers. Come up with a list of site characteristics dictated by the potential target markets' demands and desires. Then compare the two sets of characteristics.

Three Categories of Site Characteristics

Whether you start with a development idea or a site, the process of matching a particular site with a specific development idea requires you to examine the same basic criteria. Site characteristics play a vital role in determining the type of development best suited for that unique site. In discussing the wide variety of site characteristics that influence project design and construction, the remainder of this chapter will address a development idea in search of a site.

You must examine a sometimes bewildering number of site characteristics to decide how well a certain type of development fits a particular location. Begin researching such a large amount of information by organizing it. Think of all the information as falling into one of three main categories: physical, legal and political, and offsite factors. Figure 3.1 Three Categories of Site Characteristics shows the type of information covered by each category.

Site characteristics in each of these categories will either be advantageous or detrimental to your project's development capacity and master plan concept. If detrimental, classify the characteristic as a project constraint; then weigh the methods and cost of mitigation against its impact on potential profit and the possible value of the site's positive characteristics. You can sometimes transform a project constraint into a project amenity (such as using a wetlands area as open space, giving houses privacy and attractive views). Advantageous characteristics are often classified as project opportunities. Evaluate each for its potential appeal to the target market and investigate ways to capitalize on this opportunity for maximum benefit to the project.

Members of the project team are a valuable resource for comparing a potential site's characteristics with the target market's preferences and the requirements for project design and construction. Planners, designers, engineers, and environmental and financial experts each have their own unique view of a project. Have the team develop a list of critical primary site characteristics and outline potential regulations that may affect the develop-

FIGURE 3.1. Three Categories of Site Characteristics

Category	Types of Information
Physical Factors	**Geotechnical Conditions:** Soil type and characteristics, depth to bedrock, percolation rate, hydrological characteristics, depth to water table, and sinkhole and radon potential from underlying strata
	Topographical Conditions: Desirable and undesirable slopes, elevations, sinkholes, and presence of floodplains
	Site Features: Location, water bodies, wetlands, hills and mountains, rock outcroppings, tree and vegetative cover, drainage patterns and channels, and views
	Hazards: Buried storage tanks, hazardous materials, pesticide and other chemical deposits, and high-tension power lines
	Improvements: Presence of installed utilities, roads, buildings, fences, bridges, terrace structures, boat ramps, and docks
	Site History: Prior land uses and the presence of historical or archaeological artifacts
Legal and Political Factors	**Regulatory Conditions:** Federal, state, and local regulations; guidelines in comprehensive land use plan if applicable; past and current zoning, future zoning, potential rights-of-way, and utility easements; adopted building, life, health, safety, fire protection, and landscape codes; location within any jurisdictions covered by special building codes (earthquake zones, coastal plains, hurricane zones, and historic districts)
	Political Conditions: Number and types of neighborhood associations and special interest groups interested in the property, local voting jurisdictions, and local community attitudes toward development
Off-Site Factors	Noise; offensive odors; desirable and undesirable adjacent land uses; traffic conditions; type and condition of infrastructure; and availability of public transportation, schools, and other community services

ment. They can also help you judge the potential community response and formulate strategies for presenting your new project in the best possible light to various community groups.

Physical Factors

Physical factors include all tangible site characteristics affecting project marketability, design, engineering, or construction. You can further divide this category into geotechnical conditions, topographical conditions, prominent site features, hazards, improvements, and site history.

Geotechnical conditions primarily involve the chemical and physical properties of soil and water. Topographical conditions refer to the site's slope and elevation. Site features include any prominent features such as vegetation and water bodies. Hazards describes any deleterious site condition such as buried hazardous materials. Buildings or infrastructure installed on site are included in site improvements. Finally, the category of site history includes prior land uses and any possible archaeological artifacts or historical structures present on the site.

Geotechnical Conditions

Geotechnical conditions include the geological, soil, and hydrological characteristics of your site. They affect one of the most costly aspects of a land development project—the site development work. Geotechnical conditions influence the type of infrastructure required for stormwater management, types of roads and building foundations, and the design and construction of utilities. If the geotechnical conditions on your proposed site are poor for development purposes, the cost of installing infrastructure can place the homes in a price range beyond the reach of the target market. At the very least, the cost of developing the site can render the profit from the successful sale of the project marginal or nonexistent.

Geology. The first important geological condition to consider is the type and depth of bedrock present on the site. Bedrock, the solid rock material underlying surface soils, is present at various depths below the earth's surface. For residential construction, the depth to bedrock generally has a significant effect on road building and structural foundations only when near the surface. In some areas, however, bedrock can contribute to the movement of surface land masses. For instance, sinkholes can form when water dissolves surficial layers of fractured limestone, collapsing surface soils downward. Figure 3.2 Geology Map shows the type of information typically depicted for the geology of a site.

Information on Geotechnical Conditions. In most cases, you can collect geological information to evaluate the site's development capacity from a few readily available public sources. You can get maps depicting the geology of your site from the offices of the U.S. Geological Survey. Any condition that would significantly affect the building plans for your site

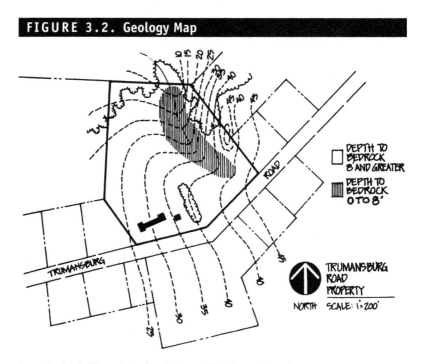

FIGURE 3.2. Geology Map

Source: Reprinted with permission from Environmental Design and Research, p.c.

is described in these maps and accompanying reports. The maps also list and show the type of bedrock and other underlying strata, allowing you to find it on your site. In some areas you can find similar maps and studies in the county engineer's office.

If negative characteristics are discovered in this preliminary phase of information gathering, consult an engineer to assess the impact on the site's development capacity. A registered professional engineer eventually has to properly design the master plan layout to receive approval from the local permitting authority. But in this preliminary phase you are primarily concerned with evaluating the site's potential to be properly engineered.

Soils. The type of soil can affect many aspects of site development and building construction. A large parcel of land may have several different soil types deposited by various natural events such as glaciers, rivers, earthquakes, and forest decay. Soils are classified into groups according to the amount of sand, silt, and clay present in the deposit. The amount of each affects the properties of the soil. You will primarily be interested in how the soil behaves under the stress created by excavation, compaction, or the load from buildings or roads. Other important aspects are the way water moves through the soil and whether the soil expands or shrinks under wet and dry conditions.

In addition, you must know the soil profile for each type of soil deposit on your site. Soil profiles are diagrams that describe the layers of soil in the vertical direction at a given location. The soils can change in one location because they are deposited in layers over time. The profile essentially gives you the physical and chemical characteristics of each soil type and its depth in inches at a certain location. Figure 3.3 Soil Profile shows the kind of information a typical profile contains about soil composition and depth.

From this profile you can determine potential problems from soils beneath the surface of your site. For example, you may have determined from walking the site that the soils are

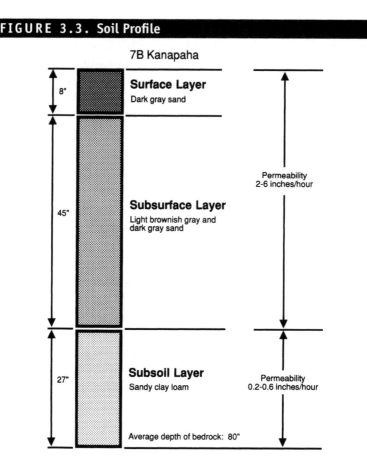

FIGURE 3.3. Soil Profile

7B Kanapaha

8"

Surface Layer
Dark gray sand

45"

Subsurface Layer
Light brownish gray and
dark gray sand

Permeability
2-6 inches/hour

27"

Subsoil Layer
Sandy clay loam

Permeability
0.2-0.6 inches/hour

Average depth of bedrock: 80"

predominantly sandy. From this you would assume these soils are well drained, a property of sandy soils. However, a layer of clay could exist at some depth, causing the filtering action of the water to slow considerably at that point and resulting in poor drainage conditions on the site.

In evaluating soil types, you look for the presence of surface or subsurface conditions that would cause the soil to move or collapse. The soil profile can reveal the existence of any soils under the surface that might cause these problems. For example, the presence of shrinking and swelling clays in an area where heavy rainfall often follows long periods of drought indicates a great potential for foundation settlement and shifting.

Information on Soils. You can find the soils on your site and the description of their properties through several public sources. Either the U.S. Natural Resources Conservation Service (NRSC), U.S. Geological Survey (USGS), or your county has classified and mapped the soils on your site. One parcel of land can contain many different kinds of soils and soil series profiles. If you find that more than one type of soil exists on your site, you need to understand which ones are best suited for roads, buildings, and drainage. The reports accompanying the maps and soil data will describe the properties of the soils as they affect these concerns. Figure 3.4 Soil Map shows how several different soil series can be found on one site.

Topographical Conditions
The slopes of a site influence where you can most cost-effectively place buildings and roads. Too steep or too flat

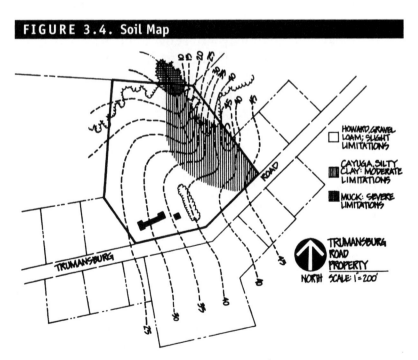

FIGURE 3.4. Soil Map

Source: Reprinted with permission from Environmental Design and Research, p.c.

slopes must be engineered to create the correct angle for your intended use. A topographic map can provide an accurate picture of the existing slope of your site; look for one that shows not only your site but also the surrounding area. Drainage patterns around the site could drastically affect the type of stormwater management systems you need for adequate drainage.

Topographic Map. A topographic map shows the site's existing contours and their elevations. It also usually indicates the location of several specific places on the site and their respective elevations, called spot elevations. Spot elevations can appear at random around the site to indicate slopes, or they can appear in special locations such as corners and low or high places. The topographic map can also convey the presence of sinkholes, caves, and drainage canals. Figure 3.5 Topographic Map with Spot Elevations shows the typical information found in most topographic studies. Note the X's that indicate spot elevations on this map.

A topographic map may also show some heavily marked lines called basin divides. In Figure 3.5, the basin divides appear as dashed lines that do not correspond with the contour lines. Instead, they show the boundaries of large areas within which water tends to drain toward the center, creating a basin-like formation. Basin divides form ridges or long lines of high points for the site; they help determine the general pattern of surface runoff and the areas to which water naturally runs. If these destinations represent the low places on the site but are not located within floodplains or designated wetlands, they will be excellent places to locate stormwater retention and detention areas.

However, if these destinations are located within floodplains or wetlands, you will probably have to divert water that naturally flows to these areas. When this occurs, consult with an engineer before going any further with your site review. If you can divert the water, you must first evaluate the cost of doing so. Floodplains or wetlands on your site means some lost development capacity in terms of unit density. Also, your profit

FIGURE 3.5. Topographic Map with Spot Elevations

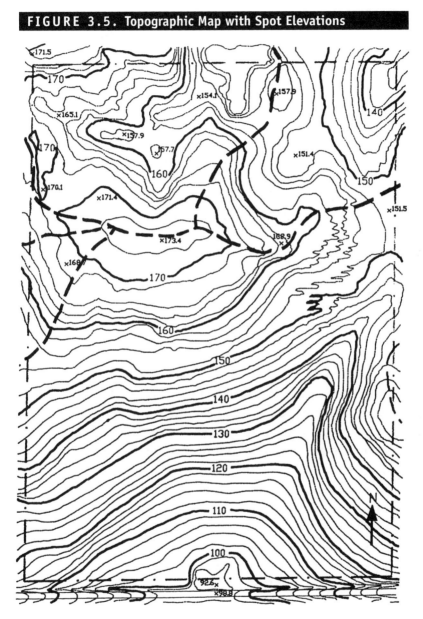

Note: This map is not drawn to scale.

could be affected if the site development costs associated with earthwork and infrastructure increase significantly. First determine if the potential marketability of the site and the subsequent profit realized warrant the costs associated with mitigating the site condition. In severe cases it may be impossible to both successfully engineering the site and still realize a profit.

Information on Topography. You can acquire topographic maps from several sources. The county engineer's office may have both topographic maps and maps of flood-prone areas for the entire county. Maps can also be ordered from USGS offices in Denver; Reston, Virginia; and Menlo Park, California. The engineer or surveyor who last surveyed the land might also have maps; many local tax rolls provide the name of the company and the date of the last survey. Any of these sources are sufficient for conducting a preliminary review to eliminate undesirable sites from your selection process.

Site Features

The site's prominent physical features include the attributes of its location and appearance. Location, one of the most important features, is critical to project marketability. Vegetation, water bodies, and special land forms all influence a site's appearance; several other factors influence the adequacy of its location. For example, at this point you may be looking for a heavily wooded site to support your idea of providing a natural setting with maximum privacy. If you are marketing homes to young families, the site's location in an excellent school district may be of utmost importance. Chapter 4 provides a more indepth discussion of these factors.

Site Location. When you began looking for a site, location was likely among your first considerations. What makes a good location? The answer is simple: A site in an area that appeals to your intended target market.

To choose a site favorable to your target market, review the group's particular concerns and lifestyle characteristics. All target groups want to live where their property will hold its value and where security and services are adequate. But beyond these considerations, you can find some distinct differences among various groups. For instance, groups with younger children often place a premium on the area's school district. Other young professionals may want close proximity to downtown offices. On the other hand, retired groups are more concerned with nearby service and recreational amenities.

Make a list of your target market's demands and desires; include services, amenities, and workplaces. Next, establish how far it prefers to travel to reach these items. Then you can determine whether the site meets most of these criteria by creating a table that lists actual travel distances to each pertinent service, amenity, and workplace. Finally, compare the actual and preferred distances to determine the adequacy of the location for your target market. Figure 3.6 Location and Travel Distances shows a typical list. The distances are rated with a plus or minus to indicate whether they have a positive or negative impact on the project's location based on the target market's preferences. As part of this analysis, be sure to consider the type, size, and density of the local community.

Keep in mind that certain areas of a city or county have locally accepted designations. These so-called territories are important to discover and understand so you can evaluate their effect on project marketability. Territorial designations such as downtown, uptown, university area, waterfront, or bay area carry specific connotations for local residents. If your project falls within one of these acknowledged territories, evaluate the image associated with it. A favorably regarded territory can give you a great marketing tool to attract buyers and actually increase the value of the homes you offer.

However, even if the general public views a certain territory favorably, one group may find it more desirable than another. For instance, locating within the urban waterfront in a large city may appeal more to singles than to married couples with children. The urban waterfront area may have been

FIGURE 3.6. Location and Travel Distances

	Actual Distances[a] (miles)	Adequacy for Target Market[b]
Services		
Major shopping center	5.5	+
Daycare facilities	5.5	+
Convenience shopping	2.3	+
Gas and car service	11.0	−
Banks	5.5	+
Hospital	7.2	+
Amenities		
Restaurants	5.5	+
Churches	3.0	+
Museum	11.5	−
Park	7.0	−
Swimming	7.0	−
Work		
Downtown	12.5	+
University area	7.2	+
Industrial park	15.0	−

a. Actual distances from a hypothetical site to services, amenities, and work.
b. Ratings are based on the target market's preferences for these distances. The evaluation of adequacy also takes into account the type, size, and density of the community.

recently restored and contain shops, restaurants, and clubs. These characteristics plus its proximity to downtown make it especially attractive to young working professionals. Its emphasis on shopping and entertainment may limit its appeal to married couples with children, who consider it merely a place to visit.

Site Appearance. Judge your site's physical appearance for its ability to contribute favorably to the desired image of your new development. For example, changing the amount and type of vegetation significantly to make the site more appealing will affect site development costs. A parcel of land devoid of trees with no mature vegetation demands a certain amount of imported landscaping, which can become expensive. On the other hand, if you are planning a high-density development on a parcel of land with thick vegetation and numerous large trees, the costs of clearing can become prohibitive.

Walk the Site. The project team should walk the site together to discuss how to lay out the lots and streets to capitalize on the site's positive aspects. Note the amount and type of vegetation, extent of the tree canopy, presence of water amenities, and any important focal points and views. Team members can also evaluate any negative aspects of the site, such as an unsightly view to an adjacent land use, and discuss cost-effective solutions such as screening. Team members should keep in mind hidden aspects such as soil type, soil permeability, and the presence of rocky underlayment discovered when the geotechnical information was gathered. The design of the streets and building placement should acknowledge both the surface features and the subsurface conditions.

The physical features of your site can have either a negative or positive effect on your project's success. For instance, if a creek runs through the parcel, restrictions may limit how close you can build to it, which may negatively impact unit density. However, the lots closest to the creek may command a much higher sales price, making up for the decreased density while adding an aesthetically pleasing element to the entire development. The target group's preferences for such features as heavily wooded rather than cleared lots or a more formal rather than natural image can help you decide the appropriateness of the site's features. You and your project team should evaluate the positive or negative contribution each condition makes in relation to development cost and project marketability.

Hazards

As important as location and appearance may be, they are only part of your decision when selecting a site. You also need to ensure that other conditions, even those that are less readily apparent, make the site usable for your intended development.

At this point, you must conduct a careful title search to determine if former uses have contributed to a problem with hazardous wastes or materials storage.

If any evidence of hazardous materials is found on your site, you will be responsible for the cost of its cleanup—unless you can prove you are an innocent landowner. An innocent landowner is one who purchased the land after the site was contaminated, was unaware of the contamination, and took all necessary precautions to ensure the site was clean before purchase. As part of taking necessary precautions, you must conduct a proper inquiry into the site's former uses. The presence of environmental pollution from hazardous materials effectively renders a site unmarketable, and the cost of proving your innocence or subsequently paying for cleanup can be financially disastrous.

To investigate a site for possible hazardous materials, follow the standards of practice for environmental site assessment published by the American Society for Testing and Materials (ASTM). This standard offers guidelines for you to follow in conducting "due diligence" to avoid liability for potential environmental contamination. The standard has two parts, which are listed and described in Figure 3.7 ASTM Environmental Due Diligence Processes.

As a first step, you should conduct a records review, including the above-mentioned title search. Consider hiring an environmental professional to conduct this data search; that person's work may be more thorough, cost-effective, and possibly more legally credible. Numerous companies review government records to identify prior land uses and any potential hazardous waste problems. For a reasonable fee, they will provide you with a written report and maps of any known environmental liabilities on the property. As part of the search, either investigate on your own or have your consultant investigate all previous zoning and thoroughly research all former owners of your site and adjoining properties.

Once satisfied that none of the former site uses have caused contamination, hire an environmental professional to conduct a Phase I study. Note that the ASTM standard of practice does

---

FIGURE 3.7. ASTM Environmental Due Diligence Processes

1. Type: Transaction Screen Process
   Source Document: ASTM Document E 1528
   Performed by: User (owner)
   Content: Questionnaire completed by owner, site visits, and records review

2. Type: Phase I Environmental Site Assessment Process
   Source Document: ASTM Document E 1527
   Performed by: Environmental professional (for example, civil engineer, soil scientist, or biologist)
   Content: Records review, site reconnaissance, interviews with current owners, evaluation, and written report

---

not cover radon, asbestos, lead, or wetlands. However, following the ASTM standard for environmental assessment can help you eliminate potentially dangerous sites and, if contamination is later discovered on the site, help you to avoid liability. In addition, your lender may require these reports as part of your loan application documents. Chapter 5 Major Environmental Regulations Affecting Development provides more information on environmental issues relating to land development.

Improvements
Many times undeveloped land acquires certain improvements due to former site uses or a development project that was begun but not completed. These improvements can range from a cleared right-of-way for a road to buildings and installed utilities. Evaluate any improvements for their possible contribution to or negative impact on the success of your project. If existing roads are not properly located or buildings are unusable, factor in the cost of demolition and removal.

Site History
Investigating the former uses of a site will allow you to determine if the land has any historic or archaeological significance. Some sites could have historic structures still standing. For others, although the structures may have disappeared, the foundations or even the location of the foundations are considered

significant. In some areas, sites in known historic districts require a historic preservation survey.

If you are considering a site in an area with archaeological significance, you may need a professional archaeologist to conduct a survey that clears the site or certain areas of it for development. Depending on your site's location, the local government or the state may require both an archaeological survey and a clearance from the state's historic preservation department.

Legal and Political Factors

Legal factors include laws, codes, ordinances, and zoning restrictions at the federal, state, and local level that dictate the way you can develop the site. Each parcel of land falls under the rules of the jurisdiction in which it is located. Carefully study these rules for their impact on the density and kind of development you want. Political factors relate to the community's attitude toward development and its willingness to accept your project.

Land development requires a number of permits and approvals from agencies at the federal, state, and local level. Understanding the complexity of the regulations that cover your project is in itself an education. The more you understand about the potential requirements, the greater your chances for project success. Armed with this knowledge, you can eliminate potentially difficult sites at an early stage. If you decide to proceed, understanding the regulations that affect your site can allow you to plan for the added cost of dealing with them—including the length of time needed to obtain approvals. In addition, you can more fully understand the costs associated with providing information to obtain the various necessary approvals and permits.

Zoning

Of the various legal requirements, the zoning for your parcel of land is critically important and must be correct for your intended use. A zoning classification describes the permitted use of the site. This legal description dictates the type of development and the placement of buildings. It sets limits on the type and number of units, building height, setbacks and easements, and percentage of the site covered by buildings. The requirements of your project must match restrictions in the zoning classification.

If the current zoning of the site is appropriate for your intended use, you should be able to go forward with your development as long as you follow the restrictions on type, number of units, and placement of roads and buildings listed in the zoning classification. Figure 3.8 Zoning Classification Restrictions shows the typical kinds of information found in a residential zoning classification.

Change in Zoning Classification. If the current zoning is inappropriate, seek a change in zoning classification. For example, undeveloped land in suburban or exurban areas often carries an agricultural classification. Before you obtain a permit for development, you must submit a request to change this to the proper zoning classification for your project.

Review the requirements of each residential zoning classification in your local zoning ordinance to determine which one best suits your project. Then decide how its chances are to succeed; talk with the city or county planning department and familiarize yourself with any laws that may affect your request.

FIGURE 3.8. Zoning Classification Restrictions

Residential Single-Family, Class I

Maximum density	4 units per acre
Minimum lot area	10,000 square feet
Minimum lot width (at building line)	65 feet
Minimum lot depth	155 feet
Minimum side-yard setback (interior)	15 feet
Minimum side-yard setback (street)	15 feet
Maximum percentage lot coverage	20%
Maximum building height	35 feet

Variance. Suppose the zoning is appropriate but a few adjustments are needed in its dimensional restrictions. You might get permission for a change in a zoning restriction on height and building placement (for instance, altering a required setback or height limitation by a few feet) if you can demonstrate that applying zoning requirements to your site creates a hardship. For example, if you demonstrate that in one or two places the building you propose needs to encroach upon a setback by 1 or 2 feet, you could receive permission to do so if it means your entire project cannot go forward otherwise. Under this circumstance, you may petition the local authority to approve a slight change in the dimensional requirement, one which does not constitute a health, safety, or environmental problem. This kind of a change in the dimensions of the design standards is called a variance and is not easy to obtain. Talk with the local planning department to assess the difficulty of obtaining any needed variances for your site.

Planned Growth

Local governments continue to seek a greater role in the design of their cities and townships to ensure that each area has adequate infrastructure, functions well, and has a pleasant appearance. In the early 1980s, some local areas enacted growth management laws to accomplish this. Growth management describes methods of controlling the pace, timing, and location of development relative to infrastructure availability and the physical nature of the development, including lot size, density, and street widths.

The concept of growth management is not new, but it's been receiving increased attention for its role in managing local development. Growth management laws originally began at the local level in states like Oregon, New Jersey, and Florida, where large influxes of population over a short period taxed local government's ability to keep up with the immediate demand for infrastructure and public services.

Growth management laws can be enacted at the state and local level. These laws center around the idea that local government should manage growth to ensure the proper use of community resources. That way local government can prevent the overloading of infrastructure; control the timing, location, and fiscal impacts of rapid development; and have greater influence over the design of new neighborhoods.

Comprehensive Land Use Plan

In many areas, you will have to familiarize yourself with the local comprehensive land use plan. These local master plans describe the community's vision of itself in 10 or 20 years. They are intended to provide long-term guidelines for all elements of future residential, commercial, institutional, and industrial development. They can also cover parks, roads, utilities, police and fire protection, schools, and other necessary support services required by the community. They can indicate what specific zoning changes might be acceptable in each area in the future.

You need to understand the community's vision as described in its comprehensive plan so that you can propose an appropriate project. If zoning or other growth controls are inconsistent with that vision, you may be able to change them. Comprehensive plans sometimes also provide guidelines and rules designed to protect the area's environmental quality. These can include provisions regulating development within certain watershed areas, along certain recognized bodies of water, and within sensitive ecosystems. You should know the local plan so you can include some of its elements in your own development or construct arguments that mitigate the lack of those elements.

The Purpose of Comprehensive Plans. The growing use of comprehensive plans and increased regulation of land development results from two major concerns: the quality of the environment and the impact of uncontrolled growth on quality of life. The first concern has led to an array of environmental regulations on land development. The second has addressed such quality-of-life issues as a community's ability to provide adequate schools, roads, fire and police protection, and other services. Be aware that the local, state, and federal government all can require approvals and permits to regulate environmental protection and manage growth. Comprehensive plans manifest this activity at the local level.

Comprehensive Plans and Zoning. Local comprehensive plans have varying degrees of power over zoning changes. In many areas they are simply guidelines for growth. In others they may more directly influence development by actually limiting the allowable zoning classifications. In a few states such as Oregon, New Jersey, and Florida, a state agency reviews and approves local plans to make sure they follow the intent of the state's growth management laws. Once the local plans are approved by the state agency review board, they determine the future zoning and infrastructure for every parcel of land in that area.

The comprehensive plan might be a legal document that establishes intent pertaining to how an area might be developed. For example, it might specify a limit on vehicles using existing roads or simply designate a certain area industrial or residential. In that case, the zoning you request must conform in every way with the intent of the plan. In other areas, the comprehensive plan might merely be a guideline for the uses a variety of zoning classifications might fit.

A local area's comprehensive plan can raise several important zoning considerations. For example, if a community adopts a new comprehensive plan, it will likely include new guidelines for zoning ordinances and a map. In some cases, however, if the zoning does not conform to the proposed land use described in the comprehensive plan, the plan could weaken the validity of a current zoning classification. Under these circumstances, you should use the comprehensive plan to support a petition for a zoning change. At the same time, the comprehensive plan could prevent you from obtaining a new zoning classification for a parcel of land if that classification does not conform with plan provisions.

If the zoning classification you require does not conform with the local comprehensive plan, you must determine the plan's strength in land development in that area. In any case, it is best to become thoroughly familiar with the plan, even when it's merely a planning tool with no legal power over zoning changes. Having your proposed zoning change conform with the ideas found in the plan will strengthen your position.

Subdivision Ordinances

After you feel confident that you can secure the correct zoning classification for your intended parcel of land, you should obtain a copy of the local subdivision ordinance. Most residential development requires dividing an undeveloped parcel of land into smaller pieces or lots. Providing roads and utilities is also required. For this reason, local governments have adopted subdivision ordinances that provide design and construction standards that must be met to obtain project approval. These standards regulate the dimensions and geometry of lots, dimensions of all setbacks, and amount of buildable area.

They also regulate the dimensions and geometry of streets, curb and gutter design, infrastructure design for stormwater management, and utility placement and design. In some local jurisdictions, zoning and subdivision regulations are combined into a unified development ordinance.

Infrastructure Requirements. Many local comprehensive plans provide for project approval based on the presence and capacity of various types of required infrastructure. Some local laws require that appropriate infrastructure be in place before a project moves forward. Sometimes referred to as concurrency laws, these require you to determine if the city or county has installed accessible power, gas, potable water, sanitary sewer, and stormwater mains and if they have the capacity to service your project. You must also determine the condition and design capacity of the roads that would serve your project and the impact your project would have on their service capacity. If your parcel of land falls within an area where services are overloaded or not yet present, the local government may have the authority to refuse to allow your project.

Contributing Infrastructure. In some areas of the country you can win project approval by supplying missing infrastructure. For example, if the project requires a turning lane on the frontage road for safe ingress and egress, you can offer to construct it, then dedicate it to the city or county for maintenance. However, with local budgets tight, don't be surprised if your offer to construct certain types of infrastructure is refused because the local government lacks the funds for maintenance.

All the same, review costs to determine whether the project can bear some kind of contribution of infrastructure when this becomes part of negotiating project approval with the local government. In the past this procedure has been accomplished by oral agreements in meetings and review processes. Now many areas use written contracts that spell out infrastructure contributions and allowances for a planned development.

Infill and Redevelopment Development. In some local areas, project approval becomes easier when the project is located where infrastructure already exists. In the past, development moved away from the center of town, creating suburbs, and communities extended the infrastructure to service new projects. When cities began to face the increasing costs of supplying infrastructure to new developments, attitudes began to change toward extending development outward in an unlimited fashion. This concept of saving costs associated with providing new infrastructure is part of the reason that infill development is encouraged today.

Infill development refers to the construction of new projects on undeveloped parcels of land found interspersed among previously developed areas. It can also mean an adaptive reuse of a previously developed parcel of land (redevelopment). Infill projects generally have infrastructure already in place. In heavily developed areas, first determine whether the existing infrastructure design capacity can handle new development, before assuming you have all the services required.

Contiguous Property

Besides the zoning classification and subdivision ordinance requirements particular to your own site, consider those of surrounding properties. Because their development potential can greatly influence the market value of your site, you should determine regulatory requirements for both. Make sure the surrounding land will be developed for uses that complement the master plan for your project. Also evaluate the character of existing development around your project. Regional tolerances vary for the degree of uniformity of surrounding properties. For example, in many areas of the country, a luxury home development can be placed adjacent to a mobile home community without fear of target market disapproval. In other areas, this cannot be done with any success.

Overlapping Regulations

One of the challenges of understanding and complying with regulations is the large number of agencies that have jurisdiction over your project. In many parts of the country, federal, state, and local regulatory agencies have overlapping jurisdictions and standards. Frequently they fail to provide a single source of information, and one particular development activity may require multiple permits from several different agencies. That's especially true of any activity affecting the environment. In addition, one agency's standards often turn out to be more stringent than another's.

Approaching the Problem. First develop a complete list of agencies that grant permits for each particular development activity your project requires. Then review the requirements for each permit and approval to understand the standards set forth and pinpoint any areas where they overlap or conflict. Once you know this, you can determine which set of standards governs in situations where jurisdictions overlap. Adhering to the most stringent standards—in effect complying with the standards at all levels—often proves the safest approach.

Gathering Information. Because of the increasing complexity of regulations affecting development, many local governments have designed programs to streamline the initial information-gathering phase. In some cases, the city or county may have a manual or list that outlines steps in the permitting process of associated departments and agencies. In other cases department representatives hold an initial meeting with a developer and discuss permitting and approval requirements for developing the intended parcel of land. These initial meetings—sometimes called first-step programs or preapplication meetings—save time for all parties.

If the local area does not have a first-step program, you need to meet with each department separately. If you can bring representatives of each department together for an initial meeting about the requirements placed on your project, you can in effect initiate your own first-step program. Regardless of the organizational structure of the city or county, you should begin at the local level in your search for permitting and approval requirements. Local departments such as the county engineer, planning, and public works offices usually have a working knowledge of the permits required at all levels for various development activities.

Political Factors

In today's atmosphere of heightened citizen awareness and participation in local government decision making, gaining a reputation as a good neighbor benefits your project's success. Take time to evaluate the political factors surrounding your project. To do this, you need to determine how the community perceives the project's impacts on the surrounding area. Community acceptance of a new development can be critical to your schedule. Understanding the concerns of all affected groups allows you to develop an appropriate strategy with the goal being to reach consensus among groups that may potentially object to your development.

Community's Attitude. The community's attitude can aid or slow the local government's progress toward project approval. Elected city and county commissioners pay close attention to the concerns of their constituency, oftentimes through public hearings. You need to present your project as a positive addition to the community. Figure 3.9 Sample Review Process for Petition for Change in a Zoning and Land Use Plan shows a flow chart of a typical procedure for obtaining a zoning reclassification. Notice the number of places where a public hearing can occur in the review process.

Community's Reaction. The potential problems with community acceptance of your project vary. That area may have special meaning to groups in the local community, causing them to view with some apprehension any changes represented by new development. Your project may suffer from being the last one proposed in a highly developed area. People in the community may perceive your new project in a less-than-positive light because they are concerned about the potential for increased traffic and population or harm to the environment. Understanding the potential response to your project can help you ward off any negative campaigns against its approval and allow you to work toward gaining community support.

Mitigating Strategy. To gain community support, first determine the likely reaction to your project from special interest groups and surrounding neighborhood associations. Attend their meetings or send representatives. Learn about their misgivings. Negative attitudes often develop because people are misinformed or uninformed. Provide information that places your project in a positive light and shows how your development plans respond to their concerns. This requires time and effort but will pay off in the long run. Listen to people's questions and doubts and attempt to address their legitimate concerns, and you can be seen as a good neighbor.

Perhaps you face a negative reaction to part of your development, say the number of units or the location of the entrance. Develop strategies and trade-offs to lessen this

FIGURE 3.9. Sample Review Process for Petition for Change in a Zoning and Land Use Plan

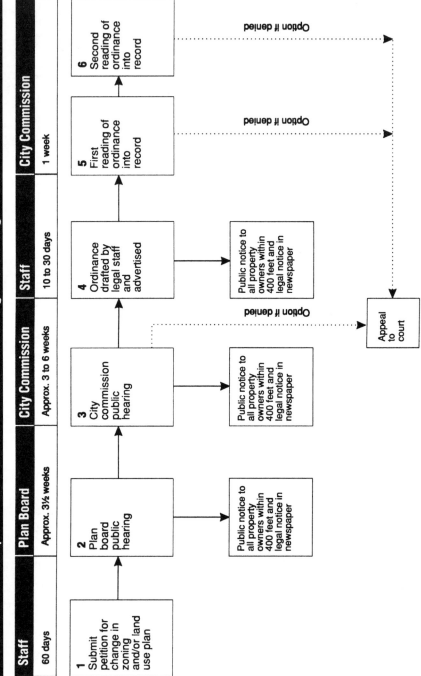

negative perception and gain community approval. Meet with city and county planners to determine how to approach the community and its concerns. At the meetings, listen for ways to assuage public concerns. For example, if a contiguous neighborhood association expresses concern about losing the privacy provided by your site's mature vegetation, perhaps you can provide a more extensive buffer than is required by zoning restrictions. Leaving a 50-foot strip of trees instead of the required 20 feet may appease the neighborhood association while enhancing the value of the adjoining lots on your own property.

If opposition to your project continues in spite of your best efforts, evaluate whether to go forward. Many times you cannot get a complete consensus among opposing groups. If other site selection criteria are favorable to your project and the market potential looks promising, consider budgeting the time and money necessary for dealing with the protracted opposition. If you have not purchased the land already, negotiate a flexible purchase contract contingent upon final approval by the local government.

Offsite Factors

Offsite factors can either enhance or detract from your project's marketability. Locating near a park, waterfront area, or popular shopping district might increase the development's desirability. That's especially true if your target group considers the adjacent land uses to be highly favorable. Having sufficient utilities available to the homeowner provides another positive offsite factor. What about the condition of roads and streets around the development—another critical factor to consider.

Negative Offsite Factors

The presence of negative offsite factors tends to influence project viability more than the absence of positive ones. Each target market has varying tolerances for negative offsite factors, which include the security associated with an area, undesirable environmental impacts from adjacent or nearby land uses, and other land uses perceived to promote crime, health hazards, or traffic problems.

Undesirable land uses may produce offensive odors, generate too much noise, or provide unwanted views. Carefully gauge the potential impact of proximity to such undesirable factors as industrial land uses, transmission lines, and landfills. If negative offsite factors are present, decide whether you can protect the project by buffering noise, providing safe access, or obscuring bad views. Next, carefully evaluate each negative offsite physical characteristic for its impact on the intended target market. You should also consider the methods and costs of mitigating the negative characteristic.

Special Studies

As you initially determine project feasibility, you may need to conduct a variety of special studies to discover specific site constraints. These studies could cover any physical, legal and political, and offsite factors for the site. Local government or lenders may mandate a particular study in some cases. Requirements for special studies have increased due to the proliferation of environmental and growth management regulations. The following special studies represent some of the more common ones you may have to perform initially to determine the likelihood of your project's approval. Where your project is located primarily influences the exact kind and number of special studies required.

Environmental Impact Studies

The environmental impact statement (EIS) is a comprehensive study that evaluates the project's impact on all aspects of the environment, including water quality, air quality, noise, wildlife and botanical ecosystems, and social and economic conditions. Many states have mandatory requirements for filing these studies for certain types of projects. Depending on the state, these may include large residential projects with regional impact and those located in areas designated as environmentally sensitive. Under federal law, an EIS can be required for federal or private projects with substantial federal involvement. The National Environmental Policy Act (NEPA) controls the EIS process for projects supported with federal funds.

Have this study conducted by a professional environmental specialist with previous experience in producing environmental impact statements. Where an EIS is not essential, consider conducting a lower level of analysis in the form of an environmental assessment. This can provide information to your lender, other investors, and the local government to show your project complies with good standards of practice for environmental protection.

Stormwater Management Plan

Local governments have historically provided infrastructure for the disposal of stormwater runoff. However, fiscal constraints make local government no longer a sure bet for providing stormwater management systems for your project. While you may sometimes be able to discharge all or a portion of site runoff into infrastructure provided by the local government, many parts of the country require the developer to provide that infrastructure. And, because of increased environmental problems with stormwater runoff and local government's inability to fund adequate infrastructure, you will most likely need to submit a stormwater management plan before a zoning reclassification is issued.

Even in areas where this may not be so, particular situations may warrant one. These situations include sites located in a sensitive watershed area or an area where past development's inadequate stormwater management has created flooding problems. A site that contains or is adjacent to wetlands also requires a stormwater management plan. Figure 3.10 Stormwater Management Checklist provides a list of preliminary questions you should answer before deciding whether your site is feasible for the intended project.

Wetlands Review

If your site contains areas that appear to be wetlands, determine their location to evaluate the potential impact on your devel-

FIGURE 3.10. Stormwater Management Checklist

☐ Does the property contain any designated wetlands?
☐ Is the property adjacent to any designated wetlands?
☐ Is a floodplain boundary located on the property?
☐ What classification is the floodplain? 100-year? 25-year?
☐ What are the local restrictions for discharging water into a floodplain?
☐ Does the property contain any low-lying areas suitable for stormwater disposal?
☐ Is the area adequate for stormwater disposal and containment?
☐ Is the drainage in the watershed used as a source of drinking water?
☐ Are the slopes and types of soils conducive to open systems?
☐ Can you discharge any stormwater into city or county infrastructure? How much?
☐ What is the design storm for calculating stormwater runoff?
☐ Does your state administer the National Pollutant Discharge Elimination System (NPDES) program or do you need to obtain NPDES permits from the federal Environmental Protection Agency?
☐ Do local standards require measures to clean stormwater before it is discharged?

opment. At this point you do not need a surveyed wetlands boundary. Instead, you need to know the approximate location and coverage of wetlands on your site. First determine if federally regulated wetlands are present. Your environmental consultant can assist with this analysis.

Next, together with your environmental consultant, determine whether you have any state-regulated wetlands. Many states have programs that determine and classify wetlands according to size, amount and type of water retained, and plants and animals present. Then obtain an approved classification of the wetlands from the proper state agency and review the wetland boundaries to see if state and federal boundaries correspond or appear different. If you intend to dredge or fill wetlands as part of your development activities, you must determine the extent of dredging, the amount of fill, and the proper agencies that permit those activities.

Traffic Studies

Besides having an impact on the environment, all projects contribute to the vehicular loading or amount of traffic on roads and streets. The county or city engineer maintains a standard by which to measure your project's impact on the existing road system. This standard will be measured in average daily traffic (ADT) or vehicles per day (VPD). The number of units you propose determines the number of ADT or VPD. The city or county engineer can then determine the impact ADT and VPD will have on the design capacity of the frontage road. Even if the local government does not require a traffic study, these numbers are important because neighbors frequently oppose a new development based on the number of cars it will load onto the existing roads and streets.

Tree Surveys

Local tree preservation and landscape ordinances are quite common now. They provide standards and codes for installing landscaping and saving or replacing natural vegetation. They also usually contain a list of tree species and associated diameters that must be protected. To meet ordinance requirements, you often must first conduct a tree survey, specifically locating all pertinent mature trees on your intended site. If you plan to leave large areas of trees undisturbed, try to avoid expensive tree inventories in those areas to reduce your initial costs. Different ordinances have different requirements for how many and which trees you can ultimately move, so be sure to check your local ordinances before taking any action.

Sources of Information for Special Studies

Where to find information about special studies varies from location to location. However, the best place to begin is with local authorities. If the community in which you plan to develop does not have an organized orientation or first-step program, meet with the county or city planner who has responsibility over the district where your project is located. Planners have a general overview of an area's problems and the procedures involved. They can then direct you to the various relevant departments, and you can again set up meetings to learn about their requirements.

For environmental regulations, you can also get help locally from the county or city. In addition, many federal agencies have regional or local offices. These are excellent sources of information on a range of environmental regulations that could affect your development activities. Another good source is the state department of environmental regulation. A few phone calls can help you understand the various types and locations of regulatory agencies that may be involved. For additional sources of information, see Figure 3.11 Sources of Information for Special Studies.

FIGURE 3.11. Sources of Information for Special Studies

Topic	Source
Zoning and Land Use Plans	County or city planning department Public library Local college library Local economic development office
Topographic, Plat, and Hydrological Maps	County or city engineer's office Map library at local college Regional utility company Previous surveys by local surveyor U.S. Geological Survey
Utilities	County or city public works department Regional utility company County or city engineer's office Local surveyor's office
Roads and Streets	County or city engineer's office Map library at local college Local surveyor's office
Traffic Counts	County or city engineer's office Recent market studies produced by county or city
Tree or Landscape Ordinance	County or city planning department Public library

Geographic Information Systems

In some areas, the local government has or is in the process of computerizing in one place its information on all local physical, legal and political, and offsite factors. The system often contains overlays of plat, topographic, and hydrological maps of a particular parcel of land. Information found on the tax rolls and in some cases demographic information are also included. This system is called a geographic information system or GIS.

GIS allows a user to key in an address or a site's tax parcel number and access a variety of maps and information about it. Where this system is in place, it can save the developer a great deal of time. Since it eliminates the necessity of gathering this information from a multitude of offices, it can also save the city or county time and money. GIS will likely become more common for larger cities and counties in the future as systems are perfected and production costs lowered.

In addition to county and city uses, many larger architecture, engineering, and planning firms also use GIS systems. These systems standardize information and map scales, allowing information to be easily transferred from city or county sources to the firm and back for changes and approvals.

Evaluating Preliminary Site Data

In deciding whether a particular site can support a known type of development, you and your project team should determine the most critical set of site characteristics to investigate. Assume at this point that you know enough about the target market to understand a few basic requirements for the development, such as the number, cost, and sales price of the units; lot sizes; required amenities and their costs; and basic master plan layouts. These basic requirements will drive the type of preliminary site information needed as you decide whether to purchase the site or develop a previously owned one. You should also have conceptual guidelines for the range of costs associated with land purchase and improvements for the type of product you intend to offer. Now you are ready to evaluate the site information.

Organizing Site Data

In determining the amount and type of information you need to make a final decision about your site, you first need a thorough understanding of how each piece contributes to project success. To begin, organize information requirements into physical, legal and political, and offsite factors. After gathering each piece of preliminary data, evaluate its effect on the other important project parameters.

Collecting preliminary site information focuses your search on only the information required for land purchase or project fit. Use your project team to the fullest. Since so much information may be collected as part of this process, avoid gathering extraneous information, which will hold down project costs. The type of information you gather influences certain aspects of your project. Figure 3.12 Site Selection Process illustrates some of the various types of information that may be gathered and what each determines and influences.

FIGURE 3.12. Site Selection Process

Type of Information	Determines	Influences
Market study	Type and size of master plan, target market characteristics	Parcel size, location, physical features
Market and financial feasibility studies	Density of units required for profit, lot size, type of project amenities	Parcel size, land price, physical features
Review of physical factors	Feasibility of master plan, density of units	Parcel size, location, land price
Review of legal and political factors	Density and type of units allowed, code requirements, feasibility of master plan	Parcel size, location
Review of offsite factors	Master plan design, type of target market	Project cost

Decision Matrix

Whether you begin with a site or a master plan concept, you are testing the fit of a particular site with a particular market idea. This can involve many characteristics, any of which can influence the other. For preliminary investigations, try to work with a limited set of parameters but choose them carefully for their importance to project success. To do so, use some method of ordering the information about each parameter and evaluating the effect of each on the other.

A decision matrix offers one method for testing the fit of a master plan concept. In a decision matrix, you assign each site characteristic a weighted average that reflects its relative importance. The weighted averages can be ranked according to cost, desirability, undesirability, demand, and target market preferences. To design a decision matrix, identify the following items:

- essential demands of the target market
- essential site characteristics necessary to support those demands
- essential physical, legal and political, and offsite factors necessary to accomplish the master plan concept and program
- unessential but desirable requirements of the target market

Target Market Characteristics. As one example, suppose you have identified a target group with the following characteristics: active, married professional adults; income range of $90,000 to $125,000 per year; 50 to 65 years old; anticipating retirement within several years or recently retired; and children no longer at home. This group anticipates at least one major life change in the form of retirement. The cost of college expenses for their children has taken or is currently taking a significant toll on their finances.

Consider this a move-down group. They no longer need the same amount of space as when their children were home. They have equity in their current homes, which they can use to lower mortgage payments for their new homes. They are looking for ways to decrease their monthly expenses while maintaining a similar standard of living. Figure 3.13 Target Market Characteristics outlines this group's demands and desires. Use this approach to outline the demands and desires of your own particular target market.

Site Characteristics. Reviewing this group's market characteristics reveals some primary concerns about your site. Holding down land acquisition and development costs is a significant goal. The price of homes for this group may range from $150,000 to $200,000, so you can only realize an adequate profit if you hold down the development costs. Since the quality of the school district does not affect this group,

---

FIGURE 3.13. Target Market Characteristics

Demographic Data
- 50 to 65 years old
- Married
- No children at home
- $90,000 to $125,000 income
- Professionals

Psychographic Data
- Anticipating major life change
- Concerned about money for retirement
- Worried about having to settle for less in a home
- No time for home maintenance because of work or travel
- Children will visit occasionally

Demands
- Lower mortgage rate than currently paying
- Smaller, low-maintenance lots
- Flexible rooms

Desires
- Quality image
- Reduced maintenance requirements
- Recreational amenities
- Safe, secure environment

---

you have more flexibility in choosing site locations. This may also lower land costs because land located in desirable school districts frequently commands a higher price.

This targeted group may prefer the land to have mature vegetation rather than wait for imported landscaping to mature. Not having to rely on imported landscaping can also hold down your project costs. This group will likely be more willing to live farther away from the primary working district than young professionals would be, but it still wants nearby services, shopping, and medical facilities. Finally, as experienced home buyers, members of this group are more aware of site characteristics that can affect their own costs. For example, they may be concerned about energy efficiency produced by proper solar orientation of the homes, soil conditions that may lead to foundation settlement or the presence of radon gas, and potential flood conditions.

Figure 3.14 Criteria for Site Selection shows a list of critical site characteristics related to the demands and desires of the target market. Again, use these criteria to determine the critical site characteristics for your own target market.

Creating the Matrix. From this preliminary study of the way target market characteristics translate into site characteristics, you can then design a site selection matrix. As one example, Figure 3.15 Site Selection Matrix identifies three potential sites. It first lists the site selection characteristics and ranks them with 1 to 3 points for each site, 3 being the best rank. The figure next assigns each characteristic a weight of importance based on its critical influence on the development as determined by your analysis of market demand. This ranking ranges from 1 to 5 points, with 5 being the most important.

You can then score each site by multiplying rank by weight for each characteristic. The highest possible score in each category is 15 points. Then total the scores in each category; consider the site with the highest score the most desirable. Notice that some characteristics are found on almost any list while others directly relate to the target market. Also, a site may be

FIGURE 3.14. Criteria for Site Selection

Location: Is the site located in an area that can serve the target market? Is the site located in a desirable area that can hold its value?

Size: Does the site have the minimum amount of acres required for the planned development while not being too large?

Acquisition Cost: What is the total cost of land with adequate buildable area to support the planned development?

Number of Owners: How many different parcels and owners of the site would have to agree to sell? Can you obtain a clear title to each property?

Zoning: Does past, present, and future zoning potential present any problems for the required density and use?

Former Site Uses: Will previous uses of the site require additional development costs to mitigate or in any way adversely affect the quality of life?

Topography: Do the natural contours support or hinder the planned development? Does the site drain naturally? Does the site provide topographic relief or views?

Soil Conditions: Will the soil conditions adversely affect development costs?

Flood Potential, Wetlands: Is the site located in a floodplain? Does the site require Federal Emergency Management Agency (FEMA) permitting or wetlands review and permitting?

Vegetation: Does the site possess desirable mature vegetation? What percentage of the site is covered with vegetation? If site vegetation is inadequate, what is the cost of importing landscape materials?

Existing Utilities: Are city or county utilities present and available for use? If public utilities are unavailable, can your project afford privately installed utilities?

Existing Roads: Are existing frontage roads in good condition? Can they handle both access and the impact of the planned development? Do the frontage roads have easy access to freeway or major arterial roads?

Proximity to Services: Is the site located within an acceptable travel distance to required services?

Proximity to Amenities: Is the site located within an acceptable travel distance to any desired amenities?

Adjacent Property Uses: What are the adjacent properties used for? Will they adversely or favorably affect the quality of life and value of property?

Adjacent Property Values: Are the surrounding property values of comparable worth or better?

eliminated if it receives a very low score or zero for one or more key characteristics like code compliance even if it receives high scores for the other characteristics.

Starting with the Site

If you already own a site that you believe has potential for residential development, use your decision matrix to choose an appropriate target market. A preliminary review of the site characteristics can determine potentially suitable target markets. The most important site characteristics to study in the beginning are location, size, amount of buildable area, and zoning criteria.

FIGURE 3.15. Site Selection Matrix

Criteria	Weight	Site 1	Site 2	Site 3
Location	5	5	15	10
Size	5	5	15	10
Acquisition cost	4	12	8	4
Number of owners	1	2	3	2
Zoning	4	8	12	8
Former site uses	1	2	3	2
Topography	1	3	1	2
Soil conditions	2	4	4	4
Flood potential, wetlands	4	8	12	12
Vegetation	2	6	4	6
Existing utilities	3	3	9	6
Existing roads	2	4	6	4
Proximity to services	2	2	6	4
Proximity to amenities	2	2	6	4
Adjacent property uses	3	6	6	9
Adjacent property values	3	3	9	9
Total Points		**75**	**119**	**96**

Note: Use the following steps to create this matrix: 1. Rank the criteria from 1 to 3 points for each site, with 3 being the best rank. 2. Assign the criteria a weight of importance for the target market from 1 to 5 points, with 5 being the most important. 3. Multiply rank by weight for each criterion and site. 4. Total the scores for each site; the one with the highest score is the most desirable.

For example, a site located near the downtown workplace and near good traffic arteries may be a prime location for a condominium or townhouse development marketed to single, young professionals. A site located away from the downtown work area and near suburban services and amenities with high aesthetic appeal may be more appropriate for development as a retirement community.

The site's location factors can help determine its suitability for different target groups. After generating a list of potential target markets, carefully review each group's location demands for compatibility. Check size, buildable area, physical appearance, and zoning criteria accordingly.

Then determine the site's capacity for the type of development you have in mind; compare it with the company's financial and personnel capacity. To do that, design a decision matrix similar to the one shown in Figure 3.15 in which you rank the important site characteristics your potential target market requires against your site's actual characteristics. This way, you can once again test the fit of the site's characteristics and your master plan concept with the demands of a particular target market.

Site Selection and the Target Market

The type of information used in selecting a site for a development depends on both target market characteristics and the site itself. Each development idea has certain requirements, and your project team should evaluate the site's fit with the program's master plan requirements to identify characteristics critical for site selection.

Once you have decided a particular parcel of land suits a specific idea for a new development, your team is ready to conduct a more extensive site analysis. This analysis provides the direction for the final layout of the master plan and the associated costs of development. The type of information gathered during site selection can guide you and the team in making definitive design and cost decisions during the subsequent site analysis.

4

Site
Analysis

Once you decide a particular site suits your new development idea, you must to perform a thorough analysis of its characteristics for their influence on the final layout. Your preliminary investigation showed no significant physical, legal and political, or offsite factors that would prevent your project from going forward and realizing a profit. You are satisfied that any problems discovered in the preliminary investigation can be cost-effectively managed. Remember, no site is completely free of characteristics that pose project constraints. If you are confident about the marketability of your idea and its compatibility with the site in general, you should be able to produce a successful master plan.

The detailed site analysis represents a critical stage in land development. Now is when you discover any previously undetected constraints that may significantly change some aspect of your master plan. Now is also the time to decide specifically how to capitalize on the site's unique features. Information from the site analysis guides the design team's decisions as it produces the final master plan. The master plan synthesizes your development idea's design components with a unique set of site characteristics. This chapter describes how to gather and analyze the additional site data and use it to produce the final master plan.

Gathering Additional Data

Although you already have a concept for your new development in mind, you may not yet have fully considered specific site characteristics. To engineer the site for streets and utilities, and to develop the final lot layout, you must now fully document all site conditions affecting project design. Their location and type will determine in part the location and configuration of the project's streets and houses.

Project Design

The detailed site investigation should confirm the location of buildable and unbuildable areas, natural circulation patterns related to topography, drainage patterns, and important views. The design decisions, in turn, will incorporate this information. Although you should avoid designing the master plan according only to site dictates, your project design team can take the ideas behind the master plan concept and adapt them to the site. Acknowledging natural features produces a more interesting project design and presents opportunities for design amenities not previously apparent.

Project Costs

Investigating site conditions can also help you manage project costs more effectively. You'll find it more cost-effective to discover the potential effect site conditions can have on the final master plan layout before you produce the final design and construction documents or actually start the work. Producing design and construction documents when you know the site conditions is far less costly than making changes later as each unforeseen site condition appears.

Increased costs due to these unforeseen site conditions can result in additional architect's and engineer's fees, removal and replacement of installed work, and additional labor and materials. Unless your budget takes this additional work into account, cash-flow and profit predictions might become invalid. Accounting for these before work is underway gives greater assurance that cash flow predictions and schedules are accurate. That makes it one of the best reasons for justifying the time and cost of a careful site analysis.

Also remember, as data are collected, that each piece of data can influence the others. Once you have completed the detailed site analysis, you need to synthesize all data into a coherent form in which critical factors outweigh lesser ones. Critical factors include any site conditions that affect project costs and profits or target market demands. For example, if your project is located in a highly desirable area, the project can afford to bear some added costs for developing on poor site conditions due to the area's higher lot sales prices.

Site Analysis Tools

To begin the site analysis, obtain the most current and definitive documentation of the site's existing conditions. First review the maps and reports you obtained from the county or city, public utilities, and other public sources in your preliminary investigation. These can include floodplain, flood-prone area, topographic, soil, hydrological, and utility maps. Plat maps, tax role maps, and old surveys may also be included. Plat maps show the official subdivided parcels of land for planning or tax purposes. The tax office may also have maps for assessing taxes. You can then use all the maps you have already collected from various sources during site selection for the first phase of site analysis.

Current Maps

Because local government budgets are tight, the maps they produce may not be current or to the degree of accuracy required by your site analysis. Find out whether a significant amount of development has occurred since each map was produced. This could affect the boundaries of floodplains and frequently flooded areas and the location of existing and proposed infrastructure. If you think a map has outdated information, first check with the planning department. While it may not have a more current map, the local planner may know of any changes in the area since the latest maps were produced. Even if the map information seems current, check with the planning department for the latest development and infrastructure plans in your site area.

Drawings and Tests

Once you have gathered all the information available, it becomes apparent which new drawings and tests you'll need to commission from various professionals. In most cases that means having new maps and drawings produced; others will require only professional interpretation of existing data from other sources. When you have to create your own maps during site analysis, always have them drawn to the same scale. That way, you can turn your maps of individual site conditions into overlays and create one consolidated map of all site conditions.

To start the process, divide the kinds of information you need for your analysis into the original categories you listed in selecting your site: physical, legal and political, and offsite factors. Your development team can then accurately assess the types of new information required to produce the documents for your project's final master plan.

Land Survey

In gathering new documents, you should commission a new or updated land survey and legal description for the site. A land survey, a type of site drawing, produced by a registered surveyor or engineer, establishes legal boundaries of a property. It's considered part of the legal description of the property, so you'll need to commission a new one to ensure that information is current and consistent. A legal description describes in writing the location of the site boundaries in terms of their length, direction, angle, and other established legal landmarks. This new survey and legal description will establish the actual boundaries of your site and provide the exact dimensions that all maps and drawings must follow.

If the drawing is produced by hand, having the survey drawn at the same scale as the topographic map allows your civil engineer to more cost-effectively produce a base map of the combined information. All subsequent maps can then become overlays to this base map. If your design team uses computer-aided drafting, overlays and changes are easily accomplished. The survey should display a scale, indicate north, and show the presence of any benchmarks. It should also show the location of contiguous streets, property, and alleys. Any existing structures or roads on the property, the location of easements and rights-of-way, and any unique site features should also appear.

Physical Factors

You are now ready to document and evaluate indepth the site's specific physical characteristics. In your preliminary analysis you determined the basic characteristics of drainage patterns, slope, soil conditions, and any floodplains and wetlands to determine the broad perimeters of what is buildable and unbuildable. Now you must specify the exact locations of those various conditions. Evaluate both surface and subsurface conditions simultaneously. Together they will determine the location and cost of installing roads, utilities, and buildings.

Soils, topography, and prominent site features are interrelated in terms of where you place roads, utilities, and buildings. Locate each of these elements of your master plan on soils that will be conducive to construction and on slopes that are within the minimum and maximum range for the intended use as stipulated by local codes and design standards. You will decrease site development costs significantly if you can locate buildings and infrastructure on appropriate soils and slopes. At the same time, factor in the location of desirable physical features such as mature vegetation and water bodies as you make your final decisions on road, utility, and building placement.

Topography

The original source of topographic information you most likely used in your preliminary investigation was U.S. Geological Survey maps. The USGS produces these maps at scales of 1:2,000 or 1 inch equals 2,000 feet. You now need a topographic map produced at a larger scale of anywhere from 1:30 to 1:200; the size and shape of your site will determine the maximum scale of your map. Producing this map requires the services of a registered surveyor or engineer. Figure 4.1 Data for New Topographic Map shows the range of data your new map should show.

Slope Analysis. The new topographic map allows you to perform an accurate slope analysis of your site and determine the best areas for streets, buildings, and infrastructure. Test these locations against your conceptual layout of the master plan to see where changes are needed to accommodate site conditions. Cross-check the buildable areas determined by slope with the soil information for those locations to understand any potential problems related to poor soil conditions. Figure 4.2 Topographic Map shows a visual picture of a site's slope characteristics.

A slope analysis expresses the grade as a percentage of drop from one high point to one low point. An easy way to remember this is by the expression "rise over run." For example, if a street is to be 120 feet long, the beginning elevation is at 135 feet, and the ending elevation is at 130 feet, the resulting grade is as follows:

135 feet − 130 feet = 5 feet (the rise)
5 feet (the rise) divided by 120 feet (the run) =
0.04167 or a grade of 4.2 percent

FIGURE 4.1. Data for New Topographic Map

1. Date map was produced
2. Project's name and location
3. Owner's name
4. Engineer's or surveyor's name and professional registration seal
5. North indication
6. Scale
7. Property lines
8. Outlines of all existing roads, structures, and infrastructure
9. Outlines of hydrological features, including old drainage channels with invert elevations
10. Location and general configuration of rocks, ledges, outcroppings, sinkholes, and ridges
11. Bench marks and appropriate spot elevations
12. Marked contour intervals at 2 to 10 feet, depending on size of property and scale of map

---

FIGURE 4.2. Topographic Map

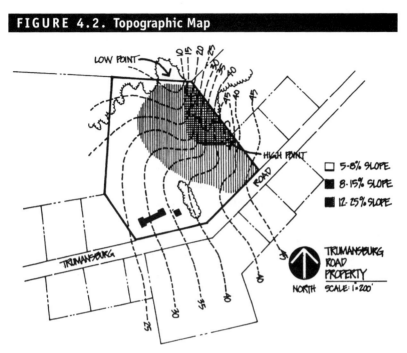

Source: Reprinted with permission from Environmental Design and Research, p.c.

Oftentimes you'll find a slope analysis has already been calculated and presented for specific areas in soil surveys from the U.S. Natural Resources Conservation Service (NRCS).

Design Guidelines for Slopes. Design guidelines establish minimum and maximum grades as being most desirable for each category of land use. Recommended design guidelines are based on the slopes that are most conducive to the intended use as well as the least expensive for construction costs. For example, a design standard may recommend a grade of between 2 and 3 percent for a grassy area intended for recreational use. In the example above, a 4.2 percent grade is too steep for such a recreational area. However, that 4.2 percent grade does fall within the 0.5 to 8 percent range recommended for street grades.

Design guidelines for slopes are published by many professional organizations, including the American Institute of

Architects and the American Society of Landscape Architects. In some places the local landscape ordinance establishes the grades for various outdoor uses. Although these can differ from code to code and location to location, Figure 4.3 Desirable Grades shows a short list of average ranges for different uses.

In choosing where to locate buildings, streets, and utilities, you must consider not only aesthetics and the basic fit with your master plan's concept but also cost and efficiency. If possible, try to locate buildings, streets, and utilities in areas containing appropriate topography for the intended use. By doing so, you minimize the amount of cut and fill (excavation and imported dirt) and decrease site development costs. Installing infrastructure and buildings on appropriate slopes also tends to produce a more pleasing design because natural landforms are not severely altered.

Soils and Subsurface Conditions

As your team evaluates the site's topography, it should also document soil and subsurface conditions so the civil engineer can know the exact nature and location of any critical site conditions. The site appears promising based on data provided by engineering maps from the U.S. Geological Survey and other sources. Now, after gathering the maps and data, you must run tests to verify the information you gathered from these sources.

FIGURE 4.3. Desirable Grades

Use	Maximum Percentage	Minimum Percentage
Drainage swale	33	1
Grassy bank	50	N/A
Grassy recreational areas	3	2
Sidewalks	8	1
Entry walks	4	1
Streets	8	0.50

Soils. Your engineer can review the soil maps and data to determine what tests you need to confirm the various soil conditions on your site. The engineer can define the locations more accurately by spot testing soils at prescribed intervals. Then compare these new data with the soil map obtained from the county, the U.S. Geological Survey, or the NRCS. Once the soils on your site are known and verified in the field, a registered soil scientist or engineer can evaluate their potential for facilitating your construction plans.

The type of soil present on the site affects drainage conditions. The engineer will probably recommend conducting a percolation rate test, which indicates how fast water moves downward through the soil to the underlying aquifer. The engineer will also spot test to determine the depth of the water table. You must understand how water moves through the soils before you can design adequate stormwater and septic systems. The depth of the water table determines the depth to which stormwater holding ponds can be dug and the amount of groundwater you must remove when buildings and infrastructure are installed.

Other Subsurface Conditions. Areas where earthquakes are common have special construction codes that help to prevent damage from seismic activity. You can obtain seismic maps for various parts of the United States from the U.S. Geological Survey. In colder climates you need to address soil conditions relative to potential foundation and structural damage attributed to frost and permafrost. These special conditions affect building placement, foundation type, and road construction. These conditions require you to follow special building codes and usually mean extra construction costs.

Hydrology and Drainage Requirements

At this point you also need to study the hydrological features and conditions affecting site drainage to determine whether they significantly affect your planned number of units and lot placement. You will also want to know what measures, if any, you should use to preserve the quality of existing hydrological features. Understanding hydrological patterns can help you determine the most efficient stormwater management systems and can prevent undesirable flooding or ponding of water. These considerations require examining both off- and on-site conditions.

Hydrology Map. A hydrology map shows the existing contours of the site and the pattern of flow from those contours. You can produce your own by drawing arrows perpendicular to the contours found on your topography map. The more arrows you use, the more accurate your picture of the overall drainage pattern will be. The hydrology map will show those destinations on your site to which water flows naturally. You want to avoid locating buildings and utilities in these areas, as they will be difficult to engineer for proper drainage. However, as long as they are not classified as floodplains or wetlands, these are good places for retention and detention ponds. Figure 4.4 Hydrology Map, shows the type of information found on a hydrology map, including the depth to the water table and flow direction on the site.

The topographic map should also show any natural obstacles that may interrupt the drainage pattern, such as outcroppings or swampy or concave areas of land. Consider these facts in evaluating the drainage pattern. If you reproduce this hydrology map at the same scale as your conceptual master plan, you can discover how the drainage patterns impact project design and adjust the layout if necessary. During this process you can also begin to see the potential areas for retention or detention ponds

Aerial Photos. Many local governments regularly take aerial photographs of their entire jurisdictions; you can obtain copies from the local planning or engineer's office. Often the photos have been taken over a number of years and show conditions and land uses for your site and the surrounding area over time.

FIGURE 4.4. Hydrology Map

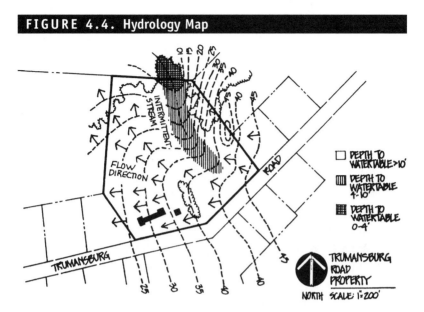

Source: Reprinted with permission from Environmental Design and Research, p.c.

Use these photos to understand the extent of tree cover or the boundaries of water bodies, which, in turn, helps you check for flooding potential. Since aerial photos are frequently taken during different times of the year, you can visually inspect the site and contiguous properties for conditions during wet and dry seasons. Doing this helps you evaluate the potential for standing water or flooding, which may not appear on hydrological maps.

Offsite Drainage. Besides analyzing on-site drainage patterns, developers have become increasingly concerned about offsite drainage. If your site is located in an already developed area, check with the county engineer to determine if stormwater from other properties enters your site. If this is the case, your engineer must consider that stormwater as well as the amount generated by your project when designing your stormwater management system.

The planning department may know of any significant problems in the area from outdated stormwater systems. Have your engineer review civil drawings for adjacent projects. The engineer can also visually inspect the properties and compare them to the existing topographic maps to evaluate the effectiveness of adjacent properties' stormwater management systems. That will help determine the approximate amount of runoff your stormwater facilities must handle from other properties.

Special Locations. In your preliminary investigation, you determined the location of your site with respect to a specific watershed area, aquifer, or designated floodplain. If your project is located in an area where the watershed supplies drinking water or a recreational lake, you may have to contend with additional requirements for stormwater discharge. Laws already in place may impose these requirements or you could face opposition from citizen groups that could slow down the progress of your development. You might be required to take such extra measures as cleaning the water before it is deposited in the ground or limiting the number of units in your project to decrease the amount of stormwater discharge.

Coastal Areas. Other factors can influence your methods for handling stormwater and the location of buildings in these types of sensitive areas. For example, the boundaries of floodplain and tidal surge areas in coastal regions determine safety factors related to storm surge and wave velocity. Coastal areas may limit the number of units or where buildings are placed. If you locate in one such area, you can find storm surge and other data for coastal regions, including hurricane data, from the National Oceanic and Atmospheric Administration (NOAA).

Floodplains. The National Flood Insurance Program (NFIP), which is designed to reduce federal costs for flood disaster relief, requires participating communities to establish restrictions for building within designated floodplain areas. The minimum type of flood required as an NFIP standard is the 100-year flood.

Floods are designated by their intensity and amount by descriptive categories of 5-year, 10-year, 20-year, and so on. A 100-year flood does not mean that a flood of an amount and intensity sufficient to cover the land up to the 100-year floodplain boundary will occur once in 100 years. Instead, a 100-year flood designation means that in any given year there exists a 1 percent chance that flooding can occur to such an amount and intensity; these categories are noted on the floodplain map. In many areas, local conditions have necessitated more stringent restrictions on the minimum standards for flood-year designations. These standards prevail if they are more restrictive than the NFIP standards.

The Federal Emergency Management Agency (FEMA) has established floodplain maps that depict the boundaries and, in some cases, the actual elevation of the 100-year flood. These maps are used to determine insurance rates and areas where minimum construction standards must be met. If your county has produced floodplain maps, compare the locations of floodplains and the date of the information on FEMA maps with the county floodplain maps. If the boundaries are different, use the most current map.

The most current maps usually show the floodplain boundary at the distance it stood from the center of the floodplain when the map data was collected. As land becomes more densely developed, the floodplain boundary naturally moves outward. Any additional development since the map was produced has increased runoff and thus the area prone to flood. In all likelihood, the floodplain boundary extends even further out than what is shown on the map. For these reasons, you should always use the most current maps.

Using a freeboard factor can also prevent the possibility of underdesigned stormwater management systems. Freeboard factors are safety measures in equations used to calculate water volume. These factors, expressed in feet above the design flood level, take into account various uncertain conditions that can lead to greater flood heights. Remember that the volume of water affects the boundary of the floodplains. Using measures such as freeboard factors provides you with a margin of safety in determining potential flooding. Your civil engineer and city and county ordinances can assist you in establishing both off- and on-site potential flood conditions.

Stormwater Runoff

At this stage, you can calculate the approximate volume and rate of stormwater runoff that your project will generate. Consider both off- and on-site patterns and conditions. The amount and speed of runoff affects the type of system you can use for its disposal; that, in turn, affects its cost. As part of your information gathering, consult local regulatory requirements affecting the discharge and disposal of stormwater. Existing codes and regulations that apply to your site and the proximity of hydrological features in need of protection may affect the methods used to control the amount and rate of stormwater runoff. Chapter 7 discusses methods for calculating stormwater volume.

Site Features

While your site's special features need not blindly dictate the layout of the master plan, they should significantly influence its overall concept. The site's features present both opportunities and constraints to the project's marketability and costs. Since site features can affect other project considerations, the development team should visit the site together to examine each one. This approach can save a great deal of time when you're ready to make the final design decisions for your master plan concept.

Project Opportunities

You can greatly enhance the aesthetic appeal of your project by using cost-effective measures to preserve desirable views and natural vegetation. Make sure your master plan layout capitalizes on any features that can contribute to the natural beauty of the project. The designer on your project team can produce a site analysis map that locates the site's important physical features. Figure 4.5 Site Analysis Map shows the kind of information this type of study should include.

FIGURE 4.5. Site Analysis Map

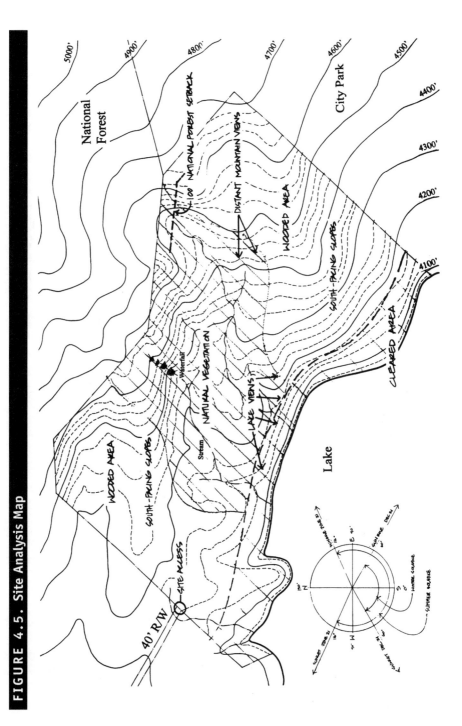

By comparing the location of physical features on the site analysis map with topography and other subsurface conditions, your team can discover where you may need to adjust the configuration of lots and streets. A team effort in fine-tuning design ideas and technical considerations means more quality in the final product—and a point to emphasize in your marketing strategy.

Views and Vantage Points. Your team should mark the major views, vantage points, and other foci on the site analysis map to ensure the layout takes optimum advantage of each. This will allow you to maximize the number of premium lots that can be sold at higher prices. For example, Figure 4.5 shows a wooded area in the northwest portion of the site. The land slopes toward the middle of the site and a waterfall; the southern portion of the site borders a lake. The goal in designing this community will be to maximize the views from the greatest number of lots to the two water amenities or the woods.

Vegetation. Evaluate the site's vegetative cover to determine the type of trees and low-lying woody plants it supports naturally. Note any specimen trees or other desirable vegetation for possible use in your landscaping plan. Compare this information with the local landscape ordinance so you know which trees must be protected. Determine where trees and other vegetation must be removed to accommodate the master plan, and estimate the associated costs. This includes the cost of tree removal permits required by local landscape code. You should also estimate the cost of importing landscape material into areas that have no vegetation.

Remember if a type of tree, woody plant, or ground cover has grown on the site in its natural condition, this means it is receiving enough water and nourishment to flourish. Carefully evaluate these kinds of vegetation as potential landscape material. Examine the ease of transplanting and the feasibility of leaving them in place. Using preexisting plants decreases the cost of importing plants and saves on maintenance costs by reducing water, fertilizer, pesticide, and herbicide requirements. Your team should try to save as much desirable vegetation as possible by making slight adjustments to the master plan or making greater use of existing vegetation instead of importing exotics.

Existing Water Bodies. The presence of streams, washes, lakes, ponds, and river frontage can have a positive effect on the marketability of your site. But you must first evaluate the quality of the water, the potential for flooding, and the presence of any regulatory constraints in locating buildings nearby. You also need to understand the size, depth, and direction of flow. This can help determine whether the site has standing water year-round or needs some artificial means of aeration before the water body can become a project amenity. Your team should note the potential uses of the water amenity and design for them accordingly. This includes whether the amenity is visual only, has recreational possibilities, or can be used either seasonally or year-round.

Mark the location of any water bodies on the site analysis map and evaluate the master plan for its ability to maximize both physical and visual access to the water. For example, note the waterfall and lake clearly delineated on the site analysis map in Figure 4.5. If you have not yet taken proper advantage of the water amenities, review the master plan for potential layout changes. Figure 4.6 Visual Access to Water Amenity shows how you can change the master plan to increase the entire project's access to water amenities without compromising project density or image.

Part A of Figure 4.6 shows the plan adapted to 16 lots with an average size of 11 acres. In this adaptation, seven lots have visual access to the lake. Part B shows the same site with an equal number of lots (16). Each lot is 5 to 6 acres. Three lots front the lake, five have a view of it, and one has a view of the new pond. An additional three lots overlook the waterfall.

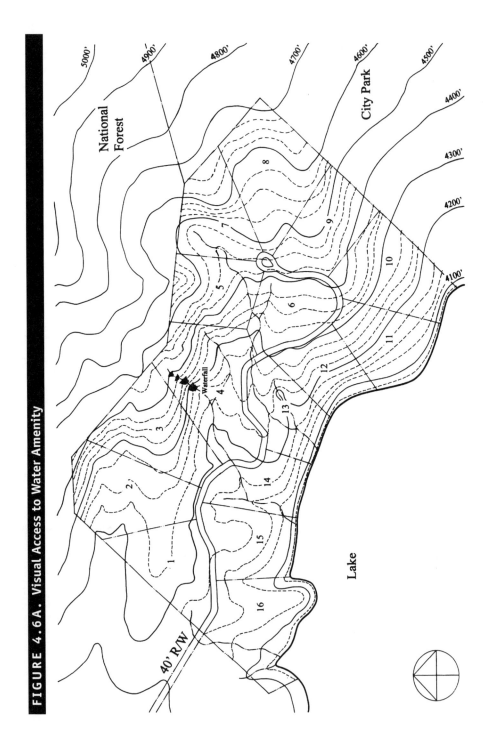

FIGURE 4.6A. Visual Access to Water Amenity

FIGURE 4.6B. Visual Access to Water Amenity

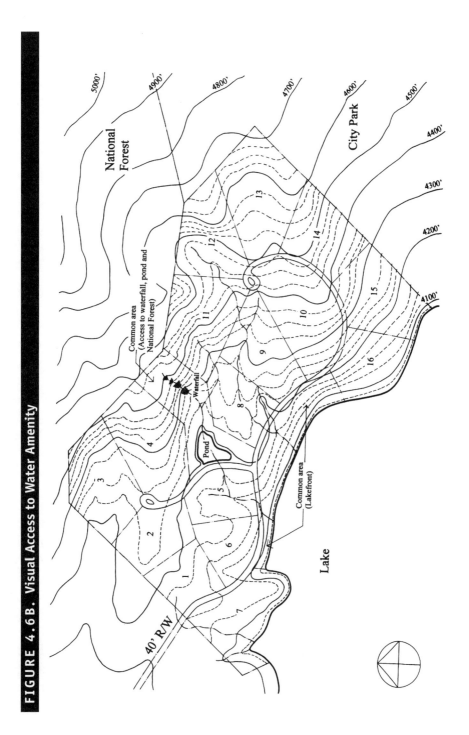

Plan B also provides two common areas, one bordering the lake and one at the waterfall. Both offer access to a national forest.

Other Unique Site Features. If the site contains any unusual physical features, evaluate their potential to use them to increase aesthetic appeal. These features can include water bodies, rock outcroppings and formations, rocky underlayment, mountains, hills, cliffs, or sharp changes in slope. The presence of large rocks under the surface can complicate site work and increase costs. However, after rocks are removed you can sometimes use them for landscaping or creatively stack them in one place to create a visual amenity or privacy buffer. This both decreases the cost of rock removal and provides an extra project amenity.

Project Constraints

All sites have a variety of project constraints. How can you minimize their negative effects on project parameters while seeking ways to use them as marketing advantages? Nature preserves, wetlands, and various types of protected ecosystems require preservation, which can decrease potential project density as it increases development costs. However, if you preserve these areas as project amenities, they can become an effective marketing strategy with wide appeal to your target market group.

Wetlands. Wetlands offer an excellent example of the marketing value of a project constraint. While this feature limits development, the view across a natural preserve can definitely enhance the market value of adjacent lots. Regardless whether the wetlands are actually wet year-round, a view of a natural landscape is more desirable than one of buildings or a parking lot. Be sure to publicize the methods and care taken to preserve the wetlands to promote your sensitive handling of land.

Preserving certain types of wetlands, such as coastal marshes or cypress swamps, can offer residents a greater involvement with nature. Many target groups place this high on their lists of desires in a development. You can also use your sensitive handling of the wetlands to promote your image as a good neighbor in the community. As one example of this technique, Figure 4.7 Courtyard Clusters shows wetlands as shaded areas scattered throughout. The master plan placed the houses in clusters on buildable areas and used wetlands as buffers between the clusters.

Waterways and Drainage Easements. If your project has existing waterways or drainage easements, these features also tend to decrease project density and affect the layout of the master plan. But you can use the presence of easements and other waterways to provide additional buffering space to adjacent lots. Creative planting along the easements can add privacy. In

FIGURE 4.7. Courtyard Clusters

Source: Reprinted with permission from Tim R. Newell, Land Planning/Landscape Architecture.

this way, proper alignment of lots along the waterways can increase their value to buyers.

Open Space. Some sites carry open space requirements as part of their zoning restrictions. Open space requirements set aside a certain area of the site to be left in its natural condition, resulting in a decrease in density. These areas can be heavily vegetated or contain surface water. As a result, open space requirements decrease the density of a project. If you have large unbuildable areas on your site, enhance their value by marketing them as parks or nature preserves. Place hike-and-bike paths through them if possible to provide a cost-effective and desirable project amenity. If this is not permitted, align the walkways along the perimeter and maximize the number of lots with visual access to the nature preserve.

Climate. Regional climatic conditions can affect the orientation of houses and lots, home design, and building materials. You enhance the marketability of your project when the master plan and chosen housing types reflect regional climate. Climatic conditions can also significantly affect construction schedules through days lost to inclement weather. Therefore, understanding climatic conditions can help produce accurate schedules and thus accurate projections of cash flow requirements. Figure 4.8 Climate Data for Benzie County, Michigan, illustrates the type of climate information necessary for design and scheduling decisions. You can obtain climate data for your site from the state weather bureau or the U.S. National Climatological Data Center of NOAA.

Climatic conditions include prevailing winds, solar orientation, temperature, humidity, and precipitation. Figure 4.9 Climate Map shows a visual image of the existing climatic conditions for a site. The amount, frequency, and intensity of rainfall can affect the type of construction methods used for open stormwater management systems. The direction of prevailing winds and solar orientation directly influence building place-

FIGURE 4.8. Climate Data for Benzie County, Michigan

Average annual rainfall	32 inches
Days with at least 1.0 inches precipitation	5
Days with at least .5 inches precipitation	18
Average annual snowfall	122 inches
Average temperature	46 degrees F
Average January minimum temperature	16 degrees F
Average July minimum temperature	70 degrees F
Number of days over 90 degrees F	6
Number of days under 32 degrees F	142

ment and design of windows and overhangs. Temperature and humidity influence the design of building mass, foundations, and heating and cooling systems. The amount of snow and rain determines roof slopes and dimensions of overhangs. Chapter 9 Selecting Housing Types will discuss in greater detail the effect of climate on project design and construction.

Regulatory Requirements

As you gather and analyze information about the physical factors on your site, you need to further examine regulatory requirements affecting your project. First determine the number and type of permits required from local, state, and federal agencies and the procedures for obtaining them. A keen awareness of these procedures can help you allot enough time in the schedule to obtain the permissions needed to build your project. This awareness will also allow you to set aside enough financial resources in your pro forma analysis to support the predicted cash flow for that amount of time.

Zoning

From your preliminary investigation, you have determined that your site is likely to meet zoning requirements in one of two ways: either the current zoning is appropriate for your intended use or you may feel confident of receiving the correct zoning classification change. Be sure to match the restrictions in the

FIGURE 4.9. Climate Map

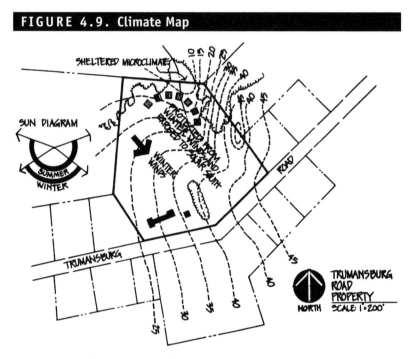

Source: Reprinted with permission from Environmental Design and Research, p.c.

desired zoning classification with the project's requirements so you can clearly see whether you can access existing infrastructure to request a zoning change or negotiate a variance.

Design Standards

Each zoning classification contains a list of design standards that includes building height restrictions, minimum dimensions for setbacks, percentage of the site covered by buildings, and other special requirements. Review these standards for their impact on the master plan concept and make sure the number and configuration of lots and streets comply.

Density. Zoning classifications and requirements primarily address desired project density. Density is expressed as number of units per acre, percentage of site covered by buildings, or Floor Area Ratio (FAR). The most common standard for density in residential zoning is the number of units per acre; however, FAR is more commonly used for multifamily and commercial zoning classifications. FAR shows the amount of area covered by all the buildings' floor plans added together and divided by the total amount of site area.

If the zoning classification has an open space requirement, carefully consider how this may affect your project density. The requirement may specify the open space as a percentage of total land area or actually delineate the location. Note that open space, parking, environmental, regulatory, and other requirements may make the density permitted by the zoning difficult or impossible to achieve.

Permitted Uses. Each zoning classification contains a list of permitted buildings that may be placed on the site. Permitted uses frequently include support services or amenities. The permitted uses list also describes the types of use allowed for buildings on the site. Residential zoning may encompass single-family homes; multifamily; adult congregate living; and institutional living facilities. While single-family uses are usually self-explanatory, you must take the time to carefully understand the exact meaning of the higher density zoning classifications commonly used for multifamily development.

Check the permitted uses for your site and the contiguous property. For example, imagine you intend to build high-end townhouses on your site and the adjacent property's zoning classification allows for a higher density or different type of use such as an adult congregate living facility. You must evaluate the effect of that potential use on your site's desirability to the target market.

Contiguous Property. Also determine the potential effect development of contiguous property could have on your new community. Will its current zoning remain the same if it is developed? If not, consult the planning office to determine what its appropriate future zoning will likely be. Then use that zoning classification to evaluate the impact future adjacent land uses might have on your project. By mapping out your site and the surrounding property, you can determine if any of your boundaries might require extra buffering from adjoining property uses. The map in Figure 4.10, Use of Contiguous Property shows various uses of adjacent property. Notice the different areas that are zoned for residential or commercial use and agricultural or open space. Each could have a positive or negative impact on your own development.

Special or Conditional Uses. Many times residential zoning classifications list uses that are permitted but require a special or conditional use permit. Examples of special or conditional land uses that may be permitted within a residential zoning classification are daycare centers, schools, and churches. The zoning ordinance may specify standards that must be met to obtain a conditional use permit, such as lot

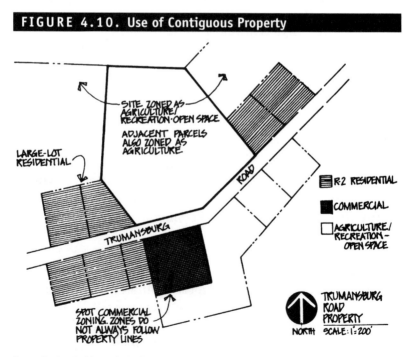

FIGURE 4.10. Use of Contiguous Property

Source: Reprinted with permission from Environmental Design and Research, p.c.

size requirements or buffering and landscape requirements. You may have such facilities or uses planned for your project. Find out whether you need any special conditional use permits for your site and whether your planned uses are appropriate for those permits.

Mixed-Use or Planned Unit Development. Many parcels of land fall under a mixed-use or Planned Unit Development (PUD) category of zoning. If the zoning classification is a type of PUD, it may be called planned residential development, planned community, or planned residential community. Mixed-use categories also have several different names. Although each local government has its own name for these zoning categories, the central idea remains the same.

PUDs were established to allow greater flexibility and a wider range of creative solutions in land use and so increase the quality of development. PUDs permit you to plan a site in an integrated fashion rather than parcel by parcel as required by typical zoning. Usually this zoning classification also allows a variety of compatible uses to come together in one designated area. The idea is to create a neighborhood or small-town atmosphere where residential, commercial, service, and cultural uses combine to form a new community. By allowing a range of housing unit types with appropriate retail and service buildings, PUDs are ideal for creating a fully integrated new community.

Often the zoning ordinance specifies a PUD classification without assigning it to any particular pieces of property. Instead, the PUD classification is used as a "floating" or overlay zone for which the landowner or developer applies. As part of its flexibility, the PUD classification gives the developer more latitude in lot layout. In addition, many zoning classifications permit PUDs to have smaller lot sizes and more flexibility in street design standards. In some areas, PUDs allow for an increased density of residential units as long as certain specified goals are met. In return for this flexibility, however, most PUD ordinances require detailed site analysis and approval by the local government. This requires a significant amount of time and work to navigate the approval process.

In conventional residential zoning, your master plan must follow all the specified design standards; if these are met, your site plan can usually receive approval. With the PUD classification, however, the design standards may not be as specific as those used for conventional residential zoning. In this situation, you as the developer need to meet with the planning department and thoroughly understand the goals and guidelines of the design standards for a PUD project. You can then have the master plan designed and submitted for various departments to review. The developer also usually makes a presentation of the concept to the local city or county commission. The commission or planning department can recommend changes to the plan before granting approval or reject the plan. In other words, the approval process for PUDs can result in a series of design changes, meetings, and hearings.

This basically means that, if you develop land in a PUD, more time and effort are required to understand acceptable types of design standards and approaches. With a PUD, you have no step-by-step path to follow to project approval as compared with the process of complying with specific zoning classification restrictions. In this case, the site analysis becomes even more important as a tool to sell your ideas to the local government. In spite of the extra time and effort involved, most developers generally consider the additional design flexibility and product marketability that they gain with a PUD classification as being well worth the trouble.

Since areas developed through this method are more carefully monitored and can be more flexibly designed, the PUD approval process can increase the quality of both the surrounding and developed areas. This factor in turn tends to increase the marketability of your project's location to any target market group. You may also have more latitude in achieving some aspects of your master plan concept in return for adhering to other important guidelines requested by the local government. In fact, developers are often attracted to PUDs by this flexibility and the increased quality of the surrounding environment that results.

Subdivision Review Process

Residential development projects must complete multiple review processes. Besides the procedure required for a zoning change approval or site plan approval for a PUD, the master plan must go through the subdivision review process. After you are certain of obtaining the desired zoning, you are ready for the subdivision approval process. If you are developing in a PUD, you may find your project exempt from some of the requirements of the subdivision ordinance.

Your preliminary investigation should have determined the design standards required by the subdivision ordinance. These include size and configuration of lots, street dimensions and geometry, road construction standards, utility placement, length of dead-end streets, street names, environmental and site constraints, and open space requirements.

At this point, you need to review these standards in detail and, if necessary, adjust the master plan to ensure it complies with these standards. You should produce a preliminary plat map to submit for the approval of the public works, transportation, fire protection, and landscape or environmental offices, as well as the utility companies. This step is usually part of a typical subdivision review process. Each department or office has unique concerns about how your design will affect its ability to provide adequate service to your development as well as conduct proper maintenance of the specific infrastructure. Based on their comments and reviews, you then make the necessary changes to the drawing you'll submit to the review body (planning commission or board) for approval.

In some cities or counties, this is done before submittal to any planning bodies. In others, it occurs after presentation to the planning board or commission. Figure 4.11 Sample Subdivision Review Process shows project approval steps for a residential development's final subdivided plat plan.

Notice that, compared with the process for obtaining a zoning classification change shown in Figure 3.9, this process for obtaining approvals from the various departments does not usually include public notices or hearings. Public notices are required, however, in many locations, although this varies from

FIGURE 4.11. Sample Subdivision Review Process

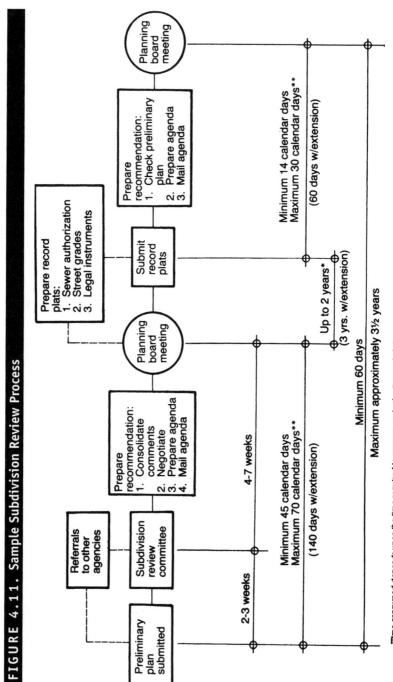

*Time consumed depends upon the time required to prepare and submit record plats.
**Automatic approval after this time period.

location to location. Without public notices the process is sometimes shorter and more straightforward than the zoning classification process and carries less chance for failure. Of course, when planning boards or county commissioners meet, citizens can attend and voice concerns. That means even a straightforward subdivision review process can face pressures from local citizens.

Environmental Approvals

As part of a detailed analysis of the regulations governing your site, you need to further evaluate how environmental regulations will affect your project, including project parameters, requirements for special development and construction practices, permitting, and associated costs. First, determine if your site falls within any special federal, state, or local environmentally regulated districts. If so, study each one to understand the proper building codes, design standards, and requirements for project approval. This chapter outlines some of the more important environmental requirements for development. Chapter 5 Major Environmental Regulations Affecting Development will cover specific requirements and obligations.

Flood Management Districts. As mentioned earlier, if the local community participates in the National Flood Insurance Program, you must locate buildings, sanitary sewers, and dispose of stormwater runoff on your site in compliance with NFIP regulations. Also, if the community participates in NFIP, FEMA will have already designated and mapped the area as a floodplain. Locating in these regulated districts can affect the type of construction allowed. For example, if you build in the 100-year floodplain, the finished elevation of the lowest floor must be at or above the flood elevation for the 100-year flood. This is also true if you have permission to build on or near reclaimed wetlands, constructed wetlands, or natural wetlands.

Coastal Districts. If your project is located in a coastal area, you must take extra steps with permitting and construction. Special permits and building codes affect building placement

and construction in coastal areas. Sites located on land designated as part of the Coastal Barrier Resources System cannot
obtain federal assistance for dredging and filling, maintaining
shorelines, infrastructure, and flood insurance. Obtaining a
Veterans Administration or Federal Housing Administration
guaranteed mortgage is also virtually impossible for property located on a coastal barrier island. Furthermore, each
state has special building codes that dictate the type, location,
and timing of construction in these areas. Usually you must
locate buildings at a prescribed distance from the 100-year
storm surge and behind and away from protective dune
barriers.

Superfund Areas. Superfund areas are designated parcels of
land where hazardous wastes have been handled improperly,
posing health, safety, and welfare problems to residents in the
immediate area. The federal Comprehensive Environmental
Response, Compensation and Liability Act (CERCLA or
Superfund) imposes strict liability for cleanup on property pur-
chasers, even if they contributed nothing to the contamination but failed to conduct a proper due diligence inquiry into
site conditions at the time of purchase. Hazardous waste questions about a property should follow established standards of
inquiry, such as those published by the American Society for
Testing and Materials (ASTM).

After you have evaluated the property as a possible CER-
CLA-regulated site according to the procedure outlined in
Chapter 3, do the same for the surrounding property. Locating near a hazardous waste site is not conducive to project marketability. Many state laws regulate hazardous waste liability,
so be sure to check state regulations as well.

State Regulated Districts. Each state has particular environmental concerns resulting in specially designated areas or
districts. These include radon-prone areas, threatened
and endangered wildlife and plants, nature preserves, protected
aquifer regions, and air quality nonattainment areas. For
example, many states with high levels of radon are adopting

radon-resistant construction codes (see Chapter 5 for more about radon). Your state department in charge of environmental quality control will have a list of specially designated areas that might affect development and construction.

Building Codes

Most local areas have adopted building codes containing the range of acceptable standards for construction performance and methods. Most local areas adopt one of the three national model building codes—the Uniform Building Code, Standard Building Code, and National Building Code—which cover most aspects of construction and design. Occupancy loads, building separation, corridor lengths, service access, fire protection, and heating and cooling requirements are some of the design considerations specified in these codes. In addition, an area may have a local code that adds to or strengthens the adopted national building code requirements. Always follow the local code because it will include national codes and in certain areas may have even more stringent standards.

Other codes such as life, health, and safety codes rule over special considerations such as providing access for disabled persons and fire protection. The local building permit and inspection department has a complete list of all the area's adopted codes. Unlike zoning code ordinance restrictions, you cannot alter building code dimensions and standards for any reason.

Offsite Factors

When selecting your site, you identified and evaluated the major target market characteristics that affected location. You also carefully discovered and evaluated any negative offsite factors for their impact on the site's marketability. Any positive offsite factors were also considered for their contribution to the project's success. Now that you have selected the site, you need to evaluate in greater detail the effect offsite factors will have on design decisions.

Frontage Roads and Sidewalks

Now is the time to discover the exact conditions of all frontage roads to determine the requirements for providing safe ingress and egress for your new project. Consider both the quality and design capacity of the roads. Determine whether your entrances will need turning lanes or traffic lights. Also determine the appropriate sight lines, vision corridors, and other measures you should employ to increase safe ingress and egress for your project. If the frontage road has sidewalks, find out who maintains them and where you can add landscaping. Be sure to estimate the additional project costs for installing and maintaining streets and sidewalks if you are required to do so by the local government.

Utilities

Your preliminary investigation located and evaluated existing utilities' capacity to accept additional volume from your project. At this point you should be able to locate on your site map all utilities, including potable water, electricity, gas, telephone, sanitary sewer, stormwater mains, and cable television. Figure 4.12 Utilities Map shows the type of drawing you need to create in order to locate all existing utilities on your site. Notice, for example, how clearly the map indicates the placement of water and sewer lines and utility easements for overhead and electrical wires.

Next, determine the best locations for tap-ins, hook-ups, and discharge points. The object here is to minimize your own infrastructure costs by designing the most efficient routes for lines in terms of site grading and infrastructure length. For lines that require minimum slopes to function by gravity, find areas on your site where topography does not provide that minimum slope. Then adjust the configuration of your conceptual master plan or relocate lines to accommodate the installation of gravity-fed infrastructure if grading cannot accomplish the job.

Installing utilities requires clearing, grubbing, and excavating. For this reason, it's best to locate utilities in places with no mature vegetation, although this is not always possible because of the required project density and optimum location

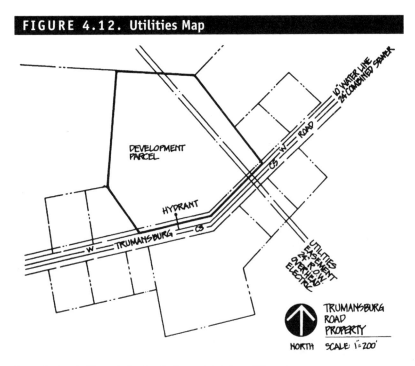

FIGURE 4.12. Utilities Map

Source: Reprinted with permission from Environmental Design and Research, p.c.

of lots. Therefore, carefully evaluate how much it will cost to install utility infrastructure in areas with mature vegetation. Also make sure no specimen trees and privacy barriers are destroyed by any clearing required for utility installation.

Sometimes utilities may not be immediately accessible to your property. If this is the case, determine the requirements and costs for permits or special permission for crossing existing frontage roads, using existing easements, or bringing lines through neighboring properties. You also want to know if you must install and dedicate any improvements to supply the utilities to your infrastructure. Finally, account for any tap fees, impact fees, and special assessment fees related to obtaining the required utilities for your project. Some local governments may also require you to contribute to an escrow fund for streets and utilities.

Applying Site Analysis to the Master Plan

Once you have documented the actual location of all pertinent site conditions, you and your design team can work back
and forth to produce a final master plan that most closely
approximates your original ideas and shows a sensitive and
efficient use of the site and its resources. Although a site has
only one set of given conditions, your team can produce several
viable solutions as a response to those conditions.

Producing Multiple Solutions

Figure 4.13 Existing Site Conditions shows a 77-acre site whose
prominent features include existing irrigation ditches, evenly
sloping ground from the northwest to southeast corner, and a
view to a series of prominent mountain peaks to the west (not
shown on the map). The site borders a four-lane highway to the
east, two-lane roads to the north and south, and low-density

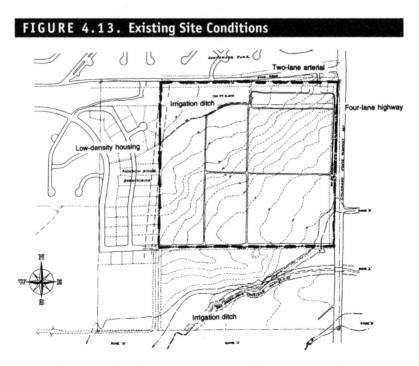

FIGURE 4.13. Existing Site Conditions

Source: Reprinted with permission from Andres Duany and Elizabeth Plater-Zyberk, Architects, Inc.

housing to the north and west. Three viable solutions were produced for this site as shown in Figures 4.14 Scheme A, 4.15 Scheme B, and 4.16 Scheme C.

Each of the three responses located the commercial retail uses along the eastern edge for the dual purpose of buffering the housing to the west and attracting commerce from the highway. Scheme A employs radiating streets aligned on a north-south axis with a view to four prominent mountain peaks on the western horizon. In this plan, the neighborhood is connected with a horseshoe loop. Scheme B maintains the existing grid-like network of roads and fields as a framework. But this plan also incorporates the existing drainage flows and topography into the street design and site plan. Scheme C is based on the regional precedent of the western grid for a frontier town. The grid establishes a diagonal series of parks running from the northwest to southeast corner. Each master plan includes subneighborhood focal points of small greens and civic sites.

FIGURE 4.14. Scheme A: Horseshoe Loop

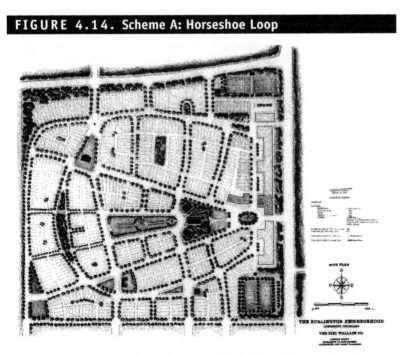

Source: Reprinted with permission from Andres Duany and Elizabeth Plater-Zyberk, Architects, Inc.

FIGURE 4.15. Scheme B: Grid with Existing Topography and Drainage

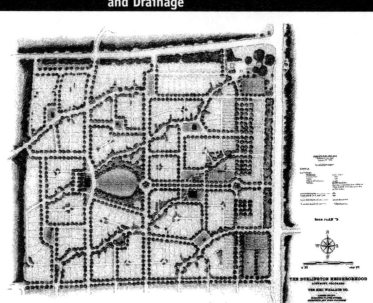

Source: Reprinted with permission from Andres Duany and Elizabeth Plater-Zyberk, Architects, Inc.

FIGURE 4.16. Scheme C: Western Grid

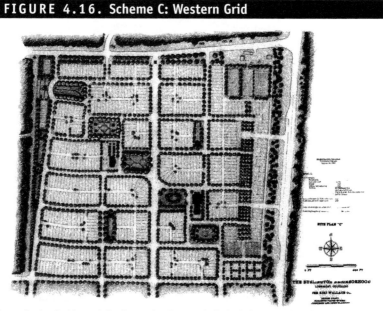

Source: Reprinted with permission from Andres Duany and Elizabeth Plater-Zyberk, Architects, Inc.

FIGURE 4.17. Scheme A, B, and C Results (in lineal feet)

Scheme A: Horseshoe Loop

Lot Frontages	
Residential	12,985
Retail	330
Office and industrial	975
Total Street Lengths	18,290
Total Alley Lengths	8,050
Residential units at 24 feet wide per unit	541

Scheme B: Grid with Existing Topography and Drainage

Lot Frontages	
Residential	14,015
Retail	230
Office and industrial	1,140
Total Street Lengths	18,645
Total Alley Lengths	7,560
Residential units at 24 feet wide per unit	576

Scheme C: Western Grid

Lot Frontages	
Residential	12,535
Retail	260
Office and industrial	750
Total Street Lengths	17,460
Total Alley Lengths	7,355
Residential units at 24 feet wide per unit	522

Source: Reprinted with permission from Andres Duany and Elizabeth Plater-Zyberk, Architects, Inc.

Selecting a Final Concept

The three schemes all began with the goal of creating a neotraditional neighborhood as the generating idea behind the master plan. From the figures, you can see that the idea behind the master plan and the integration of the particular site characteristics produced three different results in both form and number of units. The results are shown in Figure 4.17 Scheme A, B, and C Results. Scheme A with the median number of 541 units was eventually chosen because the developer believed the mountain views and horseshoe loop would have a strong aesthetic appeal to the target market. However, as this example clearly demonstrates, more than one solution—in fact, several—can work effectively for any given set of site characteristics. Financial feasibility and the target market's preferences should be the deciding factors in choosing final concept.

A detailed analysis of the physical, legal and political, and offsite factors of your site is critical to accomplishing the ideas represented by your master plan concept. Your team originally developed these ideas to meet the demands and desires of your target market. When the appropriate site was chosen, its unique set of characteristics played an important role in the final design decisions behind the master plan. In this way, by working back and forth between your ideas and the characteristics of your site, you can create a new development that cost-effectively works with the features of the site—and retains the original ideas that were so important to target market appeal.

5

Major Environmental Regulations Affecting Development

Transforming a parcel of raw land into land that accommodates buildings and infrastructure inevitably changes the physical environment. The methods of acquiring raw materials for manufacturing building products, the manufacturing processes themselves, and the process of disposing of building materials also affect the environment. Because of this, these activities, as well as the use of energy and water in materials manufacturing and construction, are increasingly coming under government review.

Transforming the Physical Environment

Because land development transforms the physical environment, developers must be mindful of their methods of changing raw land into new developments. As part of this process, developers are expected to manage solid waste generation, air and water quality, noise, vegetation, and wildlife populations. Figure 5.1 Environmental Impacts of Development shows eight broad environmental categories affected by land development. These categories are listed in the requirements for environmental impact statements submitted to the U.S. Environmental Protection Agency (EPA). Regardless of the scale of the project, developing any parcel of land makes permanent changes in each of these categories. That means land develop-

FIGURE 5.1. Environmental Impacts of Development

- **Land:** Affects wildlife habitats, alters natural drainage patterns, and changes natural vegetation
- **Water:** Adds sediment and other pollutants to natural water systems
- **Air:** Affects air quality
- **Noise:** Affects noise levels
- **Biological Communities:** Alters species population and composition

- **Human (Social) Aspects:** Changes populations in local areas
- **Local Economy:** Adds demand for infrastructure
- **Other Natural Resources:** Increases use of natural amenities such as lakes and rivers

Note: EPA requirements for environmental impact statements address these categories.

ment activities can involve the full spectrum of environmental issues.

Regulatory Climate

Since the National Environmental Policy Act (NEPA) was passed in 1969, public concern about environmental quality has prompted a wealth of environmental laws and regulations directly concerned with land development. This increase in regulations in turn has forced the already complex process of land development to confront an expanded set of project requirements. Furthermore, this current regulatory climate is not expected to abate in the foreseeable future.

Most builders and developers know that the attributes of a clean environment enhance project value in the marketplace. We all desire clean air and water, beautiful scenery, and a feeling of harmony with nature—especially in the places we live. But as developers struggle to comply with the complexity of overlapping federal, state, and local environmental laws, regulations, and ordinances, these efforts can quickly drive up project expenditures. Increased expenditures translate into cash outlays for more permits, testing, and feasibility studies, as well as longer project schedules. Not fully understanding the range of regulatory requirements can also result in costly delays.

For all these reasons, land that remains available for development usually carries environmental constraints that offer major challenges to prospective developers. As a developer, you can deal most effectively with increased regulatory restrictions by increasing your awareness of environmental laws. This knowledge can guide your team as it tries to develop creative and cost-effective solutions for environmental constraints on the site.

Creative Alternatives

The growth in environmental regulations has, in the last decade, lengthened the time required to get residential projects approved. In dealing with environmental regulations, keep in mind the following goals:

1. Understand the reason for the law.
2. Understand the requirements of the law.
3. Determine the cost of complying with the law.
4. Look for ways to transform compliance with the law into a marketing advantage for your project.

For your project to achieve success, you must understand federal, state, and local regulations and thoroughly review how environmental regulations affect all the activities required to realize your master plan concept. As the developer you are responsible for knowing, complying with, and communicating the laws to your employees. To accomplish this, you must rely heavily on your project team to monitor the environmental impacts associated with each area of expertise. Each professional can then offer suggestions about site development, design, and construction methods that are environmentally sensitive or that creatively resolve environmental constraints.

Environmental Permitting

One of the first tasks for your development team is assessing the number and type of environmental permits required for your project. This can vary widely from state to state. Many different agencies can house the permitting authorities, and the application procedures for each can differ widely.

The Environmental Protection Agency (EPA) has an extensive website containing a variety of information such as fact sheets on land development practices affecting the environment, summaries of environmental laws, and mitigation practices. Look for the list of all federal, state, and regional offices along with the names of current directors. This kind of information can help you prepare for meetings with pertinent agencies and offices about your own project and its potential impacts.

Reviewing Project Impact

As mentioned in Chapters 3 and 4, the best place to start your review of environmental regulations and agencies is at the local government level. County engineers, public works officials, building officials, and planners can tell you the range and number of permits relevant to your project. In some states they will direct you to a regional office of the state's environmental regulatory agency. For rural counties, you might be directed to the district conservation office.

At this stage, your team should investigate and identify potential problems with your development proposal to suggest strategies that might preempt an agency refusal. Then review these with the local government office. This office will also go over your project requirements to determine the various agencies from which you will obtain permits. In other cases, you may need to pay a visit to each agency to determine if any of your land development activities require a permit from that particular agency.

After you and your team have met with each pertinent agency and finished this preliminary review of your project's requirements, assess the impact compliance will have on your time and costs. This review should be part of the initial site selection research completed before land is purchased or the idea for a new development finalized. Figure 5.2 Environmental Permitting Checklist provides a list of questions your project

---

FIGURE 5.2. Environmental Permitting Checklist

☐ List the development and construction activities for your project that affect any of the eight categories in Figure 5.1.
☐ List the federal, state, and local permits needed for these various activities.
☐ List the names and locations of the permitting authorities for each of these activities.
☐ Obtain the application package from each of the permitting authorities.
☐ List the requirements and format of the application for each of the permits.
☐ List the types of reports or tests that must accompany the application.
☐ List the consultants who must perform the studies and professionals who must sign or place a professional seal on reports and tests.
☐ Estimate the costs associated with meetings, application procedures, studies, tests, and permits.
☐ Create a flowchart depicting the deadlines and amount of time allotted for submission, review, and appeal for each application process.

---

team should ask when first evaluating the kinds of environmental permits required for your project.

Submittal Process
Describing every process required for each federal, state, and local permitting authority is beyond the scope of this discussion. However, there's a relatively standard approach for moving through the process. It involves basically four steps: application procedure, agency review, approval or disapproval, and appeal. Each step requires a commitment of time and preparation of information and materials by the development team.

Application Procedure. Before you submit your application, make sure you have correctly identified the agency with legal authority to issue a permit for the activity under consideration. Make an initial contact by arranging a pre-application meeting to help establish the steps involved in applying for a permit for a particular project activity. This will also clear up any doubts about possible redundancy in permits from agencies with overlapping jurisdiction. Some agencies will require you to attend such a meeting. Whenever possible, hold one even with those agencies that have no such requirement. Doing so will save you time and money in the long run because it explains the application procedure.

Carefully check the submission and approval timing for each agency to coordinate all required permit submissions and to prevent one permit from expiring before others are approved. The pre-application meeting also establishes a positive working relationship with agency officials and the preferred methods of resolving issues if no such procedure exists.

Agency Review. The agency review generally consists of three phases: first level of completeness, second level of completeness, and legal review. When the agency initially reviews your submission packet for completeness, it evaluates whether the packet contains all necessary documents. If it does not, you must either resubmit the entire packet or supply missing information. This can cause costly project delays. You can avoid delays due to incomplete information or misunderstood requirements by thoroughly reviewing the application requirements for submission with the person you contact in the pre-application meeting.

Once the packet is complete, the agency then usually gives the application a date that establishes the official start of the permitting process. From this point on, the agency must either approve or disapprove your application within a set period of time. Remember that the time established for approval begins only after your application is submitted and approved for completeness.

Various departments within the agency conduct the second-level review. It evaluates whether your submission packet has enough supporting information to determine if your proposed design and construction methods meet all applicable codes and standards. During this portion of the review, the agency may again ask you for additional information. This could include revisions to drawings and maps or other tests and reports. Finally, the legal review determines whether the application is consistent with existing regulations and if a permit may be issued.

Approval or Appeal. After completing this process, the agency either approves, approves with conditions, or disapproves the permit. If disapproved or approved with unacceptable conditions, you must either go through the agency's established appeal process or make the required changes and resubmit. Most agencies have a written appeals process that you follow when you have an issue to resolve. If not, clarify the appeals process during your pre-application meeting. In scheduling time for project approval, make sure your cash flow can cover the possible extensions required for any appeals processes.

Key Areas
The following discussion covers some of the most common areas of environmental permitting, including wetlands, hazardous wastes, water and air quality, noise, radon, and plants and wildlife. In some cases, your development may require a variety of permits for the various activities affecting each category. In addition, remember that laws and regulations are in a state of flux for each of these areas, so you must understand how requirements may change both nationally and for the state and local area in which your project is located. That's why it's critical to keep current on pending federal, state and local environmental legislation.

The Internet can keep you informed of laws and regulations affecting land development. You can find any government document ever printed by accessing the website for the Government Printing Office. The National Archives and Records Administration provides all regulations and laws by title and number in the Code of Federal Regulations. Each law or regulation carries the prefix CFR, the title, and the number. You may read the regulation in its entirety, access a brief summary, find the regulation by subject, and look at a history of amendments for any of the regulations you need. The Environmental Protection Agency maintains a website that provides the high points of all laws and regulations pertaining to environmental protection. Finally, many private entities such as environmental law firms and national organizations involved with land development keep websites through which you can obtain information directly or subscribe to newsletters on a specific subject that concerns issues directly affecting land development.

Wetlands

Developing land containing wetlands brings heavy regulatory scrutiny at the federal, state, and local level. Figure 5.3 Major Federal Wetlands Statutes gives a short history of important laws protecting wetlands. However, the primary federal program, the Clean Water Act Section 404 program, requires a permit for the placement of fill in wetlands areas. To obtain a Section 404 permit you must show that you have no "practicable alternatives" and that filling in the wetlands will not cause significant degradation of the aquatic ecosystem. If your project can meet these tests, then you must provide mitigation for any fills that are permitted.

Regulations

The U.S. Army Corps of Engineers (Corps) and EPA jointly administer the Section 404 program. This means that, although the Corps administers the program, EPA can veto any permit decision that the Corps makes. Moreover, EPA wrote the 404(b)(1) Guidelines, the substantive standards for permit review, which the Corps must follow. The U.S. Fish and Wildlife Service and the National Marine Fisheries Service can also issue written comments on Section 404 permit applications, but they have no direct permitting authority. That means their comments are advisory in nature and not binding on the Corps.

EPA and the Corps both define wetlands as follows:

those areas that are inundated or saturated by surface or groundwater at a frequency and duration sufficient to support, and that under normal circumstances do support, a prevalence of vegetation typically adapted for life in saturated soil conditions. Wetlands generally include swamps, marshes, bogs, and similar areas.

FIGURE 5.3. Major Federal Wetlands Statutes

The Rivers and Harbors Act of 1899: This act prohibited the unauthorized obstruction or alteration of any navigable water of the United States. Under this law, excavating material or depositing fill in navigable waters is prohibited without a permit from the Corps. In 1968 the scope of the Corps review was broadened to include an evaluation of the effect of dredge and fill activities on wildlife, fish, conservation, pollution, aesthetics, biological communities, and the general public interest.

Federal Water Pollution Control Act (FWPCA) of 1972: This act prohibited the discharge of pollutants into navigable waters without a permit. It was the first statute to formally address dredging and filling activities in wetlands. Section 404 of the act regulated discharge of dredge and fill material in the "waters of the U.S.," which EPA has defined to include wetlands.

Marine Protection Research and Sanctuaries Act of 1972: Section 303 authorized the Corps to issue permits for the transport of dredged material for ocean disposal.

1977 Clean Water Act (Amended the FWPCA): The Section 404 permit system was revised at this time to specifically authorize nationwide permits.

Emergency Wetlands Resources Act of 1986: This act promotes the conservation of wetlands resources and helps fulfill obligations under the international migratory bird treaty through public acquisition of woodlands. The Corps and EPA jointly enforce the requirement under this statute.

North American Wetlands Conservation Act of 1989 (as amended in 1990 and 1994): This act clarifies national goals for the restoration and maintenance of chemical, physical, and biological integrity of the nation's waters. It provides funding for implementation of the North American Waterfowl Management Plan and the Tripartite Agreement on wetlands among Canada, Mexico, and the United States.

Implicitly, this definition requires the presence of three ecological parameters for an area to meet the definition. First, the area must have wetlands hydrology, either inundation from a river, stream, or other water body, or from groundwater. Second, the areas must have hydric soils or soils that are saturated for a significant period during the growing season. Third, the area must have hydrophytic vegetation or vegetation adapted for life in saturated soil conditions. This definition can be interpreted broadly and often includes areas that are not actually wet for long periods of time.

Early on, you need to determine whether your site has federally regulated wetlands. Check with your local county engineer's office, the nearest EPA division, and Army Corps of Engineer's office. If a wetland exists, you will find it located on maps of the area your site occupies. Once you realize the project requires a Section 404 permit, contact the district office of the Corps to find out the procedure for applying for a permit. The Corps can issue two types of dredge and fill permits: general and individual.

General permits are those issued under regulations that authorize the placement of fill for clearly specified categories of activities considered to have little or no significant environmental impact on wetlands or other aquatic sites. They can be issued on a nationwide or regional basis, and if your project complies with the stated criteria, they do not require an individual permit.

The following are three important general permits for developers:

1. Nationwide Permit (NWP) #12: Utility Line Backfill and Bedding
2. NWP #14: Road Crossings
3. NWP #26: Headwaters and Isolated Waters Discharges

In general, these three permits require the submittal of a preconstruction notification (PCN) and a wetlands delineation. The wetlands delineation shows the location and perimeters of areas on your site.

NWP #12 allows for the discharge of backfill or bedding material for utility lines, provided the discharge does not change the wetlands' reconstruction bottom contours. NWP #14 allows for the placement of fill for road crossings, provided the fill covers no more than one-third of an acre or 200 lineal feet.

NWP #26 is more complicated and allows the placement of up to 10 acres of fill into "isolated waters or headwaters or their

Newpoint BEAUFORT, SC

This 54-acre community was developed according to a plan and an architectural code that drew on local examples.

Developer: The Newpoint Company, Vince Graham and Bob Turner
Architect/Planner: Gerald Cowart

Village Homes DAVIS, CA

Village Homes, built in Davis, CA, in the 1970s, was a forerunner of today's "sustainable development" movement. Forty percent of the 60-acre site is dedicated to agriculture and green space.

Developer/Planner: Judy and Michael Corbett

Natural drainage is used to reduce infrastructure costs and to distribute stormwater to the agricultural areas.

Homes are grouped close to cul-de-sacs, while the rear yards open onto larger common areas leading to the village green.

Community agriculture includes orchards and community gardens as well as vineyards.

Town of Tioga   GAINESVILLE, FL

Town of Tioga is a 280-acre traditional neighborhood development underway in Gainesville, FL. When completed, it will include more than 500 single-family homes as well as retail, institutional, and recreational uses.

Developer: The Dibros Corporation

Existing trees have been conserved wherever possible at Town of Tioga, including these trees that originally lined an unpaved farm road.

Harbor Town MEMPHIS, TN

Harbor Town, located on an island adjacent to downtown Memphis, is one of the most complete neotraditional developments. It contains 350 apartments, over 500 single-family homes, and a commercial district.

Developer: Henry Turley Company   *Planner:* RTKL Associates

Fields of St. Croix   LAKE ELMO, MN

The Fields of St. Croix is a 226-acre conservation community that includes 90 homes, farmland, and restored native prairie.

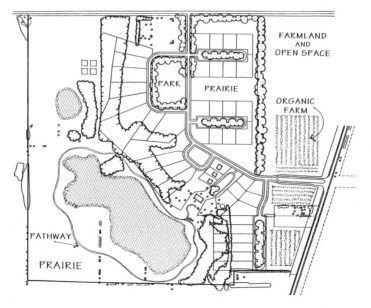

Developer/Planner: Robert Engstrom Companies

Examples of Infill Housing

A significant amount of new housing is being built as "infill" developments on small vacant parcels or in redeveloping older neighborhoods.

In Seattle, rehabilitation of an older apartment building was coupled with construction of a new parking garage below these new townhouses. Victoria Townhomes, Seattle, WA.
Developer: Lorig Associates
Architect/Land Planner: Mithun Partners

This development in central Austin placed 16 semi-attached homes on a 1.3 acre site. Tonkawa Bluff City Homes, Austin, TX.
Developer: Overland Property Company
Architect: Kipp Flores & Follmer Architects

This condominium development, Slater's Lane, contains two-story units over other two-story units in a style that echoes the historic townhouse pattern of Alexandria, VA. Slater's Lane, Alexandria, VA.
Developer/Builder: Madison Homes
Architect: Torti Gallas and Partners CHK, Inc.

adjacent wetlands," although proposals to fill more than an acre or two typically require an individual permit. Isolated waters and wetlands have no physical connection to navigable waters. Headwaters are the point on a noontide stream or river above which the average annual flow is less than 5 cubic feet per second.

The NWP #26 permit requires the submittal of a predischarge notification, including a wetlands delineation to the Corps. It then determines whether an individual permit might be required. This is the most commonly used permit in land development; you will likely apply for this if your land is near or contains wetland areas.

In 1993, the National Wildlife Federation sued the federal government about what it considered to be widespread use of NWF #26. The resulting "Tulloch Rule" was adopted by the Corps in direct response to the lawsuit. The Tulloch Rule curtailed many of the dredge and fill practices by clarifying the "fallback" or "redeposit" of dredged materials, including small amounts termed "incidental fallback." Basically, it significantly tightened the restrictions with which you must comply in obtaining a NWP #26.

However, a district court subsequently struck down this rule, prompting a new series of lawsuits. The results are twofold. Because of the Tulloch Rule, developers created new dredge and fill techniques to comply with the intent and letter of the law. On the other hand, renewed efforts by special interest groups have increased the EPA's efforts to tighten regulations on dredge and fill activities around wetlands. To navigate these issues successfully you must remain current on both the regulations in place and impending court decisions on wetlands.

Your project might require an individual permit authorizing the placement of fill into water or wetlands. An individual permit requires more time and effort by you and your team. Figure 5.4 Individual Permit Process outlines application steps.

Mitigation—avoiding, minimizing, or compensating for impacts—is required in the issuance of individual permits. Compensation usually means enhancing existing wetlands or

---

FIGURE 5.4. Individual Permit Process

Public Notice. Corps issues Public Notice within 15 days of receiving all permit information.

Comment Period. All applicable agencies review permit application and comments. Corps decides if an Environmental Impact Statement is required.

Public Hearing. Citizens may request a public hearing. (Normally these are not held.)

Permit Evaluation. The Corps evaluates permit application based on all reviews, hearings, and comments that have gone before.

Environmental Assessment and Statement of Finding. The "Statement of Finding" document explains how the permit application decision was formulated and is made available to the public.

---

creating new ones to replace one that's impacted. Mitigation decisions are on a case-by-case basis, so check requirements at the federal, state, and local levels to understand how mitigation methods and cost will affect your project.

Many state and local governments also regulate development in and around wetlands. State and local definitions of wetlands and standards for permit issuance may differ from those at the federal level. Be prepared to resolve inconsistencies among federal, state, and local regulations if your development plans include filling wetlands. If you cannot resolve the inconsistencies, you should make sure that you have complied with the requirements for each level of government by complying with the strictest ones.

Violations of wetlands regulations include ignoring permit conditions or failing to obtain a permit. The regulations can hold many parties responsible for violations, including the owner, developer, contractor, and subcontractor. The first action, usually an administrative order, requires compliance within a particular time frame. Violations can be defined as civil or criminal. A violation may be deemed criminal if its severe enough, there is prior knowledge that the activity is illegal, or it's a repetition of an illegal activity. Penalties may include heavy fines, work stoppage, corrective measures, or imprisonment.

Project Impacts

If your project contains areas that appear to be wetlands, first determine if they meet the definitions provided by the federal, state, and local agencies granting permits for activities within wetlands. Check with each agency to review its respective definitions. An Advanced Identification of Disposal Areas (AIDA) worksheet, available from your local EPA or Corps office, describes a planning process used to identify wetlands and other waters suitable or unsuitable for dredge and fill activities. This can serve as a preliminary indication of factors likely to be considered during review of a Section 404 permit application. Think of the AIDA process as a tool that does not guarantee either permit approval or denial. It merely serves as a useful guide that allows you as a developer to pre-identify potential problems before you apply for a permit.

Next, locate approximate wetlands boundaries; the wetlands could be part of a wetlands inventory so a map may show these general boundaries.

Some wetlands appear on the National Wetlands Inventory maps produced by the U.S. Fish and Wildlife Service. However, because this inventory is incomplete not all states will have these maps. Moreover, because the maps' scale is too small, you may be unable to accurately pinpoint the actual boundaries on your project. If wetlands seem to appear on or near your project on these maps, you may want to hire a consultant to help you delineate the boundaries.

Once you have identified an area as wetlands, determine whether the activities you plan to conduct there are subject to regulation. The two most common forms of development activities subject to regulation are land clearing or dredging activities and the placement of fill-in wetlands. While federal law technically covers only the discharge of dredge and fill material into the waters of the United States, which includes most wetlands, it has been interpreted as encompassing other activities such as land clearing and dredging. Fill material refers to any material used primarily to either replace water with dry land or to change the bottom elevation of a body of water. Figure 5.5 Development Activities in Waters or Wetlands Requiring Dredge and Fill Permits describes the different types of activities you might be considering for your project.

Hazardous Wastes

Developers undertake another important responsibility—hazardous wastes—when selecting an appropriate site. When clearing your site of environmental problems associated with hazardous wastes, the two most important regulations to be aware of are contained within the Resource Conservation and Recovery Act (RCRA) and the Comprehensive Environmental Response, Compensation and Liability Act (CERCLA).

Regulations

RCRA governs active and future facilities generating solid and hazardous wastes. As a developer, you will most likely be concerned with CERCLA, which governs abandoned sites or sites with a prior history of uses that have the potential to generate hazardous wastes. CERCLA outlines your liability as a

---

FIGURE 5.5. Development Activities in Waters or Wetlands Requiring Dredge and Fill Permits

1. Placement of fill necessary for the construction of any structure; building of any structure or impoundment requiring rock, sand, dirt, or other materials
2. Site development fill for recreation, industrial, commercial, residential, and other uses
3. Building dams, dikes, artificial islands, levees, or artificial reefs
4. Building property protection or reclamation devices such as riprap, groins, seawalls, breakwaters, and revetments
5. Beach replacement or enhancement
6. Fill for structures such as sewage treatment facilities, intake and outfall pipes associated with power plants, and underwater utility lines

---

landowner for problems caused by former land contamination from solid wastes. To assess the impact of hazardous wastes on your site, you must first understand their definitions under RCRA and CERCLA. Begin by referring to the RCRA definition for hazardous wastes and the CERCLA definitions for hazardous substances, pollutants, or contaminants.

Under RCRA, wastes are classified as hazardous if EPA lists them or if they exhibit one or more of the following characteristics: ignitability, corrosivity, reactivity, or toxicity. If a waste is neither a listed waste nor exhibits one of these four characteristics, it may still be classified as a hazardous waste under state regulations.

Under CERCLA, hazardous substances include materials designated as hazardous under the Clean Water Act, RCRA, the Clean Air Act, and the Toxic Substances Control Act of 1976. Moreover, under CERCLA, a hazardous substance can be either a product or a waste. (RCRA regulates only wastes, not products.) A waste with any amount of "hazardous substance" triggers CERCLA jurisdiction. All RCRA wastes are considered hazardous substances under CERCLA.

The Superfund Cleanup Acceleration Act of 1998 is essentially an amendment to CERCLA. This act directs the administrator of the Environmental Protection Agency to establish programs that provide grants to eligible entities such as local government units or redevelopment agencies for site characterization and assessment of brownfield facilities. This law defines a brownfield facility, with a few exceptions, as real property, the expansion or redevelopment of which is complicated by the presence of hazardous material. A brownfield is any developed or undeveloped land having a prior use in which hazardous materials were utilized. When land appears to be undeveloped, the hazardous materials could exist as underground storage tanks, contaminated soil stemming from effluent from a previous activity, or buried wastes in various types of containers.

Other provisions of the law entitle the federal government to assess the performance standards of any cleanup activities. It also clarifies a new property owner's liability in after-purchase discovery of hazardous materials. You as the developer of such a property must show proof of due diligence according to the American Society for Testing and Materials (ASTM) standards of assessment of the presence of hazardous wastes and present a complete title search clearing your land of any suspicious former uses.

Violating RCRA and CERCLA requirements has serious consequences. Under CERCLA, failure to conduct a proper inquiry into previous uses of a site or showing prior knowledge of the presence of hazardous wastes on your site will subject you to lawsuits from subsequent homeowners and the federal government. In addition, you must pay the cost of environmental cleanup as well as a series of heavy fines up to $25,000 for each day of noncompliance. Liability under CERCLA is retroactive, strict, and joint and several. The liability applies not only to cleanup costs but also to "natural resources damages." This includes contaminated drinking water sources and severe excavated land forms resulting in damage of topsoils and vegetation. Violations of RCRA can result in civil penalties, including fines up to $25,000 for each day of noncompliance, as well as criminal prosecution.

Project Impacts

Aside from a title search, what's the best way to ensure that no prior land uses on the site contributed to the generation of hazardous wastes? As described in Chapter 3, you can evaluate your site for hazardous wastes by performing an environmental site assessment study as laid out by ASTM. Proper inquiry into the site's conditions shows you used due diligence in evaluating the site for hazardous wastes. This in turn can qualify you as an innocent landowner under CERCLA in case hazardous wastes are discovered during site development.

Avoid any site located near other properties whose present or past generation of hazardous wastes could endanger homeowners' health. Investigate the water supply source and the means of conveying water to your new development. The EPA keeps a list of RCRA generators (those persons or entities that generate hazardous wastes as defined by RCRA) and RCRA

Treatment, Storage, and Disposal (TSD) facilities. The ASTM standard of practice recommends that your new development not be located within a one-mile circumference of a RCRA facility. In addition, locating near a RCRA facility will likely hurt your project marketability.

Water Quality

Land development activities can affect the quality of both groundwater and surface water through the introduction of pollutants and sediment. Surface waters are defined as oceans, streams, rivers, lakes, marshes, bogs, ponds, and channels, while groundwater refers to the underground supply of water known as the aquifer. Regulations have long protected surface waters, but groundwater protection is a concern as well because it provides much of the drinking water for the United States.

Regulations

Federal laws regulating surface water and groundwater quality seek to maintain a level sufficient to protect human health and recreational activities. For instance, if federal regulations deem the level of contaminants is too high in the local drinking water supply, a variety of measures will be taken in the area to reduce those levels. These can include curtailing land development or increasing the measures employed to protect the local water supply from project runoff. Federal laws regulating water quality also seek to protect the propagation of fish, shellfish, and wildlife. Figure 5.6 Major Federal Laws Regulating Water Quality shows the major federal laws that govern water quality.

Three important parts of the Clean Water Act are Sections 319, 401, and 402. Section 319 defines the scope of the regulations affecting water quality. Section 402, known as the Nonpoint Source Control Program, protects groundwater by reducing the surface water pollution from nonpoint sources. Section 401 requires states to certify that any federally permitted project will not degrade water quality through the discharge of runoff into surface waters. If you plan to discharge surface runoff into navigable waters, the state must certify that the

FIGURE 5.6. Major Federal Laws Regulating Water Quality

Rivers and Harbors Act of 1899: First federal regulation protecting the nation's waters for the promotion of commerce.

Water Pollution Control Act of 1948: Provides technical assistance and funds to states from the federal government to promote efforts to protect water quality.

Water Quality Act of 1965: Charged states with setting water quality standards for interstate navigable waters.

The Clean Water Act of 1972: Landmark legislation to protect and restore the physical, chemical, and biological diversity of the nation's waters, making it illegal to discharge pollutants without a permit.

Marine Protection, Research and Sanctuaries Act of 1972: Prevents unacceptable dumping into oceans.

Clean Water Act Amendments of 1977: Allowed states to assume responsibility for federal programs and strengthened controls on toxic pollutants.

Water Quality Act of 1987: Strengthened the focus on achieving water quality goals by supporting new state and local efforts to deal with polluted runoff, funding treatment plants, addressed pollution caused by urban runoff, and protected estuaries of national importance. This act strengthened the requirements for the Environmental Protection Agency-regulated permitting of development activities discharging pollutants by requiring a National Pollutant Discharge Elimination System (NPDES) permit.

Coastal Zone Act Reauthorization Amendments of 1990: Focused efforts on reducing polluted runoff in 29 coastal states.

Water Resources Development Act of 1998: This act provides measures for the restoration of rivers and watershed areas in terms of decreasing the amount of pollutants and sedimentation discharged by development activities. It also provides the funding of specific restoration projects.

discharge complies with all applicable effluent limitations and water quality standards.

Section 404 outlines the program known as the National Pollutant Discharge Elimination System (NPDES). It controls point source pollution from industrial or sewage treatment facilities; EPA also includes stormwater runoff from construction activities. Generally, if you are disturbing 5 or more acres of land, you must apply for a NPDES permit.

Your team also needs to carefully review state and local regulations on water quality to understand which activities associated with your project are regulated. Multitiered federal, state, and local regulations are common for water quality. For example, local governments sometimes have special programs for development in sensitive watershed areas, especially those with the greatest impact on the public supply of drinking water or water used for recreational purposes.

In some states, the state or district office charged with regulating water quality not only requires various permits but also coordinates permitting from all federal, state, and local agencies. Because water-quality issues are directly tied to wetlands issues, you'll sometimes find all activities affecting wetlands and water quality housed in one state agency.

Violating laws governing water quality standards can result in work stoppage, heavy fines, and having to pay for the cost of cleanup. In addition, conducting illegal activities with prior knowledge and repeated violations can be considered a criminal offense.

Project Impacts

Several development and construction activities are likely to have a major impact on water quality. Regulation of water quality focuses on any activity that changes the way water naturally drains into surface water and groundwater. Also included are any activities that discharge pollution or sediment-laden water into open stormwater retention and detention systems, sewage retention systems, drainage wells, abandoned mines, and sinkholes. Finally, Section 404 of the Clean Water Act potentially regulates any activity that discharges pollutants or decreases or enlarges the natural boundaries of surface waters through the deposit of sediment or water. These types of activities require a national pollutant discharge elimination system (NPDES) permit from the Corps of Engineers. Figure 5.7

Common Pollutants of Water Quality shows various types of pollutants and their effects on water uses.

Grading and Installing Infrastructure. During site development, grading and installing infrastructure can change the natural contours of the land, which in turn can change the natural flow of surface runoff, causing erosion. Erosion may produce a heavy sediment load in the runoff or the debris from construction activities may carry pollutants in surface runoff. Because these pollutants may eventually find their way into surface water and groundwater supplies, building codes require proper siltation barriers and erosion control devices both during and after construction. Each requires a separate local permit, and if grading and installing infrastructure affect wetlands, you'll need a federal permit as well.

Dewatering Operations. Dewatering operations are sometimes necessary when you're installing utility infrastructure and setting foundations. Dewatering basically pumps away the top layer of the water table so excavation can occur. Local governments issue permits for dewatering and subsequent discharge of the water. In some areas, that extracted water must be used for other construction operations such as wetting down imported fill.

Sanitary Sewer System. Your project's sanitary sewer system requires several permits that regulate installation and design. Building codes govern the bottom or invert elevation of pipes, the installation of sump pumps and lift stations, clean-out mechanisms, and back-flow prevention systems. Each of these operations requires permits from local governments or the state districts regulating water quality. The design of drain fields and the placement of septic tanks also require permits and must follow building code requirements.

FIGURE 5.7. Common Pollutants of Water Quality

Category	Examples	Effects	Affected	Sources
Oxygen-Demanding Materials	Sewage, paper, manufacturing wastes	Deficiencies in oxygen levels that can stunt growth and reproduction in aquatic plants and cause fish mortality	Water supply, recreation, fishing	Domestic wastes, industrial wastes, urban runoff
Infectious Agents	E. coli, salmonella	Disease in humans and animals	Water supply, recreation	Domestic wastes, agricultural runoff
Nutrients	Nitrogen phosphorous	Excessive algae growth	Water supply, recreation	Fertilizing landscape, domestic wastes, industrial wastes
Toxic Substances	Ammonia, mercury, lead	Cancer, injury, or mortality in living organisms	Water supply, recreation	Runoff with pesticides and herbicides
Thermal Pollutants	Power plant discharges	Fish mortality	Fisheries	Power plants
Sediments and Minerals	Sand, silt, clay	Aquatic plant and fish mortality	Water supply, recreation	Poor stormwater runoff design
Oil and Hazardous Substances	Oil, gasoline, petroleum by-products	Plant and animal mortality	Water supply, recreation, fishing	Poor stormwater design, highway runoff

Air Quality

Residential developers should also be aware their projects might be subject to environmental regulations under the federal Clean Air Act. The act designates as nonattainment areas those regions that fail to comply with national ambient air quality standards (NAAQS). The EPA has also set acceptable pollutants levels to protect human health and the environment. There are NAAQS for six classes of air pollutants: ozone, carbon monoxide, nitrogen dioxide, sulfur dioxide, particulate matter, and lead.

The Clean Air Act Amendments of 1990 established aggressive control requirements to address four crucial air pollution problems: urban smog, hazardous air pollution, acid rain, and depletion of the stratospheric ozone layer. The amendments also directed states to set new deadlines for submitting their State Implementation Plans. All states must submit these State Implementation Plans to establish air pollution control programs and reduce pollutants in designated nonattainment areas. Parts of the country labeled nonattainment areas are given a date by which they must be brought into compliance with levels outlined in the NAAQS.

Regulations

State Implementation Plans take into account future growth for particular air basins in a state and establish permit requirements for new sources of air pollution. Because of the stringent new pollution standards, many previously unregulated activities will now fall under air pollution control measures. It's very possible that regions that fail to meet NAAQS could become increasingly strict in allowing new development because of factors such as degraded air quality due to increased traffic.

Project Impacts

Is your new project located in or near a designated nonattainment area or marginal nonattainment area? If so, check the status of the state's SIP. Find out what various provisions aimed at cleaning up the air might mean to future planning in the area.

Check with the local air-quality agency early in the process to determine what air pollution control measures might apply during development or to your completed development. For example, many areas now regulate open burning of cleared debris. You may need permits for this, as well as for any site development work that generates hazardous air pollutants, such as operating construction equipment. Consider, too, increased traffic generated by your completed development, which may indirectly heighten pollution in the area. When you contact the local air-quality agency, the staff will prescribe appropriate air-quality control measures for the area where your project is located.

Noise Control

Noise control regulations are designed to minimize the danger to the population from a large threshold shift in noise level. This measures the difference in decibels between the lowest and highest level of sound intensity before and after noise exposure. Current EPA standards permit certain ranges of permanent threshold shifts for new projects. Noise control regulations determine the change in noise levels that may occur as the result of a proposed action, then review its effects on the population or the land exposed.

Regulations

The standards for noise control have resulted from a variety of federal acts. After Congress passed the Noise Control Act of 1972, the EPA created the Office of Noise Abatement and Control. Its funds were cut in 1981, but it left behind a number of guidelines for local noise control ordinances. Violating these standards can result in work stoppage and fines assessed for each day the violation continues. Figure 5.8 Major Federal Laws Governing Noise Pollution lists the important features of the primary laws governing noise.

Frequently local areas have standards governing the transmission of noise. These standards generally apply to any source of noise and stipulate the limit in the number of feet that audi-

FIGURE 5.8. Major Federal Laws Governing Noise Pollution

National Environmental Policy Act of 1969: This requires an environmental impact statement for all major federal projects significantly affecting the quality of the human environment, for the purpose of identifying alternative actions that avoid or minimize damage to the environment. It has a specific provision for noise control.

Noise Control Act of 1972: This act requires the EPA to compile and publish reports to identify products that are major sources of noise pollution and to provide techniques for controlling noise from such products. Construction-related products include heavy machinery, pumps, generators, compressors, power tools, pneumatic drills, vibrators, pile drivers, and jackhammers.

---

ble sound can travel. You need to know the provisions of the local noise ordinance to prevent work stoppage on your site due to unacceptable noise generation.

Project Impacts

If you plan a large-scale residential or mixed-use development, you might be required to submit an environmental impact statement to EPA. The EIS's noise pollution element determines the change in the noise environment that may occur as a result of development. It also examines development's effect on the surrounding population and animal habitats. If your project is federally funded in total or in part, you'll need an EIS that includes a noise pollution element. Be aware too of noise control standards for worker protection issued and regulated by the Occupational Safety and Health Administration (OSHA).

Radon

Certain regions of the country need to be concerned about radon, a colorless, odorless gas present in all soils and constantly being released into the atmosphere. Prolonged exposure to radon primarily increases the risk of lung cancer. Sources of radon include building materials, groundwater, and soil. Though present in all soils, the amount found there does not necessarily indicate the amount that might be transported into the home. That depends on the type of construction, the location of the building footprint, and the characteristics of the soil.

Regulations

The EPA recommends reducing indoor radon levels below 4 picocuries per liter or as low as possible, but levels can be accurately measured only after a home is built. Therefore, if your project is located in a radon-prone area, you may want to use radon-resistant construction rather than perform extensive soil testing.

Radon gets into a home by convective flow, which carries radon through cracks and openings in foundations, and by diffusion, which moves gas from areas of high concentration to low. Figure 5.9 Major Radon Entry Routes shows typical methods of radon transport into the home. In areas with high radon levels, state and local governments are adopting radon-resistant building codes. Violations can involve fines and work stoppage.

Project Impacts

Developers should use widely recognized radon-resistant construction techniques in areas where radon levels run high. To determine whether you need radon-resistant construction for your development, consider the following factors:

1. Survey existing homes in the same geological region for elevated radon levels.
2. Check your site for soils with high permeability or rock fractures.
3. Check the soils on your site for their possible derivation from rock containing high levels of uranium or radium. Data on permeability rates and geological derivation are available in soil surveys from the U.S. Department of Agriculture and U.S. Geological Survey.
4. Check your county's radon level by reviewing the EPA Map of Radon Zones available from state radon programs and EPA's national and regional offices.

FIGURE 5.9. Major Radon Entry Routes

A. Cracks in concrete slabs
B. Spaces behind brick veneer walls that rest on an uncapped hollow-block foundation
C. Pores and cracks in concrete blocks
D. Floor-wall joints
E. Exposed soil, as in a sump pump
F. Weeping (drain) tile, if drained to an open sump pump
G. Mortar joints
H. Loose-fitting pipe penetrations
I. Open tops of block walls
J. Building materials such as some rock
K. Water (from some wells)

Source: Environmental Protection Agency, *Radon Reduction Techniques for Detached Houses, Technical Guidance,* 2d ed., EP-88, Washington, DC, 1988.

How to reduce radon levels depends on the type of foundation you're planning to use. In homes with basements, crawl spaces, and slab-on-grade foundations, radon-resistant construction includes minimizing radon entry and providing for inexpensive installation of a subslab or submembrane depressurization system. This generally includes reducing the potential for cracks in concrete slabs, sealing around utility penetrations, and sealing the top of sump pumps. Another option is to provide a method for the gas to escape through a controlled route in the house. This involves venting the slab and providing a pipe (passive system) for drawing the gas upward to be vented through the roof. Some cases require an active system (adding a fan to the pipe).

For another option, consider eliminating the stack effect. The stack effect results when warm air rises through a building and escapes through openings in the upper levels, drawing radon through the house. To reduce the stack effect, eliminate openings between floors and seal the home's superstructure. For homes with crawl spaces, you can limit radon entry into the home through floor openings and ductwork as well as sealing interior spaces by a barrier installed over the crawl space floor. Figure 5.10 Methods to Reduce Radon Pathways illustrates various techniques for reducing radon in the home.

For good information on radon-resistant construction, review the EPA publication, Radon Resistant Construction Techniques for New Residential Construction: Technical Guidance. Section 304 of the Toxic Substances Control Act requires EPA to produce other publications that provide good information on radon control. Don't overlook the Internet as a great source of information about radon, radon mitigation, and radon resistant construction methods. The EPA maintains a website with extensive information on radon detection, resistant construction techniques, and mitigation.

You may also want to use subcontractors familiar with radon-resistant construction. Be aware, though, that no methods provide foolproof protection against radon. For this reason, you may want to avoid clauses in sales contracts that create contractual responsibility for radon prevention.

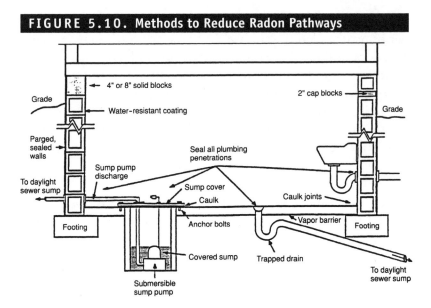

FIGURE 5.10. Methods to Reduce Radon Pathways

Source: Environmental Protection Agency, *Radon Reduction Techniques for Detached Houses, Technical Guidance,* 2d ed., EP-88, Washington, DC, 1988.

Plants and Wildlife

Protection of endangered plants and wildlife rests in the policies originally formulated by Endangered Species Act of 1973. This act defines which species are endangered and threatened by including them on a list of protected species that have legal status against habitat disruption. The designation is intended to protect species from extinction. Continually reviewed and strengthened since it passed, the Endangered Species Act has engendered a vast number of court cases, the outcomes of which have proven the strength of its rather stringent rules.

Regulations

Section 9 of the 1973 Endangered Species Act states that it is unlawful for any person to "take" any listed species anywhere in the United States. Take is defined as harass, harm, pursue, hunt, shoot, wound, kill, trap, capture, collect, or in any way disturb the animal or its habitat. Violators face fines of up to $20,000 per year, imprisonment for up to one year, or both. The Migratory Bird Act makes it unlawful to take any birds or nests or eggs of birds listed as endangered, with violations resulting in fines up to $2,000 and imprisonment for up to two years. The Bald Eagle Protection Act states that no person shall take any bald eagle, alive or dead, or its nest or eggs. Violating this act can bring fines of up to $10,000, imprisonment for up to two years, or both.

Project Impacts
As a developer you need to review EPA's list of endangered species and their designated habitats. To do that, first determine whether development activities on your site may disturb the habitats of endangered species. The list frequently changes; make sure yours is current. Then review the same criteria set by the state. You may even want to meet with the state environmental office to review them. Each state has specific habitats native to its region that may be protected under state statutes. Disturbing or destroying such habitats will probably require both federal and state permits.

New Approach to Development
Adhere to environmentally conservative regulations by using them as a basis of your home or land development design concept. Then market this idea to your customers; the idea of sustainability is embodied in the trend favoring "green" building techniques and practices. The target market for this concept is large and continues to grow.

Many aspects of creating and constructing a residential development add environmental amenities to the community. Practices such as donating common areas for hike-and-bike trails, enhancing the surroundings by appropriate landscaping, and providing lakes and ponds for community enjoyment not only improve the quality of the environment but give a project a distinct marketing edge. In some cases you may be able to turn a project constraint, such as the requirements to provide retention and detention areas for stormwater management, into a project amenity such as a lake or pond.

Examine all environmental regulatory requirements for their potential either to provide a project amenity or create a marketing advantage. Many programs, books, and Internet sites are full of information about both land development and homebuilding practices and techniques. A great number of these techniques deal with such marketable ideas as energy efficiency, improved indoor air quality, and water conservation. You might want to adopt an entire menu of green building techniques or pick and choose ones you believe to be marketable and cost-effective.

Marketing the Environment

When one development company began work on site approvals for a large residential development, it became apparent that local government considered the land environmentally sensitive. Restrictions for density and buffering from nearby wetlands threatened to make the project infeasible. The developer made a special effort to apply careful land management techniques, including preserving open space networks, using native plants for landscaping, and minimizing cut and fill. Because of these efforts, the developer got the project permitted in half the time expected.

This savings in time produced enormous savings in cash outlays for debt service on loans and salaries. The project came on-line earlier than expected and produced revenues from sales in a more timely manner. As a result, the developer had a greater amount of funds up front to protect the project's cash flow. Further, the project's environmental sensitivity provided the theme for an extremely successful marketing campaign.

When the developer had to leave more than 350 acres of land in this project untouched, the development team produced a unique master plan that capitalized on the distribution of lots adjacent to the nature preserve. The team also used this natural area to buffer the entire development from the surrounding urban areas. The developer then marketed the project as a perfect combination of modern living within a natural environment. Lot prices bordering the natural areas commanded selling prices 35 percent higher than those of similar projects in the area.

The Green Developer

Increasingly, individual development companies are using green development and building techniques in their new projects, which help to produce more sustainable communities. Sustainability refers to the practice of supplying the needs of people today without depleting resources required by persons in the future. This is accomplished through sensitive land-use practices that protect water quality and conserve the best natural features of the land. It is also done by carefully choosing materials that require less energy to produce and transport and can be easily regenerated or recycled. Building sustainable communities also involves home designs that take into account the type of materials chosen, energy efficiency, and low-maintenance features that use less water and energy.

Recognition Programs

The growing concern for producing sustainable communities has produced several programs across the country for recognizing developments that are sensitive to the environment.

One national program that recognizes environmentally sensitive development is the Building With Trees recognition program, a joint effort of the National Association of Home Builders and the National Arbor Day Foundation. The program publicly recognizes developers and builders who demonstrate excellence in working with the environment by saving, planting, or transplanting trees in new developments. The program challenges developers and builders to use a site's natural features as a focal point for the development process and offers national recognition for a job well done.

In another effort, the city of Austin, Texas, has created the Green Builder Program, which shifts building practices to those who save energy, water, and natural resources. The program seeks to promote a quality of life that is healthful and rewarding for the citizens of Austin. The core of the program revolves around water, energy, building materials, and solid wastes.

Developers and builders can participate in the program by attending a seminar, following guidelines in the Austin Green Building Guide, providing customers with green building information, and participating in continuing education on green building materials and techniques. In return, the builder receives free advertisements as a member of the Green Builder Program and technical assistance in implementing green designs and building practices.

You can access The Green Building Guide, a 400-page document, on-line at the Austin Green Building Program's website. Two other examples: the Smart Building Program in Oregon and the Rocky Mountain Institute of Basalt, Colorado's Green Development Community. Check your state or local community for any similar programs that recognize environmentally sensitive development and construction.

Environmental Awareness

Why should you as a developer and builder increase your own environmental awareness? While environmental laws and regulations are written to protect the country's natural resources, they also directly affect the cost and process of development and building and the quality of the built environment. Increasing your knowledge of environmental laws and regulations can set the foundation for your ability to follow cost-effective development and building practices, create minimal environmental impact, and meet regulatory requirements.

Making wise choices in land development practices is also the best way to offer new solutions to old environmental constraints. When you comply with regulations by offering alternative development and construction methods, you may ultimately turn potential constraints into marketable project amenities. This will enhance property values and position you as a developer committed to delivering a quality product.

6

Developing a Master Plan Concept

Models and strategies for residential land development result from prevailing characteristics of the time. Levittown, Pennsylvania, built right after World War II, is one of the first examples in the United States of a large, built-from-scratch residential neighborhood. Its target market of returning GI's and their families made the single-family house situated in a homogeneous neighborhood a fixture of that period and for many years to come. This simple model of a neighborhood consisted of the house, the front and backyard, the sidewalk, and the street repeated over and over. People used their cars to travel to other places for work, school, recreation, and shopping.

The pattern was basically an extended curved grid. The grid became an important pattern for the design concept of the suburb. In general, it was simple and easy to understand, an idea borrowed from the urban grid pattern popular at the time in most cities. It provided the home buyer with a familiar and recognizable pattern.

The suburbs began with this model and grew in response to home buyers' desire to live within driving distance of the economic and cultural advantages of the city while being protected from urban noise, pollution, and congestion. Eventually, because of increased traffic, population, and pollution, the suburbs acquired some of the same conditions as the city. Furthermore, because of their distance from the workplace, workers began to experience longer commutes, producing an increase in travel costs and time spent away from home. As a result, the attitudes of home buyers toward suburban living began to shift. These changes, as well as factors such as new technological innovations, changes in work and family life, increased crime rates, and growing environmental problems, forced developers to modify the original simple model of the suburb, creating new approaches to residential design.

Societal changes in the last half of the 20th century led to changes in the design of residential development. Remarkable change in the number of times the professional worker will likely change jobs over the life of his or her career has created a category of nomadic home buyers. Because of the transience of white-collar workers, these home buyers no longer see the purchase of a home as an assured profit-generating investment. The buyer is likely to be unable to stay in one house long enough to generate increased equity and property value. Today's family might move many times while the children are still in school. Therefore, many buyers are now choosing the lifestyle that a new home and neighborhood provide over all other concerns they might consider in a new home.

Today, buyers are more interested in the intrinsic quality of the neighborhood and the ability of the home and the community to service their needs. Home buyers evaluate their choice in a neighborhood with increased scrutiny. They want more quality for their money, represented by such things as nearby services, recreational amenities, and employment. As time at work increases, people seek more ways be at home for longer periods of time. They want employment centers to be nearby and commutes to work and services to be shorter. They also want durable materials in the home, improved customer service by the builder, lower maintenance and energy costs, and increased security. Above all, in looking for a place to live, buyers desire an affordable neighborhood with distinctive characteristics, which the generic quality of many suburbs of the past has failed to provide.

To satisfy this need, you as a developer must begin with a strong, central idea for a new development. That idea becomes the theme of the new community, offering a neighborhood that will appeal to buyers. After affordability, members of each of the target markets look for attributes with which they can personally identify. For instance, if their focus is on raising children, they look for a neighborhood that is family-oriented in its housing styles and amenities. They might prefer a greater number of neighborhood parks with excellent facilities rather than a health club or golf course. Fortunately, even small-scale developments can offer some of these elements. A viable marketing plan showcases location or one or two cost-effective services or amenities strictly targeted toward a specific type of buyer.

Initial Idea

A residential development has greater market appeal when based on an easily recognizable idea that can influence all subsequent design decisions for the project. These decisions include choice of street and lot layout, open space distribution, housing types, materials, and types of amenities, services, and landscaping. Because the design idea shapes the neighborhood's identity, it should fit perfectly with the target market's demands and desires.

Creating a clear neighborhood identity through a well-designed master plan relies on a thorough understanding of three important concepts: site characteristics, the target market's preferences, and regional context. The way you bring these three concepts together in the master plan is critical.

What is a Master Plan?

The term master plan has long been used by design professionals to describe the drawing that depicts a site plan showing the location of all streets, houses, services and amenities, and open spaces. It is the final plan that compiles all aspects of the new development into a visual form. The extension of the term into its familiar use of master-planned community has come to mean a development that was conceived around a particular idea. That idea was formulated to target specific markets. The community contains a diverse group of elements that come together to form a cohesive whole, each carefully planned to fit well with the other. This chapter will discuss the idea of the master-planned community, as well as other forms of development. The following sections will discuss the methods for producing a master plan concept, the generating idea for any new development.

Producing the Master Plan Concept

To produce a master plan concept you first must understand the relationships among all the factors you consider when completing your final design. This involves synthesizing the ideas emerging from your knowledge of site characteristics, the target market's preferences, and regional context. If you do this successfully, you will create a master plan that exhibits a unique wholeness or unity. Figure 6.1 Factors Used to Unify a Master Plan describes some of the basic considerations you must address in producing a unified master plan.

Community Identity

As you develop a master plan, constantly review each design decision for the way it contributes to the identity of your new development. You can make a new development a special place with a strong design idea that integrates different elements of the master plan. Design decisions should not conflict with one another. For example, you will undermine your original idea if you try to create a family-oriented neighborhood but use a street layout that allows for higher automobile speeds.

Make sure members of your design team understand the idea behind the new development and realize that this idea will play a crucial part in each design decision. As part of this process, you need to establish guidelines that direct the decision making of the project team. Figure 6.2 Key Elements of a Master Plan shows some of the elements of the master plan design that you can manipulate to showcase the new development's desired identity.

Site Characteristics

You can produce the final master plan only after you have done a complete inventory of the site's opportunities and constraints.

FIGURE 6.1. Factors Used to Unify a Master Plan

Site Characteristics
- Existing natural features
- Existing regulatory or physical constraints
- Location
- Size of developable land

Target Market's Preferences

Location
- Desire to be near/away from urban core
- Level of shopping and service amenities desired onsite
- Types of amenities desired onsite
- Quality of offsite roads leading to work, services, amenities
- Length of commute tolerated to each
- Quality of designated school district

Type of Development
- Natural or more formal setting
- Lot size
- Level of social interaction among neighbors promoted by development's design elements
- Types of public amenities and access routes
- Type of home designs associated with target market's demographic status

Regional Context
- Type of building material available
- Type of homes traditional to the area
- Type of design elements that will produce energy-efficient homes
- Preferred recreational amenities associated with the area

Once you have formulated the idea behind the master plan concept, the architect, land planner, or landscape architect on your project team can then identify and evaluate all project parameters necessary for design execution. At this point, the team should reevaluate the site characteristics to determine the number of units and supporting infrastructure required for both project feasibility and the target market's preferences.

The underlying idea for a new development must be compatible with the required number of units and unique site char-

FIGURE 6.2. Key Elements of a Master Plan

Element	Treatment
Entrances	Formal or informal; massive walls and signage to announce strong presence; minimal walls and signage for understated presence; defined by formal or informal, natural landscaping
Streets	Axial (developed in a straight line with a focal point at the end); based on a grid; curvilinear; connected (loop) or disconnected (cul-de-sac); formal or informal; defined by landscaping; parking allowed or not
Signage and Street Furniture	Natural materials and color palette; high-tech materials and contemporary color palette; strong or minimal presence; period, traditional, or contemporary style
Lighting	Defines streets; underscores landscaping; provides security; provides mood and atmosphere; uses period or traditional lighting standards; uses hidden or contemporary lighting standards
Buffers	Natural buffers of undisturbed vegetation; imported landscaping; berms or built buffers of fences and walls
Amenities	Natural amenities found on site such as lakes, creeks, meadows, marshes, mature vegetation, hills, and valleys; built amenities such as trails, courtyards, plazas, parks, tennis courts, swimming pools, clubhouse, gym, restaurants, and golf course

acteristics. In fact, each can influence the other. But rather than simply imposing a predetermined master plan on a given site, allow the site's natural features to mold and shape your master plan into its final form. This not only produces a more beautiful plan but oftentimes reduces costs.

Scrutinize your site's natural features to discover the ones that could be emphasized in your master plan concept or marketing strategies. Many times the land has an identity of its own because of site features that mark the land as a special place. These natural features are the ones you will want to showcase.

They can be as prominent as the ocean, a lake, or other body of water. Or they may be more subtle: rolling hills, predominant vegetation, or clean air; sometimes it only takes one large tree. It could even be a portion of the site's history in the form of a previous use such as a farm, old plantation, or campground. These types of features give a new development a sense of place that distinguishes it from others.

One of the master plan's primary goals is to create a specific identity for the new development that best achieves your requirements for number of units, use of natural features to enhance project value, and efficient site engineering. A design that showcases a site's natural features results in a development with characteristics unlike any other. This unique aspect contributes significantly to the special character of the neighborhood. Therefore, whenever you as the developer respect the natural features of the land, you produce a site-sensitive development that carries greater market appeal for target groups. (See Figures 4.14 to 4.16 for different approaches to adapting a master plan to the natural features of a site.)

Target Market's Preferences

What type of development most appeals to the target market you have selected? Answer this question by thoroughly understanding the group's demands and desires. Remember that demands represent those things that translate into master plan characteristics the group cannot live without. Desires represent those characteristics that enhance the development's appeal but whose absence may not necessarily cause the group to reject the development.

Make a list of the lifestyle characteristics of the group you are targeting. Then list the demands and desires that result from those characteristics. Include financial considerations and requirements for housing, security, recreation, and home maintenance. Also include any special or unique characteristics that distinguish the group from others. Figure 6.3 Characteristics of a Sample Target Market shows a short list of characteristics for a target group of young, married professionals with children. The more detailed you make your list, the

FIGURE 6.3. Characteristics of a Sample Target Market

Demographics
- Married with 1–2 small children
- 25–40 years old
- $90,000 to $120,000 income range
- One professional income household

Psychographics
- Life centers around work and family
- Small amount of leisure time for wage earner with family
- At-home caregiver requires services such as drop-in day care, quality preschools, sports, dance, gymnastics, music services catering to children
- Desire good neighborhood public and private schools
- Wage earner frequently brings work home
- Low interest in house and yard maintenance
- Place safety and security of children as priority
- Desire nearby family recreational opportunities
- Looking for affordability

more relevant your decisions will be about what to offer in your new development.

You can then translate each of the characteristics in Figure 6.3 into design equivalencies. Figure 6.4 Demands and Desires of a Sample Target Market shows several characteristics of the sample target market described in Figure 6.3 and illustrates how you can translate target market characteristics into design ideas tailored to specific needs.

Because the target group has a life centered around children, the master plan concept should support this whenever possible. Make providing a quality family-oriented neighborhood the central idea of your development. For example, design the street layout so that leftover open space becomes a park, and provide one park for each neighborhood. This type of amenity could be the hallmark of your development, which clearly states its master plan concept. Parks are relatively low-cost amenities, providing opportunities for children as well as adults to meet each other. Make the image and name of the development something that creates feelings of harmony, security, and quality.

FIGURE 6.4. Demands and Desires of a Sample Target Market

Characteristics
1. Wage earner has small amount of leisure time to spend with family
2. Wage earner frequently brings work home
3. Concerned about safety and security of children
4. Low interest in house and yard maintenance

Design Equivalents
1. Provide neighborhood parks, hike and bike trails, sports opportunities such as open space for soccer, neighborhood swimming pools, and tennis courts located within walking distance where possible.
2. Provide home office or flexible room such as spare bedroom or portion of gameroom.
3. Design street layout for slow vehicular speeds, provide sidewalks for pedestrian use, design dead ends such as cul-de-sacs where appropriate to prevent through traffic, provide adequate lighting for hike and bike trails and streets, consider providing security patrols or developing volunteer neighborhood watch programs.
4. Use smaller lots landscaped with native plants that require less water and fertilizer, consider providing a lawn service for front yards for one year after purchase as marketing idea, place small lots bordering open space to maximize views and give sense of privacy while minimizing homeowner's area to be maintained.

Besides site and target market characteristics, regional characteristics play an important role in the design decisions for your project. Regional context describes the types of master plan designs, materials, and styles of architecture that are used and accepted in a particular area over time. These land planning and architectural traditions often evolved in response to climate, landforms, and available materials. In many areas, these traditions have become associated so strongly with the place that it's difficult to successfully contradict them for master plan designs, materials, and housing types.

For example, the use of a colonial-style master plan and housing types common in Atlanta, Georgia, or Washington, DC, may appear out of place in Denver, Colorado, where the planning and building traditions are based on a response to a mountainous region. Regional building types and materials are usually based on the local area's history, climate, and terrain. If you can incorporate some of the important existing regional preferences into your project design, you can increase its chances for success by celebrating the development's sense of place. Therefore, carefully evaluate any new design ideas for the possible inclusion of firmly established regional preferences.

Sense of Community

Besides addressing site characteristics, the target market's preferences, and regional context, the identity of the new development should also promote activities that allow homeowners desirable social interactions. It should also promote the type of relationship members of the target market want to their yards and the outdoors. Many people enjoy gardening and doing their own landscape maintenance, while others either don't have time or prefer these activities done for them. Many people choose residential developments for the neighborhood's ability to support their own ideas of personal identity. People scrutinize residential developments for the same reason that they carefully select clothing and automobiles: to make a statement about themselves. As a result, generic treatments of developments and housing have less appeal in today's market as people search for neighborhoods that provide them with a sense of belonging. Figure 6.5 Elements Defining a Neighborhood offers a checklist of considerations you must address in producing a master plan concept with a strong neighborhood identity.

Social Interaction

The degree to which homeowners in the neighborhood desire exposure to one another defines their level of social interaction. Although few people want to live in total isolation, various target markets have different levels of interest in getting together with their neighbors. These are partly based on their stage in life, job pressures, interests, whether they have children, and the children's ages. The amount of free time available also influences the desired level of social interaction.

FIGURE 6.5. Elements Defining a Neighborhood

1. What distinguishing characteristics such as specific architectural style, type of materials, use of landscaping, and amount of mature vegetation should the neighborhood have?
2. What portion of these characteristics should you derive from the existing architectural traditions or regional context?
3. What level of social interaction does the target market demand?
4. What methods can you use within the project budget to encourage this level of social interaction? (A hike-and-bike trail is one method for encouraging low-level social interaction and a clubhouse is one method for encouraging high-level social interaction.)
5. To what extent are pedestrian-based streets and connections like hike-and-bike trails appropriate?
6. To what extent are automobile-based streets and connections like alleys appropriate?
7. What type of public spaces should you offer? (Examples include open spaces, parks, sports facilities, and town centers.)
8. How do members of the community want to access these public spaces?
9. What degree of privacy should individual lots and homes provide and how do you plan to achieve this? (For low-level privacy, landscaping is sufficient. For high-level privacy, landscape screening and walls may be used.)
10. What is the privacy gradient between personal and public spaces and how do you plan to achieve this? (For a low-level privacy gradient, use small, open front yards, houses close to the street, and sidewalks. For a high-level privacy gradient, use large front yards, landscape screening, and no sidewalks.)
11. How can landscaping and choice of materials for signage and street furniture promote the development's identity and define public and private spaces?

Once again, the target market characteristics can offer strong guidelines for the design ideas that encourage social interaction in your new project. Design choices such as the distance of the home from the street, the presence or absence of sidewalks, location of mailboxes, and neighborhood parks are some of the many design ideas that can promote or discourage social interaction.

Retired people often have more time available for the pursuit of friendships and recreational activities. Young professionals, single or married, without children may also have more free time than young professionals with school-aged children. Whereas adult-oriented pursuits may attract the first two groups, the last group may have more interest in child-oriented activities. For example, target groups without children may seek solitary pursuits such as walking or running for fitness and community pursuits such as group sports and other opportunities where people come together to make friends. Target groups with children may primarily look for opportunities to get together with other parents.

Planning for Privacy

Even when people desire a high degree of interaction at the pedestrian level, the master plan must respect the individual's privacy. You need to strike a balance between privacy requirements for backyards and interior personal spaces with devices that promote a specific level of outdoor community activity. To accomplish this, establish an appropriate privacy gradient between the individual's personal space and the public space of the neighborhood. A privacy gradient describes the transition from the most private areas of an individual's domain to the most public areas of the neighborhood. It includes transition spaces that allow a person to move from more hidden spaces into more and more open spaces.

For example, consider the following type of privacy gradient. Informal living spaces such as the kitchen or family room might be located at the very rear of the house. The formal spaces of dining and living rooms would be located at the front. The front porch forms a transition space between the individual's personal home space and the public while still being attached to the house. The distance of the front lawn from house to street is still another space in the gradient. Finally, the sidewalk and street form the most public boundaries.

Suburban Privacy Gradient. Suburban planning concepts begun in the 1950s were based on creating a large front yard with a long setback from the street. The large front yard offers little either to protect privacy or encourage social interaction.

With the front yard's exposure to the street, private activities here are inappropriate. Yet, because it places the home so far from the street, it discourages social interaction between the individual and neighbors. This model continues to persist in some areas despite its requirements for increased infrastructure and landscape maintenance and its high lot purchase costs. You will find certain target groups that prefer the long setback from the street and others who enjoy the close proximity to their neighbors afforded by a short setback.

Increasing Privacy. The more private spaces such as backyards and personal living spaces should contain architectural and landscape elements that separate them from more public spaces. Landscaping can visually seclude private outdoor spaces such as backyards; landscape buffers and architectural elements such as fences, pergolas, and screens can shield decks and pools. No matter how small or large the private spaces may be, they usually require some type of screening to create a sense of seclusion. However, the appropriate balance between seclusion and the opportunity for socializing with neighbors depends on the particular demands of the target market and the concept of your new development.

Balancing Privacy with Social Interaction. In recent years, some developers and planners have shown an interest in reclaiming the street side of homes as a more pedestrian-friendly environment that encourages walking and interaction among those who live in the neighborhood. This can be done by reducing the size of the front yard, pulling the facade of the house toward the street. The shorter distance from door to street brings the individual closer to neighbors using the sidewalks or streets. Reducing the front setback also creates an appealing sense of enclosure and human scale that makes the pedestrian feel more comfortable. This approach also maintains the individual's privacy gradient through the preservation of a transition space in the smaller front yard. Adding design elements such as front porches and sidewalks can increase the level of social interaction and yet maintain the individual's privacy gradient.

Reducing the size of the front yard also provides more space for private activities in the backyard while reducing the overall size of the lot. The degree to which you use this idea depends on the tolerance level of the target market, the size of the home, and the way in which the idea supports the neighborhood's overall identity. When applying this idea, you also need to respect regional preferences. For example, this approach might be more readily accepted in older urbanized areas where the townhouse and row house are common.

Even accounting for regional tolerances to street distance, one of the primary sources of social interaction comes from the street itself. Make the street more conducive to pedestrians by controlling its geometry. The appropriate type of geometry and alignment can reduce automobile speeds and provide pleasant vistas for people walking down the sidewalks. Using sidewalks and small setbacks to separate pedestrians from automobile traffic gives pedestrian routes a more human scale. If you reduce street widths to the minimum standard, you further enhance the human scale of the pedestrian routes and reduce the speed of automobiles. Using appropriate destinations like parks or corner stores and focal points like mailboxes, lamp posts, and benches can create a streetscape that invites pedestrian use.

In fact, your master plan concept should offer pedestrian routes with meaningful destinations to public spaces, including the neighborhood park, a clubhouse, tennis courts, schools, or a retail center. The goal is to have people use these routes for recreational access to amenities and services, and opportunities to socialize with other people. Depending on the availability of public transportation in the area, these routes may even be used for commuting to work. To draw people into public spaces, carefully design the entrances and views with proportions based on a human scale. All materials chosen for street furniture, signage, pavement, fencing, and lighting should complement the chosen idea for the new development and provide consistency in its design. Your architect and landscape architect should be able to provide you with a variety of design choices that support these ideas.

Creating a Unique Place

All developments, large and small, should strive to create a unique environment for the people who live there. You can do this by carefully arranging physical spaces and using design elements, including setbacks and street design, that carry meaning for inhabitants. To establish the unique nature of a place, use details and concepts that tie the development to a recognizable location and give it a defined regional context. You should therefore evaluate any design decision to see whether it supports the previously established idea for the new development in ways that express the neighborhood's unique attributes.

A neighborhood can follow the form of a variety of indigenous or regional models—for example, traditional neighborhood, country hamlet, or small urban district. However, the new development should not become a carbon copy of these models. Use rather than replicate the model as an informing idea by applying its important elements in creative new ways. This involves studying the way the model treats various components such as size, scale, streets, common areas, and materials.

Size and Scale. The manipulation of size and scale defines relationships among objects, buildings, open space, and people. Try to vary the scale throughout your project. Also, try to set the scale to vehicular standards where appropriate and pedestrian standards where people are likely to walk and gather. If you design your new development to follow a particular model, study the model's size and scale relationships in the lengths, widths, geometry, mass, heights of buildings, and streets to find those that can project your new development's identity. The elements in Figure 6.6 Factors Relating to Size and Scale describe the most prominent scale relationships in residential development.

Materials. Choose materials for your project that are compatible, express the image you wish to promote, and can be finished

FIGURE 6.6. Factors Relating to Size and Scale

1. **Building to Building:** Buildings next to one another should have a compatible or similar height and mass.
2. **Building to Street:** Design buildings according to whether people will encounter them primarily on foot or from automobiles. People on foot more readily relate to smaller facades and lower heights, while people traveling in automobiles more easily see larger facades and taller heights.
3. **Building to Pedestrian:** Buildings relating primarily to pedestrians should have shorter setbacks from the street, scaled-down entrances, and lower heights.
4. **Pedestrian to Street:** Streets designed for pedestrian and automobile use should provide landscaping, setbacks, or parked-car zones as buffers between pedestrians and automobiles. Also, with pedestrian streets, keep street widths and pedestrian paths to a minimum.
5. **Pedestrian to Open Space:** Open space or common areas should remain smaller, create safe pockets (more private areas like gazebos and playgrounds in public open spaces like parks), use pedestrian-scaled connections (paths) from pocket to pocket, and have entrances scaled to the human body.

---

with a well-designed color palette and texture range. Use materials that are cost-effective and able to perform well in the location; consider materials associated with the region. Materials can be classical, traditional, regional, contemporary, high-tech, or rustic, to name a few. Your choice depends on how the materials support the development's identity derived from the target market's preferences. Throughout your project, consistently use a range of materials and colors with one unifying theme. This can unify various housing types and lot distributions, making them seem part of a whole.

Land Planning and Architectural Style. Many people feel that suburban developments frequently look alike no matter where they are located. These developments fail to express a unique sense of place by repeating monotonous elements and ignoring the attributes of the location. Keep in mind that a particular land planning and architectural style can include a variety of housing types. Also, using a variety of compatible planning and architectural styles can project a recognizable community identity while offering a range of design flexibility rather than strict monotony. Within these styles a mixture of different housing types and lot sizes can promote variety and yet appear consistent through the use of unifying details, materials, and colors.

For example, suppose you base your development on a small-town theme in an area where Victorian architecture reigns. You have elected to honor the regional context by referring to Victorian architecture but do not want to simply replicate it. In addition, you want to offer a variety of housing types and create a neighborhood tied to the spirit of the local area.

In this situation, if the buildings are of similar size and scale you may be able to place detached single-family units, townhouses, and apartments in the same development or even on the same street without creating chaos. It's important to use details from the same architectural style. These details can include such items as window treatments, trim, porches, entries, and roof pitches. A compatible range of colors and materials can also aid in tying these different housing types together. By acknowledging appropriate scale relationships between housing types, you can further create consistency without compromising variety and interest. Avoid abrupt changes in the size and scale of adjacent buildings as one way to produce an appropriate relationship of scale.

Natural Features. Using the right combination of size, scale, streets, common areas, and materials helps to create a neighborhood with a distinct character. If these elements are compatible with one another, they will all reinforce the idea behind your master plan. Acknowledging the natural attributes of the location can help create a neighborhood distinct from others. This goes beyond the evaluation of site features you conducted to select your site and analyze how specific natural features affect cost and engineering.

Frequently, when people perceive a development or certain area of town as having a unique character, it comes partly from the way buildings and spaces have acknowledged an existing natural feature. This is one reason people are attracted to such places as the seaside, waterfront, mountains, and desert.

Once you've chosen a site, try to incorporate any natural features into your design. Consider including a prevalent tree species in your development's name and using it as part of the logo that appears on all marketing materials. You might use a single specimen tree in the same manner. Perhaps your site has a stream or creek, a series of small lakes or hills, a valley, or a view of a distant mountain. Any of these could help create a unique identity.

Buildings, streets, and common areas in these locations tend to capitalize on the land's natural features through their views. Architectural features such as windows, porches, and entryways open up building facades, creating a connection between interior spaces and the surrounding environment. This technique tends to give the buildings a specific appearance. In addition, building shapes are often adapted to particular climatic requirements. Through these devices, the area's natural features become part of the development's environment and vice versa.

While not all sites have the drama of an ocean or mountain view, each site may have its own unique characteristics. When a street deviates from an expected pattern to curve around a large specimen tree or when buildings part to reveal a glimpse of a meadow or creek, the development takes on a character unique to that particular location. Inventory your site's resources to find opportunities that add interest to your development. When you incorporate important natural features into the design of your new project, the results can have greater market appeal because they offer something no other development possesses.

Finalizing the Master Plan

Once you have acknowledged the site's special characteristics, your target market's preferences, and the regional context, you are ready to finalize the master plan. As a first step, review the complete list of lifestyle characteristics and the corresponding design ideas to ensure the plan has addressed all concerns. Study each of the master plan's design elements to ensure that it helps relate the concept to the target market's preferences. Change any design elements that conflict with those preferences.

Next review the adaptation of the master plan ideas to any special site characteristics for their ability to lend a unique quality to the development. For example, if portions of your site provide a beautiful view, manipulate building placement and angle windows to maximize the number of units with this view. Review site characteristics to determine the most functional and efficient handling of circulation (the movement of pedestrians and cars within your project), utility installation, and stormwater management and to check for potential conflicts with the conceptual master plan design. This may require another review of the information in the site analysis to check concerns about topography, drainage, infrastructure, and buildable versus unbuildable areas. You may also have to realign streets to avoid unbuildable areas or to capitalize on positive natural site features.

Selecting a New Development Concept

In choosing a concept for a new development, first confirm the tolerances for number of units, as well as the target group's requirements for privacy, security, recreation, and amenities. However, balance these concerns with an awareness of the new design ideas in residential development. New designs that respond to the social and economic changes of the time may not be suitable for every target market. Test these ideas for their fit with the target market's demands, regional preferences, and your site's unique characteristics.

The degree to which you can offer services and amenities in your neighborhood depends on the profit generated from selling a certain number of units within a particular time frame. Each design decision—whether about materials, landscaping, housing types, or amenities—carries a cost-benefit ratio. The benefit derives from a potential increase in market appeal or the ability to sell houses and lots for increased prices. For each service or amenity, the benefit must outweigh its actual cost. In other words, by providing that benefit, you must increase the overall value of your project enough that sales and profits offset the cost of providing the amenity or service.

As your project team works on the master plan concept, also keep in mind that all groups generally desire some sense of belonging. A well-designed neighborhood can provide ways for the individual to connect to the neighborhood as a whole. This might be through the overall image or the physical aspect of connecting public and private spaces. People seem to need this connection regardless of the degree of social interaction they demand.

New Directions in Residential Design

The social and economic changes previously discussed have caused planners and developers to rethink urban and suburban issues. Many have formulated their own design strategies for new residential development, which in turn have become popular schools of thought. The media has focused much attention on issues such as the increasing cost and decreasing availability of land; the ability of existing infrastructure to accommodate increasing demand for utilities; uncrowded streets and highways; and environmental concerns. Public awareness of these new issues stands at an all-time high, prompting an increase in local government responses. All this adds a new layer of considerations for you as the developer.

The following sections discuss a few of the better-established responses developers and planners have made to these issues. Each briefly summarizes the design categories in which these new residential developments might fall.

The Master-Planned Community

Originally, the suburbs did not take into account the effects the automobile had on pedestrian transportation. But after concerns began to arise about the negative effects of automobile traffic on safety issues and a peaceful environment and safety, balancing the relationship between the pedestrian and automobile became a major issue. The next generation of singly designed residential developments focused on this issue, making it one of the outstanding features of the master-planned community.

This approach relies on a large collector road with branching cul-de-sacs. In it, the cul-de-sacs are usually reserved for houses and the collector road primarily for automobile traffic in and out of the neighborhood. This design also aligns houses along the cul-de-sac branches and uses landscape buffers to separate them. Figure 6.7 Collector and Cul-de-Sac Plan shows the distribution of streets and lots typical in this approach.

By eliminating through traffic, this design strategy focuses on giving the sense of a small neighborhood. However, the discontinuous nature of the streets makes it less conducive to walking. In addition, once the individual ventures beyond the cul-de-sac, the speed and large-scale requirements of automobile transportation again determine the character of the neighborhood. With the original collector and cul-de-sac plan, placing recreational amenities such as parks or tennis courts within the development would force people on foot to compete with automobiles to gain access to them—unless a specific pedestrian pathway accompanied the collector road. As a result, in developments such as the one illustrated in Figure 6.6, people usually choose to drive to amenities rather than walk.

If you use this model to design the neighborhoods in your project, try to link amenities to pedestrians. Make the small cul-de-sac pods seem less isolated by connecting them via pedestrian routes in the buffers that separate them. If you want to avoid isolated pedestrian paths, use sidewalks along appropriately scaled streets to balance automobile and pedestrian routes.

The Master-Planned Community Today

The term "master-planned community" usually refers to a relatively large residential development containing a variety of housing types, prices, amenities, services, and even commercial centers. Larger master-planned communities may contain a

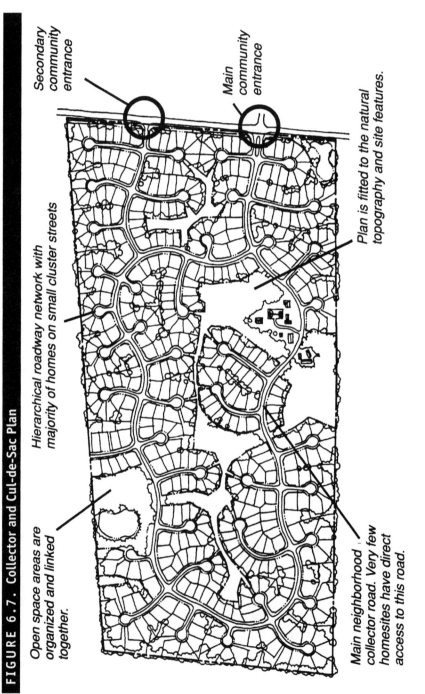

FIGURE 6.7. Collector and Cul-de-Sac Plan

Secondary community entrance

Main community entrance

Hierarchical roadway network with majority of homes on small cluster streets

Open space areas are organized and linked together.

Plan is fitted to the natural topography and site features.

Main neighborhood collector road. Very few homesites have direct access to this road.

Source: Frederick D. Jarvis, LDR International, Inc., *Site Planning and Community Design for Great Neighborhoods* (Washington, DC: Home Builder Press, National Association of Home Builders, 1993), p. 49.

compilation of neighborhoods, each designed to match the demands of a different target group. Consequently, you can find estate homes, patio homes, townhouses, and multifamily housing within one single community.

Master-planned communities have generally achieved great success in marketing and sales, especially in areas of job growth. Home buyers coming into a new area seem to be more comfortable with a development community they can readily understand. They are looking to instantaneously relate to aspects of the community. Master-planned communities have become so prevalent that many home buyers already know their attributes. Essentially, they are purchasing a familiar lifestyle that closely matches their own.

The Neo-Traditional Neighborhood

Neo-traditional neighborhoods go by many names: new towns, traditional neighborhoods, new urbanism, or neo-traditional neighborhoods. Architects and planners began in the late 1980s to form the basic principles of this development type. Several early examples exist such as the Kentlands in Gaithersburg, Maryland, and the beach resort community of Seaside, Florida. As examples of these increased, city and county planners and consumers began to notice and even request such a development as part of their local city or county plan. Some of the ideas found in these models include providing a more interactive experience between the individual and other neighbors and the residents and the community. These types of development contain time-tested ideas that have survived from original traditional small towns of the past such as Princeton, New Jersey; Carmel, California; and Annapolis, Maryland.

Elements of Neo-Traditional Neighborhoods

A variety of target markets seem to respond well to these new ideas for designing developments. Figure 6.8 Elements of Neo-Traditional Neighborhoods gives a brief list of some of the important design considerations used in these new models.

These ideas are diametrically opposed to designs based on the collector road and branching cul-de-sac. For comparison,

---

FIGURE 6.8. Elements of Neo-Traditional Neighborhoods

- Master plan attempts to provide a sense of community through its design
- Master plan usually based on a grid or modified grid system
- Few collector roads and cul-de-sacs, if any, are used
- Pedestrian traffic is as important as vehicular traffic
- Use of alleys to provide privacy and services
- Street widths and lot sizes are reduced
- Emphasis on the street side of homes for recreation, social involvement through the use of porches, sidewalks, and short distance from home to street
- Return to on-street parking
- Incorporation of residential housing located above commercial first floors of town center
- Mixing of services, single- and multifamily housing, and parks
- Commercial and residential buildings grouped together by size and scale
- Extensive use of mixed housing types, styles, and sizes held together by proportion, materials, and compatible color palette

---

refer back to Figure 6.6 and see Figure 6.9 Neo-Traditional Plan, which show examples of the two different treatments. The traditional plan can provide more units than the conventional one because of its smaller lots and accommodating street geometry. The primary difference between the two plans, however, is the traditional plan's inclusion of shared and through streets. Shared streets refer to those used by both pedestrians and automobiles. There are also more opportunities to meet and talk with neighbors through the use of connecting elements like pathways and alleys reminiscent of a small-town atmosphere, use of civic or public squares instead of simply parks, and the relationship of houses to streets.

Critics of neo-traditional neighborhoods have suggested they are too expensive to develop and, unless connected to public transportation, fail to work any better than conventionally planned developments. However, the costs do not have to be significantly higher. In fact, in some cases, such features as shorter distances and street lengths decrease infrastructure and thus the overall development costs for neo-traditional communities. In many cases, smaller lots with the same number of units as other developments allow for more open space. This can both facilitate approval for a variety of environmental permits and increase market appeal.

A neo-traditional development can work well in a variety of existing conditions. They are popular in urban areas where people more readily accept higher densities and smaller lots. They also lend themselves to smaller infill-like areas of the city. An older existing neighborhood within the city might prove ideal for renovating into a neo-traditional neighborhood.

Once again, be aware of regional biases and land availability in your project area when evaluating the viability of such a project. Remember that you do not necessarily need to follow the design principles to the letter. Consider them a menu from which to choose design ideas that enhance your project's site and your target market's lifestyle characteristics. An estimated

FIGURE 6.9. Neo-Traditional Plan

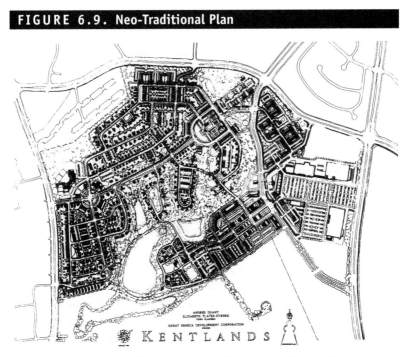

Source: Reprinted with permission from Andres Duany and Elizabeth Plater-Zyberk, Architects, Inc., and Joseph Alfandre & Company, Inc.

150 neo-traditional developments exist in the United States at the end of the 1990s; many more are planned. Figure 6.10 Neo-Traditional Neighborhoods in the United States shows a short list of residential developments that follow these principles.

Infill or Pocket Development

Residential development projects located within either suburban or urban cores are generally known as infill development and have several advantages for the developer. All types of infrastructure—schools, streets, utilities, and various services—are already in place. Sometimes they are situated close to work centers or other desirable areas. Locations that are "left over" from previous suburban development can often have the same characteristics of suitable infrastructure and the benefit of a recognizable location that carries positive associations.

Look for urban core areas that contain the small city neighborhoods built 20 to 50 years ago. Sometimes, these neighborhoods are run-down but prime for timely redevelopment because of their desirable location. Homes in these types of neighborhoods can be demolished in favor of updated ones that appeal to specific target markets. In some cases the homes can be renovated and resold as single or multifamily housing.

Urban Renewal and Residential Development

A unique type of infill or pocket development occurs when existing office or warehouse buildings outlive their usefulness and are converted to apartments or multifamily housing. Cities are increasing their efforts to revitalize downtown areas by providing theater and shopping districts, parks, and sports facilities. It has become profitable to renovate older urban buildings whose proximity to downtown work centers eliminates the need to commute, adding to their appeal.

When renovating older buildings, consider converting them to loft apartments, condominiums, or townhouses. This type of housing especially appeals to the growing workforce of single or married-with-no-children professionals. It also appeals to older, active adults who have more leisure time and wish to

**FIGURE 6.10. Neo-Traditional Neighborhoods in the
United States**

Alabama
Gorham's Bluff, Pisgah
Tannin, Orange Beach
Blount Springs

Arkansas
Brodie Creek, Little Rock
Har-Ber Meadows, Springdale

California
The Crossings, Mountainview
Laguna West, Sacramento County
Rio Vista West, San Diego

Colorado
Prospect, Longmont

Florida
Celebration, Orlando
Seaside, Walton County
Rosemary Beach, Walton County
Haile Village Center, Gainesville
Rivendell, Sarasota County
Southlake, Orlando
Tioga, Gainesville
Windsor, Vero Beach

Illinois
Kirkwood, Kirkland

Indiana
Beachwalk, Michigan City

Maryland
Kentlands, Gaithersburg

Massachusetts
Mashpee Commons, Mashpee

Mississippi
Cotton District, Starksville

New Mexico
Tierra Contenta, Santa Fe

North Carolina
Arbor Creek, Holly Springs
Southern Village, Chapel Hill
Camden Park, Chapel Hill

Ohio
Central Neighbor Plan, Cleveland

Oregon
Fairview Village, Fairview
Sunnyside Village, Clackamas County

Pennsylvania
Eagleview, Uwehlan Township
Hill District, Pittsburgh

South Carolina
Daniel Island, Charleston
Newpoint, Beaufort

Tennessee
Cordova, Harbor Town
Mid-Town Corridor, Memphis
South Bluffs, Memphis

Virginia
Belmont Forest, Loudoun County
Haymount, Caroline County

Washington
Northwest Landing, Dupont

Wisconsin
Middleton Hills, Madison
Cityworks, Milwaukee

participate in activities they enjoy. In the past, these developments have been successful primarily in older cities with a tradition of urban residential living. However, even in states that had their major growth after World War II, the pressures on suburbs, land availability, and the segmentation of target market groups are making city living a viable option for home buyers.

Infill developments can enjoy the advantages of existing infrastructure and, in some cases, may receive tax advantages from the city. On the other hand, these developments are sometimes resisted by local residents who might think they will increase traffic or destroy open space.

Development Guidelines

How will you maintain the neighborhood identity and design ideas you so carefully created over the life of the development? You need to establish a system that applies the same standard of excellence first expressed in your original master plan concept to the decisions that owners and builders will make as they help create your new development. Establishing written guidelines that direct builders and owners in housing type choices, materials, safety concerns, and land usage takes the first step toward ensuring the development evolves in a manner that keeps your original ideas intact. Those standards should address both design issues related to housing type and land use, and construction issues related to materials, methods, costs, and project management.

Architectural Guidelines

Create architectural guidelines that give the new development a consistent identity. That said, remember to develop guidelines that allow for diversity, flexibility, and interest rather than monotonous uniformity.

One option: Setting a palette of complementary colors and materials promotes diversity within a consistent theme. In the same manner, setting dimensional requirements for height, massing, and building placement can promote the identity you desire without actually specifying particular styles that produce cookie-cutter architecture. For example, instead of requiring that all buildings be American colonial in design, list various materials that might be chosen for each of the individual buildings. This way you can avoid a monotonous streetscape dominated by white Corinthian columns and red brick.

Architectural guidelines govern the style of houses and the buildings designed for retail, services, and recreation by including specifications for materials and styles. They also address how you position buildings on the land and their relationship to the street. Include within your architectural guidelines standards for landscape design related to homes, pathways, streets, retail and service centers, and common areas. Delineate types of plant materials and the party responsible for, and approved methods of, maintenance.

Well written architectural guidelines can provide owners and builders with many choices within a range of ideas. Prepare the architectural guidelines so they can be considered when owners and builders present new ideas within the context of the guidelines. The guidelines should include, but not be limited to, the list shown in Figure 6.11, Architectural Guidelines.

As the developer, you may sell lots to other builders throughout the life of the development. If this is the case, you should have provisions in your contracts that restrict other builders from going outside the written architectural guidelines. Prospective home buyers should be apprised of the guidelines and agree to honor them. Just as with your agreement with the builder, these guidelines should represent a contractual agreement between you and the homeowner so that methods such as fines and replacing nonconforming work can be enforced.

Once your neighborhood is established, let the neighborhood association and some type of review board enforce the guidelines but maintain an active role in overseeing the way development progresses. Many developers choose to participate in the various boards and committees that use qualified individuals to review new home plans and elevations. The committee ensures that the architectural guidelines are respected.

FIGURE 6.11. Architectural Guidelines

Land Use
A. Dimensions
  1. Front, side, and rear-yard setbacks
  2. Percentage of lot covered by building footprint and impervious surface
B. Site Improvements
  1. Dimensions and materials of sidewalks, front porches, driveways, decks, pools, and patios
  2. Types, dimensions, materials, and placement of outbuildings and mail-boxes allowed
  3. Landscape buffers and screening requirements between houses
  4. Sod, mowing, and tree-removal requirements
  5. Lighting standards

Building Design
A. Dimensions
  1. Minimum and maximum height and width of facade
  2. Roof pitch
  3. Finished floor elevation
B. Materials
  1. Roof
  2. Exterior finish of facade
  3. Trim and ornamentation
  4. Glazing
C. Colors
  Color pallette for all exterior finishes and site improvements

---

Some developers retain the right of final approval after all lots are sold to builders until all homes are complete.

Have the architectural guidelines clearly state which items of new construction need committee approval. The builder or owner requesting the review should submit plans, sections, and elevations to the committee and include appropriate descriptions of materials and colors. The committee also needs to review the following items:

- all additions to the building floor plan and height
- any changes in the building's facade

- any changes in exterior materials
- all attached auxiliary outdoor spaces, such as decks, patios, porches, greenhouses, pools, cabanas, and spas
- all detached outdoor spaces, such as tennis courts, gazebos, pergolas, storage sheds
- fences and gates
- new driveways or parking areas

Construction Guidelines

If your project offers lots to other builders, you'll also need guidelines to govern project management. Prequalifying builders guarantees the construction of high-quality homes, safe job sites, and cost- and time-efficiencies stemming from well-managed construction projects. Prequalify builders based on their reputation in the community and their ability to complete the work, basing the latter on their financial position and available labor. A list of preferred builders is both an excellent marketing tool and an effective way to maintain the quality of your new development.

As with architectural guidelines, you need written construction guidelines that address project management. Use written communications and meetings to let builders know the rules and clearly state and enforce the penalties for failing to comply. Builders who violate the guidelines should not be allowed to take additional jobs in the project.

Construction guidelines should also list standards for project management to ensure builders construct homes in a timely manner with the least amount of disturbance to other homeowners. The guidelines should specify standards for hours of construction, maintenance of a clean site, job safety, building to code, proper management of construction workers, and use of approved materials and methods. Figure 6.12 Construction Guidelines provides a short list of areas that such guidelines should cover.

Deed Restrictions and Covenants

Deed restrictions and covenants are items written into the original lot purchase contract. They make sure the buyer and sub-

FIGURE 6.12. Construction Guidelines

Job Access
- Establishment of temporary roads and utilities (length of time in use and restitution of natural conditions after use)
- Dust and erosion control for temporary roads and utilities

Job Site
- Cleanup measures and schedules
- Equipment and material storage
- Dust and erosion control
- Stormwater runoff control
- Noise control
- Tree protection
- Display of project signage

Project Management
- Minimum and maximum length for project completion
- Presence of job superintendent as the established point of contact
- Management of subcontractors
- Appropriate conduct of construction workers
- Daily work hours

Building Construction
- Use of approved materials and methods
- Proof of compliance with all building codes
- Timely schedules for subcontractors' follow-up work

sequent buyers will abide by specific land use rules. Attached to subdivision approval, deed restrictions and covenants ensure that a proper range of land uses is upheld. The extent of these specifications depends on the nature of your development and the target market. The intent is to ensure that your development's identity remains intact. Types of individual land uses that may require specification include maintenance of yards and other outdoor spaces, storage of large equipment, parking for boats and trailers, pet housing and control, and display of outdoor art and sculpture. A reasonable list of the types of equipment and recreational vehicles that owners can store on their lots and the stipulation of appropriate screening devices can ensure that individual land uses help to project the intended identity of the community.

Master Plans of the Future

The demands of a particular target market will always influence the master plan concept for a new development. However, external forces continue to play a significant role in design. These forces include growth-management policies, adequacy of infrastructure, increased environmental protection, and decreasing availability of land. Future land development will undoubtedly be affected by the trend of local governments trying to protect natural resources while confronting increasing costs to provide infrastructure and services.

In addressing these issues land planning seeks to ensure an adequate quality of life for all members of the development. In the coming years, land planning will undoubtedly play a stronger role in determining, for example, the density and infrastructure standards for new developments through new zoning concepts and standards. In addition, all players involved in land development—from developers, builders, planners, and engineers to architects, designers, and local government officials—need to work together to establish reasonable guidelines. Everyone in this process should have the same goal: addressing quality-of-life issues that are essential for the continued health of the local community and the business of land development.

7

Site Engineering and Stormwater Management

Site engineering shapes the slope of the land for the efficient placement of all the infrastructure needed by a new development. Essentially this process establishes proper grading for buildings, roads, utilities, erosion and sediment control, and stormwater management. Among the goals of site engineering are diverting runoff from areas where people and buildings are located and correctly placing those buildings and roads to drain runoff away from environmentally sensitive areas. To do this, the grading plan changes existing contours where necessary and attempts to balance excavated and replaced earthwork while taking into account both the master plan's requirements and the site's natural features. Site engineering also includes design and placement of all infrastructure on the site.

Without careful management, site engineering can become the most costly part of development. Have knowledgeable professional engineers and consultants do this work, but you as the developer need familiarity with site engineering concepts to coordinate the work and evaluate the feasibility of engineering proposals. This avoids a later discovery that excessive site engineering makes the master plan financially infeasible. Incorporate site engineering into your master plan design early in the process. To make this happen, you need effective communication among the design and engineering professionals on your project team.

Site Engineering Plan

To create a site engineering plan or civil engineering drawing, you must adapt your master plan concept to the physical characteristics of the existing site. Much of the information you'll need comes from a thorough inventory of characteristics discovered during your site analysis. Figure 7.1 Site Engineering Goals outlines the objectives you want to accomplish in engineering your project.

Components

The site engineering plan includes details about grading, stormwater management, and erosion and sediment control. Work together with the engineers and design professionals on your project team to determine the best approach to site engineering based on soil characteristics, topography, and the physical features of your site.

From the topographic map and the analysis of the site's physical features you can locate the basin divides, high- and lowland areas, and prominent soil and geological characteristics. Basin divides are the ridges that form a high perimeter barrier to each of the low areas of the site. Water tends to drain toward the center of each basin. From the location of the basin divides, you can form a clear picture of the site's natural drainage. Determine, too, where any bodies of water or wetlands are on the site. In all likelihood you will have to divert stormwater away from wetlands. Discharging stormwater into surface waters requires permits and special pollution-controlling measures.

FIGURE 7.1. Site Engineering Goals

- Provide safe and functional access to all areas of use
- Divert stormwater runoff away from buildings without excessive erosion or sedimentation
- Provide for the economical installation and maintenance of utilities
- Provide for economical grading (balance cut and fill, minimize the amount of imported fill)
- Preserve the site's natural character

Next, note the depth of the water table at various points to see if it's feasible to place open retention or detention systems in certain areas. A retention system permanently contains water, while a detention system temporarily detains water until it is either discharged or infiltrates into the soil. Under the best conditions, the top of the water table should be low enough to allow a few feet of soil between it and the bottom of the retention or detention system. Some states' stormwater management statutes specify a certain number of linear feet between the bottom (invert) elevation of an open retention or detention pond and the top of the water table. This ensures that, as stormwater percolates downward through the layers of the soil profile, pollutants are filtered out before they reach the water table.

Your team also needs to understand the soil and geological conditions for each area of the site. These conditions affect the rate at which water infiltrates the soil and percolates downward, the potential for excessive soil erosion, and the feasibility of excavating for the placement of utilities. Soil types can vary greatly over a few acres on a given parcel of land. Use the soil map produced in the site analysis phase to locate variations, including those with slower percolation rates and the potential to hinder construction. These areas may require special attention during site engineering.

Master Plan
Members of the project team use this information to evaluate a location's ability to accommodate the site engineering necessary for the master plan. To do this, overlay the master plan onto the topographic map containing notations of physical features to show how site conditions relate to the location of streets, parking, utilities, buildings, and amenities. If the team has formulated the master plan with these conditions in mind, only minimal design changes should be needed. For example, you may need to move certain buildings and street alignments a few feet. However, with proper attention to the site's existing characteristics in the early design phase, the master plan concept should remain intact.

Develop a Conceptual Grading Plan

Next you need to develop a conceptual grading plan of the entire site to accommodate all major components of the master plan. A grading plan shows surface and invert elevations of your stormwater management systems and utilities. It also establishes all finished floor and grade elevations for buildings and adjacent ground areas. A finished floor elevation refers to the height of the completed first floor of a building; a finished grade elevation describes the height of the completed earthwork.

The location and height of these elevations determines how much you need to change existing contours to accommodate the siting of buildings and utilities. This in turn indicates the amount of cut and fill needed to make these changes. Cut refers to excavation that lowers existing grades and slopes; fill is material deposited in certain areas to create grades with higher elevations.

Stormwater Management Plan

As you create the conceptual grading plan, also develop a conceptual stormwater management plan using various calculations to determine the volume and rate of stormwater runoff. These calculations can show the volume of stormwater your project generates within a specified amount of time and help determine the type of stormwater systems needed to carry and contain the runoff. They also allow you to size stormwater pipes, inlets, spillways, culverts, catch basins, and manholes. Finally, if you need to contain stormwater on site, stormwater calculations help you determine the sizes of retention and detention ponds.

Erosion and Sediment Control Plan

To prepare for earthwork activities during construction, you need a sediment and erosion control plan. This plan indicates what measures you intend to take to stabilize excavated areas and prevent sediment from being deposited in unwanted areas such as surface waters and adjacent properties. Your plan should show the location of any erosion control barriers and specify the type of materials to be used. To ensure effectiveness, follow proper installation techniques for all erosion and sediment control measures.

Grading Plan

The grading plan is the first construction document earthwork and site development contractors use to understand the type and scope of their work. It shows where contractors must clear the site and how much earth they must move to arrive at the correct finished grades. All major elements of your master plan should be accommodated in an efficient, cost-effective manner. To save site development costs, locate stormwater systems along the most efficient routes for discharging into public stormwater mains or for on-site retention. You should also direct your engineer to save as many mature trees as possible, including meeting the requirements of any local tree ordinance.

Cut and Fill

The finished grade should not deviate too much from the existing grade to avoid excessive cut and fill. The cut and fill process also can create unstable finished grades with the potential to erode. Importing fill quickly becomes expensive because you must buy the fill, transport it to the site, and use special measures to place and stabilize it, including constructing retaining walls, steps, and terraces. Excessive cut and fill can also remove too much natural vegetation, creating poor growing conditions for imported landscape material.

All these steps increase site development costs and create areas that require long-term maintenance. Direct your engineers to design a grading plan that achieves your goals while balancing cut and fill on the site. When you balance cut and fill, you use the same amount of material excavated (cut) on your site for your fill requirements.

Spot Elevations and Slopes

As you lay your master plan onto the topographic map, establish all spot elevations for strategic components of the master plan. A spot elevation shows the height at one particular point on the site. Place the finished elevation at the corner of all buildings, sidewalks, roads, and parking. Once you establish spot elevations for the important elements of your master plan, you will have a network of dots to connect through changes in slope. Use the spot elevations to understand the difference between the existing and required percentages of slope between each element of the master plan. This in turn establishes the amount of grading you need to change contours and conform with required slopes or changes in grade between those strategic points. A list of important project features for which you need to locate spot elevations are found in Figure 7.2 Strategic Spot Elevations.

Once you establish spot elevations, make sure the topography slopes away from each element under consideration to allow positive drainage (drainage away from the structure). If the topography fails to slope in the correct direction, determine whether you can cost-effectively engineer that particular area by changing the grade.

FIGURE 7.2. Strategic Spot Elevations

Finished Floor Elevations
- Interior corners of buildings, landings, and patios,

Finished Grade Elevations
- Within 5 feet of buildings at corners, edges of streets, drives, all other paved areas, and open stormwater systems
- Strategic points of open spaces and yards to establish correct slope

Surface Elevations
- Top of curbs, sanitary sewers, stormwater and potable water pipe cleanouts, catch basins, and manholes
- Top of walkways, drives, center lines of streets, and parking surfaces

Invert Elevations
- Bottom of swales and retention and detention ponds
- Bottom of sanitary sewer, potable water, and stormwater pipes
- Bottom of catch basins, sump pumps, and lift stations

Code Compliance

Although design guidelines for maximum and minimum slopes are published by various organizations such as the American Institute of Architects, the American Society of Landscape Architects, and the Urban Land Institute, many elements of your master plan must meet standards legally established by the state's various adopted codes. The U.S. Department of Transportation and the Highway Research Board also have standards. In some states, local governments follow standards set by the state department of transportation for roads, streets, and parking lots. In other areas, locally developed standards may be the definitive code. As you develop your site's grading plan, you will find it more cost-effective to follow the minimum standards for grading streets and utilities.

To ensure your grade changes comply with the minimum and maximum slopes allowed by code for the intended uses, select critical areas for a cross-sectional analysis. Examples could include a cross section between the house and the street (to confirm positive drainage) or the length of a sidewalk (to confirm correct slope for the intended use). In each area establish the high and low elevations and the distances between them. Using the slope calculation described in Chapter 4, find the percentage of each slope. Then check that percentage to determine whether it falls between the maximum and minimum slope required by code for that structure or the area between structures.

You may also need to check other standards in your local area besides those covering slopes. For example, the approved federal and local building and life, health, and safety codes determine standards for walkways, ramps, and those portions of recreational areas used for walking and parking. In addition, local landscape or development ordinances frequently provide restrictions and standards for slopes and construction methods used in walkways, open spaces, and recreational areas.

If your state has laws governing the design of stormwater management systems, the state statutes determine the range of correct slopes for open swales and retention and detention systems. These statutes also specify pipe slopes and invert elevations for closed systems carrying stormwater. Public works departments, the county engineer's office, or the local utility company usually establish standards for maximum and minimum slopes for all gravity-fed utility pipes.

In addition to state and local standards for stormwater management and utilities, the locally adopted building code specifies the proper perimeter grades for all buildings. Check these to determine appropriate grades for providing positive drainage around buildings and other structures. Generally, the grade should drop away from buildings by 0.25 inch per foot in the first 5 feet of distance surrounding the building, although these dimensions can differ from code to code. Be sure to refer to the local building code for the exact dimensions and slope of minimum and maximum grades for each use on your site.

Microengineering Process

As you determine the appropriate grade for your site's building and structures, you are in effect microengineering the site lot by lot. During this process, locate the finished floor and grade elevations adjacent to building footprints on the engineering drawing. Next, incorporate the microengineering of separate buildings and structures into the overall slopes established in the grading plan. Each lot or small area surrounding the individual building must flow properly into the slopes established for the overall site. The water can flow over the land into the stormwater management system with the correct grade provided at the microengineering level. Figure 7.3 Positive Drainage of Buildings illustrates the microengineering required around each structure.

After you have figured out the placement and elevation of buildings, drainage, roads, and utilities, you can then estimate their engineering costs. These costs could rise dramatically if you drastically change the existing contours through cut and fill. If you need to use extensive cut and fill to accomplish the master plan's engineering goals, weigh those costs against the benefits of placing particular buildings in certain areas to determine the overall effect on project profitability.

FIGURE 7.3. Positive Drainage of Buildings

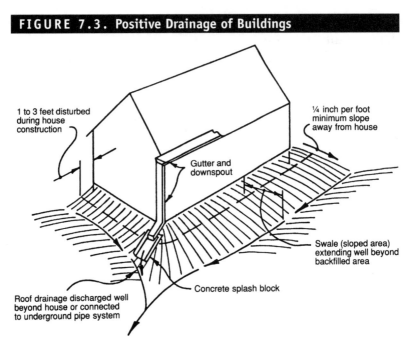

1 to 3 feet disturbed
during house
construction

¼ inch per foot
minimum slope
away from house

Gutter and
downspout

Swale (sloped area)
extending well beyond
backfilled area

Concrete splash block

Roof drainage discharged well
beyond house or connected
to underground pipe system

Source: Reprinted with permission from *Residential Drainage,* Washington Suburban Sanitary Commission, Hyattsville, Maryland, 1979 (authorized May 1994).

Once this information has been added, use it to perform cut-and-fill calculations. These determine the amount of excavated material you need to remove or imported fill you need to bring to the site to accommodate the master plan. For the conceptual grading plan, your engineer can perform preliminary cut-and-fill calculations to provide a quick and inexpensive estimate of grading costs. Figure 7.4 Types of Cut-and-Fill Calculations shows four common approaches to use at this stage of site engineering.

At this point the project team can produce the final grading plan. This plan should contain all strategic spot elevations as well as existing and proposed contour lines. Use heavy, solid lines for proposed or new contour lines and dashed or dotted lines for existing contour lines. Make sure all spot elevations of the important elements of the master plan correspond to the location of the new contours.

Use Best Management Practices

Developing a raw parcel of land makes four unique changes to the hydrology of an area: peak flow characteristics, total runoff, quality of groundwater, and quality of streams, lakes, and rivers. By placing buildings and roads on a site, you naturally increase the amount and rate of stormwater runoff because the process disturbs vegetation and covers permeable soils with impermeable surfaces. When vegetation is removed, erosion occurs faster and in a greater amount than in the natural state. This results in higher, more intense, and faster runoff than is found in natural conditions. In the past, engineers managed stormwater runoff by removing the water as quickly as possible to a discharge and containment point. Now they must also focus on the effect stormwater runoff has on the quality of groundwater and surface water used for drinking, sediment control, and on bodies of water used for recreation.

You can choose from a variety of methods to effectively manage stormwater runoff on your site. These can include the use of manufactured systems such as pipes, culverts, and catch

---

FIGURE 7.4. Types of Cut-and-Fill Calculations

Prism Method: Use this method when the excavation for a building is small and land has a uniform slope. Multiply the area of excavation by the average height of the corners to obtain the approximate volume of cut or fill.

Average-End Method: When you look at a cross section of a cut-and-fill area, the top and bottom areas are parallel planes (A_1 and A_2). Use the formula Volume = $A_1 + A_2 \div 2 \times 1$ (the distance between them) to determine the amount of cut or fill.

Contour Method: Add the area between the existing and proposed contours together and multiply the total by the distance between the contours to arrive at the amount of cut or fill.

Cross-Sectional Method: Draw sectional lines through the site plan at intervals (usually 50 feet) and measure the cut and fill of each section with a planimeter (an instrument used to measure the areas of planes). Then add the areas together to obtain the amount of cut or fill.

---

basins as well as on-site constructed systems such as ponds and ditches or swales. Balancing manufactured systems with on-site constructed systems usually results in more cost-effective methods of discharging stormwater. When you protect your site's natural features and prevent erosion and sedimentation from occurring both on your site and off, you are employing "best management practices."

The grading plan incorporates the stormwater management plan by providing appropriate slopes to accommodate gravity-fed stormwater pipes leading to discharge points. Effective control of surface runoff also requires proper slopes to carry water to containment or discharge areas. Handling surface stormwater drainage involves five considerations: costs, efficiency (using the least amount of infrastructure possible), eliminating standing water or flooding in critical places like houses and yards, controlling the rate of runoff, and controlling the pollution deposited into the surface water and groundwater.

Figure 7.5 Effect of Development on Stormwater Runoff illustrates the primary ways land development changes natural stormwater runoff conditions. Q (discharge) refers to the volume of stormwater runoff over time, typically expressed in cubic feet per second. Peak Q refers to the maximum volume discharged after a rainstorm. Base flow refers to the volume discharged to surface waters before development. Notice that development increases the maximum volume discharged (peak Q) and that this maximum volume is reached more quickly in postdevelopment than in predevelopment conditions.

In most areas, reducing the postdevelopment peak Q down to the predevelopment peak Q level is the first objective in managing stormwater runoff. This ensures that the maximum rate of discharge can pass under or through downstream structures such as bridges and culverts. You can do this in two ways. You can retain all the runoff from development on the site, which requires the increased volume to be evaporated or infiltrated. Or you can detain the increased runoff through temporary storage in a detention pond and gradually release it at the predevelopment Q rate. Detention does not reduce the total volume of water being discharged after development.

FIGURE 7.5. Effect of Development on Stormwater Runoff

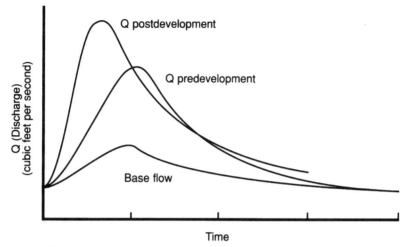

Q postdevelopment

Q predevelopment

Base flow

Q (Discharge)
(cubic feet per second)

Time

Note:

1. Discharge (Q) is the volume of water over time. Base flow is the water discharged to surface waters before development, excluding surface runoff. Peak Q is the maximum discharge after a rainstorm.

2. Postdevelopment peak Q is *higher* than predevelopment peak Q (that is, has greater volume over time).

3. Postdevelopment peak Q occurs *more quickly* than predevelopment peak Q.

4. Postdevelopment Q creates *greater total volume* of runoff than predevelopment Q (that is, the area under the curve for postdevelopment Q is greater than that for predevelopment Q).

Instead, it releases the greater volume of postdevelopment Q but at a slower rate than would happen without controls. A detention requirement based on reducing postdevelopment Q to predevelopment levels remains the most common control requirement.

Principles

In most areas you have several choices for reducing the postdevelopment peak Q to that of the predevelopment conditions. Often, local codes will dictate the methods. In areas with infrastructure at full capacity, all the stormwater runoff generated by your project must be contained on site or detained until it evaporates.

As a developer, whichever method you choose to provide effective stormwater management should be based on the principles outlined in Figure 7.6 Principles of Stormwater Management. Keep in mind that preventing problems in advance is more cost-effective than correcting them after the fact; following the principles in Figure 7.6 can help you accomplish that goal.

Types of Systems

As your stormwater management plan progresses, you can use two distinct types of systems to carry and store stormwater runoff: closed and open.

Closed Systems. Closed systems are underground conduits and other structures that carry stormwater runoff to a point of dis-

---

FIGURE 7.6. Principles of Stormwater Management

1. Every parcel of land is part of a larger watershed.
2. For more cost-effective engineering, mimic the features and functions of the site's natural drainage pattern.
3. The volume, rate, timing, and pollution load of stormwater should approximate the conditions of the undeveloped site as closely as possible. In some cases, existing pollution loads are unacceptable and must be decreased.
4. Maximize on-site storage of stormwater.
5. Depending on local requirements, avoid discharging stormwater directly into surface water or groundwater.
6. Use open systems wherever possible.
7. Plan and install stormwater management systems before beginning construction.
8. Follow the contours of the land when locating stormwater management systems.
9. Consider recycling stormwater to water golf courses and landscaping.
10. Use multiple storage ponds rather than a single storage pond.
11. Design swales and retention and detention systems with undulating rather than straight shorelines.
12. Use vegetative buffers along shorelines.
13. Design stormwater management systems for easy maintenance.

---

charge or clean sediment and pollution from the stormwater. These systems include pipes, catch basins, inlets, and underground retention and detention areas. Pipes, the most common type of closed system, must be used where open swales are unsuitable for conveying stormwater. Examples include areas with too-swift runoff, overly steep topography, or unsightly or dangerous open systems.

Open Systems. Open systems consist of retention and detention ponds and shallow swales. They may also be a constructed wetlands area on your site. In this chapter, the concentration is primarily upon swales, retention ponds, and detention ponds. Remember that retention ponds retain water at all times, while detention ponds temporarily detain it to reduce peak rates, allowing the water to discharge into surface waters at the pre-development discharge rate. Detention ponds also allow the water to infiltrate the soil. In addition, retention and detention ponds can be used as destinations for stormwater runoff.

Swales are long, narrow open channels that carry water along the surface to a containment destination. Build them with minimal slopes and closed ends to hold the water temporarily while it infiltrates the soil. When that happens, these systems are simply long, narrow detention ponds.

Standing water should appear in swales and detention ponds for only a short time after a rainstorm. Many state statutes on stormwater management specify this length of time, usually from around 70 to 80 hours after the storm. Open detention systems that retain standing water longer than specified by law are considered underdesigned; the developer must reconstruct the system to meet those standards and may be subject to fines.

If your project uses an open system as a final destination, the depth and area should be of a size to hold the volume of water calculated as the total runoff within a given period of time resulting from a particular site on your project. The open system can also be designed to contain only a specific portion of the site's total runoff, with the rest discharged to public infrastructure. Your engineer can perform these calculations by comparing the amount of paved surface from buildings and roads to the amount of unbuilt land. In some areas developers may be required to retain 100 percent of the runoff on their property. Other areas may require that 80 percent of the postdevelopment runoff stays on the property—the amount generally considered normal under natural conditions on undeveloped land.

If the local government has provided access to public stormwater systems for your project's runoff, you can keep the number of open or closed systems to a minimum because they will be used only as conduits. If you must contain a portion or the entire amount of runoff, your costs will increase along with the amount of land you'll need to support the stormwater management system. Check with the public works or engineer's office to determine whether and how much you can discharge into the public system. Be prepared for the possibility that the public system is approaching capacity, limiting your access to it.

Designing Closed Systems

After determining which areas need a closed system of pipes and inlets, you can begin to design your stormwater management system. Prepare a conceptual piping diagram and size the pipes; you'll need this information to help estimate infrastructure costs in the preliminary stages of project design. Consider the area to be drained as an isolated site. Then perform the calculations to determine Q, or the volume of runoff in cubic feet per second within a specified time period, which that area of your project will generate.

Inlets and Pipes. Once you have determined the volume and rate of runoff, prepare a layout of the inlets and pipes beginning where runoff flows and ending at the final discharge point. Inlets are openings in the ground or street covered by grates where runoff flows into a pipe. You may need to provide sediment traps at the invert elevation of an inlet or some type of filter at the opening grate. Most local areas have codes providing design standards for traps, inlets, and filters. States with stormwater management statutes also have specific standards for the number, type, and placement of inlets.

Catch Basins. When constructing a closed system, you may need to install catch basins. Catch basins are concrete structures that allow debris and sediment to settle out before runoff enters the pipe. They are usually located adjacent to streets and roads or underneath inlets in roads or parking lots. You can also place catch basins at bends in pipes and places where large volumes of water accumulate such as street intersections. Catch basins are expensive; as you plan stormwater management for your site, try to minimize the number you use. Figure 7.7 Types of Closed Stormwater Systems shows examples of catch basins.

Pipe Location. When determining the best locations for pipes, keep in mind the slope of the land and the rate of runoff. This

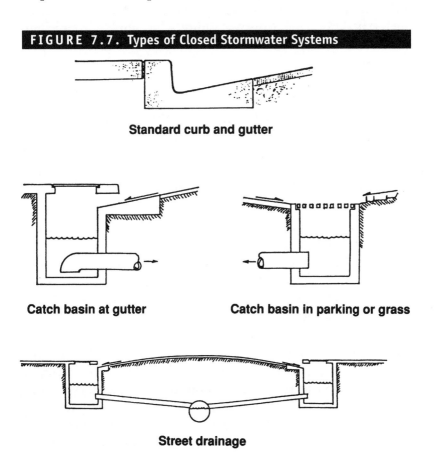

FIGURE 7.7. Types of Closed Stormwater Systems

Standard curb and gutter

Catch basin at gutter   Catch basin in parking or grass

Street drainage

should also coincide with the shortest distance from the source to the point of discharge. Make the slope of the pipes at least 1 percent to facilitate flow and self-cleaning. Generally, design standards require that you keep inlets about 100 to 200 feet apart. Align pipes along roads or parking lots where possible and never go under buildings. Draw straight lines from point to point using as few bends as possible.

Roughness Coefficient. At this point you know the slope of the pipe, the rate or velocity of the runoff flow, and the distance the runoff travels through the pipe to its final destination. As the next step in sizing the pipe, determine the roughness coefficient for the type of pipe you plan to install. Each type of pipe has an interior surface with a certain roughness, depending on its material. This value, called Manning's Roughness Coefficient, has been calculated for each type of pipe and comes with specifications for the pipe.

Pipe Sizing Nomograph. Once you have the roughness coefficient for the pipe, you can determine the size of the pipe flowing full by using a pipe sizing nomograph or chart developed by the U.S. Army Corps of Engineers. Nomographs are produced for various values of roughness. Figure 7.8 Pipe Sizing Nomograph shows the chart for a pipe with a roughness coefficient of n = 0.015.

To use the pipe sizing nomograph, select the correct chart for the known roughness coefficient of the pipe you plan to install. The left side of the chart shows the rate of runoff or discharge (Q). The right side shows an array of slopes. By drawing a straight line between the known rate of runoff (Q) and the known slope, your line crosses the middle column at a point corresponding to the diameter of the pipe. This is an easy method for sizing pipes that carry water or runoff by gravity flow. A variety of computer software has also been developed for sizing open and closed retention, detention, and conveying systems. However, if you do not have access to these, using charts and calculations can give you a good understanding of the types of systems you need on the conceptual level.

FIGURE 7.8. Pipe Sizing Nomograph

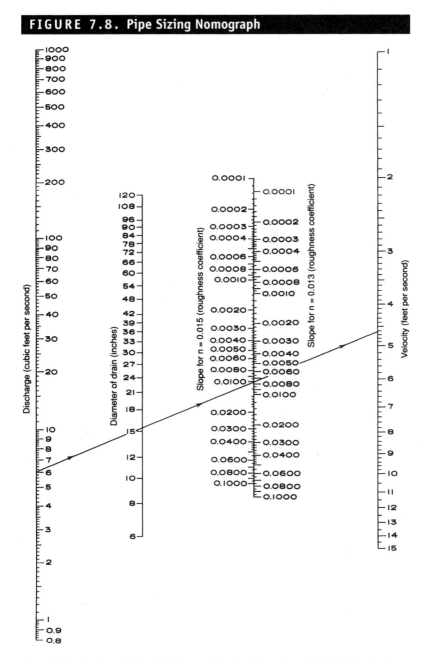

Keep the use of pipes, inlets, and catch basins to a minimum because these are expensive structures to purchase, install, and maintain. If you use closed systems such as these, you need to make the final destination of the stormwater runoff (the detention or retention pond) larger than if you used a swale to carry the runoff. Although in a closed system runoff cannot evaporate or soak into the soil, these systems are necessary where you have rapid rates of flow or insufficient room for open systems.

Designing Open Systems

Where possible, design open systems as a network of small receiving areas instead of diverting water to one large receiving area. This reduces both the size and depth of open systems, making them less intrusive. It also can provide more interesting and aesthetically pleasing ponding areas.

Controlling Costs. One of the best reasons for using open systems is that they cost less to install and maintain than closed systems. Shallow excavation and replanting are far less expensive than deep excavation and installing pipes, catch basins, and inlets. Since swales and other open systems are on the surface, you can easily fix poor filtration or clogging of the systems with minimal disturbance to the surrounding area. When closed systems become clogged, you have to excavate and repair entire segments of pipes and then replant the disturbed area. If these pipes are located beneath a street, it increases the disturbance and cost of repair.

Open Spaces. Open spaces and landscape buffers that are sometimes used for passive recreation can become temporary storage facilities for stormwater runoff since they are not in use during rainstorms. Temporary ponding for short periods does not compromise their primary functions. However, if these areas are part of the amenities you have provided in direct response to the target market's preferences, this may not be the wisest choice. It compromises their value to the users and could require costly maintenance from frequent flooding.

Undulating Boundaries. The boundaries of swales and other open systems should undulate rather than run as straight channels. Undulating boundaries provide more perimeter area for plants that filter out pollutants in the water (a littoral zone), slow the rate of water flow, and make the open system appear more natural. Undulating boundaries can also increase the lengths of open systems, which in turn creates additional opportunities for development if the system is used as a project amenity. Since open systems allow a certain amount of runoff to evaporate, increasing the length will also increase the amount evaporated.

Even small open systems are more visually interesting if designed with natural, curving boundaries. Figure 7.9 Stormwater Detention Techniques illustrates this concept.

When you design open systems as natural ponds with undulating banks, use the following guidelines to enhance their appearance and maintenance:

1. Keep standing water shallow, decreasing potential accidents when children play nearby.
2. Plant the sides and bottom area with vegetation that can live under saturated soil conditions, which improves the system's appearance when it has no standing water. This also provides a littoral zone of aquatic plants that filters additional pollutants from the water.
3. Gradually slope the sides to the bottom of the system. By doing this and planting the sides and bottom area, you make the system appear to be a natural landform. As such, this technique eliminates the necessity of fencing and barriers; without an abrupt change in elevation, no special measures are required to protect children from falling in. These guidelines also apply to any kind of swale or detention or retention pond.

FIGURE 7.9. Stormwater Detention Techniques

Standard Surface Detention

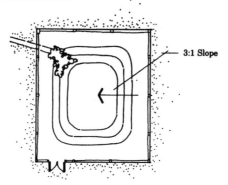

Alternate Surface Detention

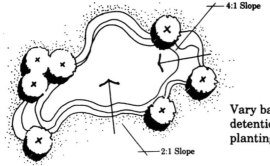

Vary banks along edge of detention area and incorporate plantings to create amenity.

Source: Donald H. Brandes, Jr., and J. Michael Luzier, *Developing Difficult Sites: Solutions for Developers and Builders* (Washington, DC: Home Builder Press, National Association of Home Builders, 1991), p. 62.

Combining Open and Closed Systems

Residential developments offer more opportunities for using open systems for stormwater management than commercial projects simply because there is more undeveloped land. This makes the volume of residential stormwater runoff lower than for commercial projects. However, developers frequently must use a combination of open and closed systems. For example, retention and detention ponds sometimes require a mix of open and closed systems to control sedimentation and rate of flow. Figure 7.10 Detention Basin Features illustrates the use of

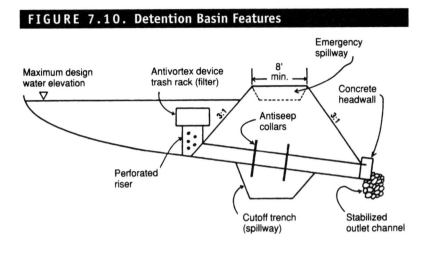

FIGURE 7.10. Detention Basin Features

several components of a closed system such as filters, spillways, and headwalls in an open-system design.

Check the rate of flow to determine if it is slow enough for you to convey the runoff over the ground in an open system. If the rate exceeds a certain value and is running over paved surfaces, you must send the runoff into a closed system; if it is running over a natural surface you can deposit it into either a closed or open system. A commonly used standard requires the developer to send stormwater runoff into a closed system if the rate is over 1.5 cubic feet per second. However, consult the county engineer or local codes to find the correct design standard for the rate of runoff for your project.

Ideally, if closed systems are necessary, you need only place them only along the streets, while allowing open systems to handle the runoff from houses and yards. You may be able to have your stormwater system consist solely of open systems. However, this approach requires streets without curbs. If the streets in your development have curbs, runoff must enter a catch basin to go through the curb and into a closed system of pipes. If the land has a significant slope, the intersections of the streets naturally collect a lot of water, requiring catch basins. So, as you plan your site's stormwater management design, use open systems where possible and supplement these with the necessary closed systems.

Stormwater Drainage Plan

An important component of your stormwater management plan is how you will handle stormwater drainage. Produce a conceptual plan for stormwater drainage early in project design along with the conceptual master plan. Once you know the layout of streets and houses, you can calculate the amount of stormwater runoff generated on-site within a certain time period by comparing the amount of built and unbuilt surfaces. Also note the locations of receiving areas such as swales and retention and detention ponds, as well as the type of open or closed systems used.

This conceptual stormwater drainage plan can show the type and amount of open and closed systems necessary for stormwater management. It can also show possible locations for receiving areas and prove the feasibility of providing cost-effective stormwater management. This allows you to adjust project density or layout if necessary to accommodate stormwater management requirements. It can also alert you to possible increased costs for engineering the project as designed.

Site Drainage Patterns

To produce the stormwater drainage plan, first you must understand the natural direction of water as it flows over the site. Study the topographic map with the master plan overlay and again locate the basin divides, which form the ridge areas of your site. The water runs to the center of the basin in a perpendicular direction. Your site may have many basins or only a portion of one, but all are actually small watershed areas. Figure 7.11 Drainage Basin shows the difference between the undashed lines of the site's contours and heavy dashed line of the basin divide.

As you study the topographical map, you can easily find the low areas where water collects by gravity. Note these as potential destinations for the discharge of stormwater runoff. Again, make sure these low areas are not located within a floodplain.

FIGURE 7.11. Drainage Basin

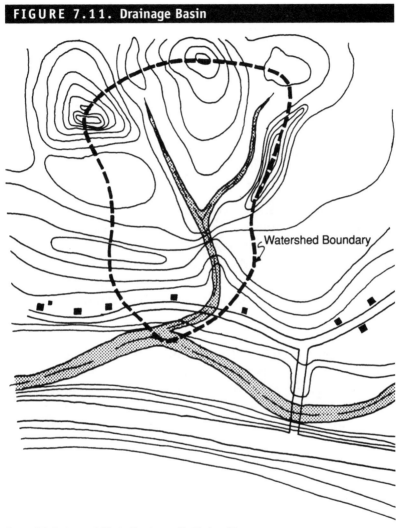

Watershed Boundary

Source: U.S. Environmental Protection Agency, Washington, DC.

Some areas may prohibit the discharge of stormwater into a 100-year floodplain. Some may even prevent you from discharging stormwater into any type of floodplain. If the low areas on your site are located within floodplains, you might have to divert water that naturally flows toward them, so check local requirements with your county engineer.

Rational Formula

Once you have located possible areas for swales and retention and detention ponds, use the rational formula to calculate the total amount of stormwater runoff your project will generate within a certain period of time. The rational formula is generally used for areas of less than 200 acres although, because it is an empirical formula, engineers differ slightly on the maximum number of acres for which it is appropriate. Larger tracts of land may be engineered in sections of 200 acres or less. Figure 7.12 Rational Formula explains the variables of the formula.

Runoff Coefficient. The average runoff coefficient (C) takes into account the amount of water that runs off the different types of surfaces on your site. Each surface has a runoff coefficient corresponding to the amount of water that runs over the surface compared with the amount that infiltrates the surface. Figure 7.13 Runoff Coefficients shows these values for a variety of different types of surfaces.

Intensity of Rainfall. Know the intensity of the rainfall (I) in your area before you begin calculating the total amount and rate of stormwater runoff for your site. The intensity of rainfall refers to the amount of rain in inches per hour that falls during a certain period for a selected location and type of storm. Rainfall intensity charts depict values of intensity for each hour within a 24-hour period and are given for different classes of storms in different geographical locations. Storms are classified as 2-, 5-, 10-, 25-, 50-, and 100-year storms. A 100-year storm means

---

FIGURE 7.12. Rational Formula

$Q = CIA$, where:

Q = maximum amount of runoff in cubic feet per second
(Q accounts for both quantity and rate.)
C = average runoff coefficient for the entire site
I = intensity of rainfall in inches per hour
A = total area to be drained in acres

FIGURE 7.13. Runoff Coefficients

	Runoff Coefficients
Description of Area	
Business	
Downtown	0.70 to 0.95
Neighborhood	0.50 to 0.70
Residential	
Single family	0.30 to 0.50
Multi-units, detached	0.40 to 0.60
Multi-units, attached	0.60 to 0.75
Residential (suburban)	0.25 to 0.40
Apartment	0.50 to 0.70
Industrial	
Light	0.50 to 0.80
Heavy	0.60 to 0.90
Parks, Cemeteries	0.10 to 0.25
Railroad Yard	0.20 to 0.35
Unimproved	0.10 to 0.30
Character of Surface	
Pavement	
Asphalt or concrete	0.70 to 0.95
Brick	0.70 to 0.85
Roofs	0.70 to 0.95
Lawns, Sandy Soil	
Flat, 2 percent	0.05 to 0.10
Average, 2 to 7 percent	0.10 to 0.15
Steep, 7 percent or more	0.15 to 0.20
Lawns, Heavy Soil	
Flat, 2 percent	0.13 to 0.17
Average, 2 to 7 percent	0.18 to 0.22
Steep, 7 percent or more	0.25 to 0.35

Source: Reprinted with permission from American Society of Civil Engineers, *Design and Construction of Sanitary and Storm Sewers,* Manual 37, 1969.

that a storm of this amount and intensity has a 1 percent chance of occurring in any given year. The specific classification of storm to use in your calculations is known as the design storm. This will be determined by the local government authority, usually the city or county engineer's office.

Most residential projects use either a 10- or 25-year design storm. You can obtain rainfall intensity charts for your area from the local weather bureau or county engineer's office. If your state has specific statutes governing the design of stormwater management systems, consult these. Figure 7.14 Rainfall Intensity Curves shows the intensity of rainfall for various types of design storms in a one-hour period for different regions of the country.

The value of Q in the rational formula shown in Figure 7.12 represents the total amount of runoff in a certain period of time that your project would generate. Use the result in other formulas to size swales and retention and detention systems. This formula can also calculate the total amount of runoff for the entire site under both predevelopment and postdevelopment conditions. This gives you a general idea of how much stormwater is generated and how much area is needed to hold it if you plan to contain all or a portion of it on site. This in turn gives you an idea of the amount of built surface area a given site can support.

Subarea Drainage Requirements

Once you are satisfied you can engineer the site for the required amount of stormwater runoff the project may generate, you can begin to microengineer smaller areas. Have your engineer recommend a way to divide the project into smaller drainage subareas. Design each site separately. The design of the master plan and the characteristics of the site itself can provide clues for making these various divisions. Essentially parcel size, soil conditions, road layouts, natural basin divides, and topography all determine the number of drainage subareas.

Streets, roads, parking lots, and buildings form natural boundaries or dams to surface runoff. Paved surface not only creates increased runoff with faster rates, it also obstructs drainage patterns. Because of this, these areas are often used as the perimeters of the smaller drainage areas. Take special care with sediment and pollution control around streets and parking lots; these sources can allow heavy metals to enter the nation's waterways and so are heavily regulated under federal law. You

FIGURE 7.14. Rainfall Intensity Curves

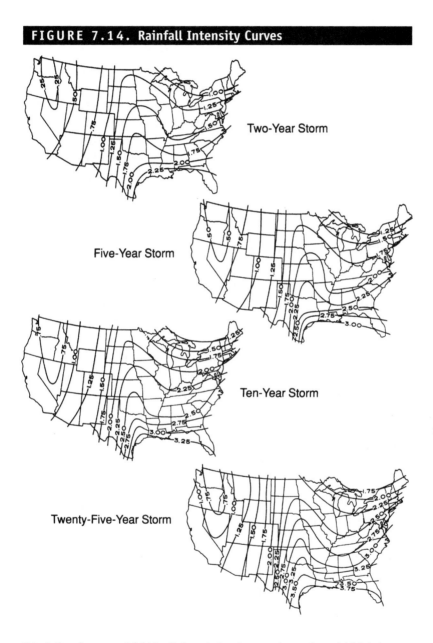

Two-Year Storm

Five-Year Storm

Ten-Year Storm

Twenty-Five-Year Storm

Note: In these four maps, rainfall intensity for each storm is measured as one-hour rainfall in inches per hour.

Source: Engineering Division, Soil Conservation Service, U.S. Department of Agriculture, *Technical Paper No. 40, Rainfall Frequency Atlas of the United States for Durations from 30 Minutes to 24 Hours and Return Periods from 1 to 100 Years, Washington, DC, 1940.*

must also divert water around these structures to avoid dangerous conditions caused by standing water.

You may be able to engineer each subarea separately with open and closed systems or by using a combination of the two. Essentially, this means each subarea handles its own stormwater runoff. This may not be possible where a great deal of built surface exists or where slope and soil conditions prevent good infiltration. Then, stormwater runoff must be conveyed out of one subarea and into another. The destination can be a retention or detention pond or a discharge point into the county or city stormwater system.

Regardless whether you're designing an open system or a closed one, differentiate between planted or natural and paved areas. Frequently, parking lots and streets require closed systems because they generate more runoff traveling at a faster rate than natural areas such as lawns. Where possible, use open swale systems for conveying stormwater with shallow depths. Do this for curbless streets and parking lots that have adjacent natural space large enough to handle the swale. Do not place open or closed systems near any trees and vegetation slated for protection; the excavation required for constructing these systems would likely force their removal.

Retention and Detention Basins

Make sure the design of your retention and detention basins follow sound stormwater management practices. Some states provide guidelines; if your state does, follow them. If not, take measures to ensure the safety of all residents, especially children, around the open system. You also need to protect the water supply from pollutants found in stormwater runoff. And, to promote project profitability, you need to make the system aesthetically pleasing and its long-term maintenance cost-effective.

System Configuration. Design the detention system as a series of small depressions with shallow depths similar to the way you design swales. Place these depressions in setback or buffer areas and plant them so they appear as natural undulations in the land. You may also use swales to connect the depressions or to act as the final destination of stormwater runoff from underground pipes.

Swales and detention areas should have longer physical configurations with undulating perimeters, which gradually reduce the velocity of flow to promote the gradual sedimentation of particles. Most heavy metals entering the aquifer or waterways come in the form of particulate matter. Swales should maximize the length of flow from source to discharge point to allow those particles to settle. At the same time, carefully design swales and detention areas with sufficient slope to prevent the reduction of flow and the subsequent creation of hydraulic dead zones.

Retention systems are more expensive to construct than detention systems and always have a standing pool of water. Turn them into a project amenity. Make them deep enough to hold the standing water needed to support active plant and animal life. This depth may be more than sufficient to contain the calculated volume of stormwater runoff. Remember that seasonal changes can cause water to evaporate. If the water level in a retention pond drops to less than 2 feet, it can kill plant and animal life and create unpleasant odors and appearances. Your retention pond may need pumps for aeration or additional water if levels drop.

Key Data and Assumptions. Design retention and detention basins based on the volume of runoff within a given time period (Q) obtained from the rational formula. You also need to use the following additional information and assumptions to size these systems:

1. Use the percolation rate of each soil type on your site in calculating the size of retention or detention ponds. You can obtain percolation rates in the soil data information found in surveys for the U.S. Department of Agriculture or the local public works or engineer's offices. In other words, you should calculate separately each area that has a soil type with different percolation rates.

2. Assume that, during a storm, water runs into the retention or detention basin and infiltrates only through the bottom of the pond. Consider the water infiltrating through the sides of the pond as insignificant for these calculations.

3. The retention and detention ponds should hold at least 80 percent of the estimated total runoff your project generates within a given period of time. Assume that the site in its undeveloped state generates a runoff rate of approximately 20 percent of this total. Then check the amount of stormwater that local or state ordinances require you to retain on your site.

4. Remember to consider the amount of runoff generated by adjacent site uses, if any, in estimating the volume of stormwater runoff you must manage.

5. Place the bottom of the retention or detention pond above the water table if possible to keep pollutants from entering directly into the aquifer. Local and state ordinances may determine the distance from the water table to the invert elevation of the pond. Projects located where the invert elevation of the retention pond can extend below the water table may need filters or membranes to alleviate potential pollution of the water table.

Calculations. The following problem sizes a retention or detention pond for a hypothetical project. Figure 7.15 Project Parameters shows the general data necessary to perform these calculations. These project parameters have been simplified for illustrative purposes and might also include data for other parameters such as sidewalks and walkways.

To calculate, find the peak discharge within a given period of time (Q). To do this, first convert the number of square feet of each surface into acres (A). (See Figure 7.15.) Then multiply the runoff coefficient for each surface (C) times the rainfall intensity (I) times the number of acres to be drained (A) or $Q = CIA$. Since roofs, drives, patios, and streets all have the same runoff coefficient, you can combine them. For simplicity, assume the rainfall intensity for these areas is one inch per

FIGURE 7.15. Project Parameters

Total site area: 60 acres
Number of houses on the site:
  3.5 houses per acre or 210 houses

Assume for each house:
  Roof area = 2,000 square feet
  Drive = 480 square feet
  Patio = 250 square feet

Assume for the development:
  Streets = 400,000 square feet

Areas	Total Square Feet	Total Acres
Roofs	420,000	9.64
Drives	100,800	2.31
Patios	52,500	1.21
Streets	400,000	9.18
Total Developed Land		22.34
Total Undeveloped Land		37.66

hour. You can then calculate the runoff for both the developed and undeveloped land as follows:

Surface	Q (cubic feet per second)	= C	I (inches per hour)	A (acres)
Roofs, drives, patios, and streets	21.22	= (0.95)	(1)	(22.34)
Undeveloped land	13.18	= (0.35)	(1)	(37.66)

As you can see in this example, the total acreage (A) for the site equals 60 and the peak discharge of runoff for the site (Q) equals 34.40 cubic feet per second. Next, to find the total effective runoff coefficient C (effective) for the entire project, divide the total Qs by the total acres:

C(effective) = Sum Q ÷ Sum A
C(effective) = 34.40 cubic feet per second ÷ 60 acres = 0.57

Sizing the retention or detention pond to contain the amount of runoff on this 60-acre project, you then use two formulas. The first calculates the volume of water going into the pond (V_i) during one hour as follows:

$$V_i = A \times C(\text{effective}) \times 1 \times T$$

where A = the total number of acres, C(effective) = the effective runoff coefficient from the rational formula, 1 = the first hour of the storm, and T = time or the number of seconds in one hour. You can then calculate the volume of water (V_i) for the 60-acre project as follows:

$$V_i = 60 \text{ acres} \times 0.57 \times 1 \times 3,600 \text{ seconds in one hour}$$
$$= 123,120 \text{ cubic feet of volume in the first hour}$$

Next, calculate the volume of water that infiltrates downward into the bottom of the pond (V_o) with the following formula:

$$V_o = \text{bottom area} \times \text{percolation rate} \times \text{time}$$

To use this formula, you must first estimate the area for the bottom of the retention or detention pond in square feet. You can then obtain the percolation rate in feet per hour from your information on soil characteristics. For this problem, assume the percolation rate is 6 feet per day, or 0.25 feet per hour, and the bottom area is 90,000 square feet. Then calculate the volume of water infiltrating into the bottom of the retention or detention pond as follows:

$$V_o = 90,000 \text{ square feet} \times 0.25 \text{ feet per hour} \times 1 \text{ hour}$$
$$= 22,500 \text{ cubic feet}$$

You can next determine the total storage volume of the retention or detention pond (V_s) by subtracting the volume of water infiltrating into the bottom of the pond (V_o) from the volume of water going into the pond (V_i) during one hour:

$$V_s = V_i - V_o$$
or
$$V_s = 123,120 \text{ cubic feet} - 22,500 \text{ cubic feet}$$
$$= 100,620 \text{ cubic feet}$$

Test your estimate of the bottom area of the pond by determining the required depth of a pond with an area of 90,000 square feet. Divide the total storage volume (V_s) by the estimated area of the pond (90,000 square feet). If the depth is acceptable, then 90,000 square feet is sufficient at that depth to hold all of Q. In this case, 100,620 cubic feet divided by 90,000 square feet = 1.12 feet of depth. A depth of less than 2 feet is still very shallow and therefore acceptable for a detention pond. However, you can also choose to make the retention or detention area smaller by increasing the depth up to an acceptable level. If you are sizing a retention pond, the depth can be greater to accommodate water storage year-round.

Work the formulas back and forth, holding one variable constant and adjusting others, until the pond achieves an acceptable area and depth. If the depth proves too great to hold the total storage volume within the 90,000 square feet, you can enlarge the area until the pond has a proper depth. The area and depth in this problem represent only one pond. This gives you an idea of the amount of land needed for containment if you held 80 percent of the runoff on your own site. If this is the amount you must contain, your actual designs should divide this large area into numerous smaller ponds. Then make sure that the total combined areas and depths of the smaller ponds equal that of the one large pond, the ponds are interconnected to provide balance, and each is designed for its contributing watershed.

Creating Project Amenities

No matter how you design the detention and retention ponds, using open systems for stormwater management automatically means you must leave a portion of the site where they are located unbuilt. This provides an opportunity to use the systems for more than one purpose. Creating project amenities or privacy buffers with these areas can add value to your project, usually at minimal cost.

In residential developments, a network of swales behind a row of houses can have the visual effect of extending each owner's property. If you place a row of trees or landscaping along the network, the open system can also form a privacy buffer. If you connect swales to a retention pond, the pond can even become a focal point for your project. Figure 7.16 Retention Pond as Project Amenity shows a system of swales connected to a centrally located retention pond.

When you locate swales and detention or retention ponds in setback areas such as the sides and backs of houses, shallow depth and additional perimeter landscaping can help to disguise them as stormwater management systems while providing visual interest. If you must use retention ponds, evaluate the cost of showcasing the pond as a water amenity. If you cannot afford large retention ponds that require expensive pumps and aeration devices to keep water levels at an appropriate depth, use a series of longer and more narrow swales as detention ponds. (See Figure 7.16.) If possible, locate these along hike-and-bike trails or in park areas. Provide perimeter landscaping to soften the edges and avoid straight lines in the design of the pond footprint.

FIGURE 7.16. Retention Pond as Project Amenity

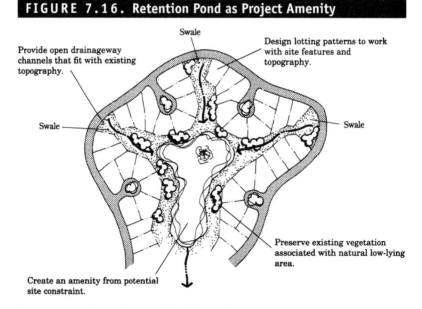

Source: Brandes and Luzier, *Developing Difficult Sites*, p. 61.

Also, when possible, locate open systems along natural drainage pathways. This choice creates a more aesthetically pleasing result because it causes the least amount of disturbance to the land. This in turn translates into lower installation costs. Figure 7.17 Natural Drainageways Left as Open Spaces shows a plan that leaves the drainage system undisturbed in open space areas. Lots aligned along this undulating area are more desirable and can command higher prices because of the privacy provided.

Erosion and Sediment Control Plan

Erosion, the movement of sediment, and its subsequent deposit are part of the natural cycle that landforms undergo as they are exposed to wind, rain, and flooding over long periods. However, land development and construction activities speed up this process through clearing, grading, and paving natural surfaces. When unstable soil is left exposed, excessive deposits of sediment are carried into surface waters and other areas where they are not wanted. This causes sedimentation to build up on adjacent properties or roads.

Erosion causes unstable landforms and the loss of valuable top soil, which can affect every phase of development and construction. Minimize erosion on your site by understanding its causes and using protective measures both during construction and for long-term maintenance. While the action of wind and rain on exposed land causes erosion, four major factors influence the amount of erosion that can occur on your site: type of soil, slope, intensity of rainfall, and amount of plant cover. The characteristics of the type of soil influences how well the soil will compact together or erode. Steeper slopes erode more quickly and in larger quantity than flatter slopes. The intensity of rainfall determines the force of the water acting upon the soil; the more intense the rainfall, the more erosion occurs. Finally, the more vegetated the area is, the less erosion occurs. Where erosion occurs, a sediment deposit will follow.

Sedimentation can occur in places where stormwater is discharged and can cause a variety of adverse effects. Besides con-

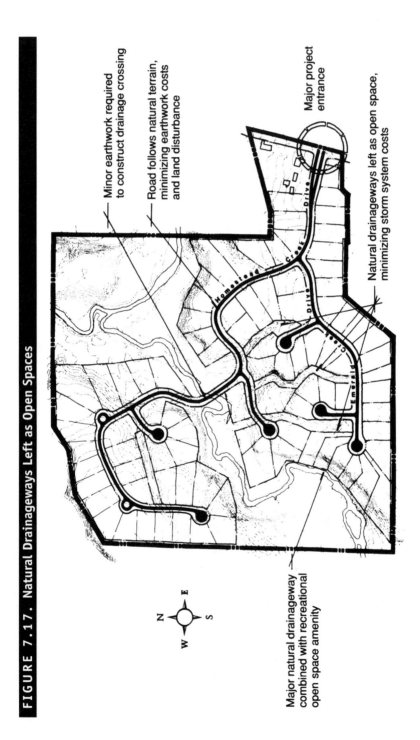

FIGURE 7.17. Natural Drainageways Left as Open Spaces

Minor earthwork required
to construct drainage crossing

Road follows natural terrain,
minimizing earthwork costs
and land disturbance

Major project
entrance

Natural drainageways left as open space,
minimizing storm system costs

Major natural drainageway
combined with recreational
open space amenity

Source: Brandes and Luzier, *Developing Difficult Sites,* p. 82.

tributing to the deposit of heavy metals, sedimentation causes water to become turbid or muddy, decreasing the amount of oxygen and light available to plants and animals. In addition, the deposit of sediment in one area can cause excess flooding and erosion downstream.

Temporary Control Measures

Erosion can occur whenever ground is disturbed. Removal of protective plants and changes in grade that leave unstable slopes can provide opportunities for wind and rain to wash soil away.

If you are building in a climate that has intense amounts of rainfall, erosion can be especially difficult to control. When disturbed, certain soil types with high concentrations of sand or collapsible properties may be much more unstable than other soils.

Bales or Fabric. Federal, state, and local regulations require erosion-control measures during construction. These regulations specify the materials and methods to use. Generally, you need to surround the work area with siltation barriers to prevent soil from eroding onto other property or in developed areas elsewhere on the site. Common siltation barriers include the use of straw bales or filter fabric at the perimeter of the work area. Figure 7.18 Straw Siltation Barriers illustrates the placement of perimeter bales.

Straw siltation barriers are effective measures for preventing sedimentation onto other property if placed close enough together. Note, though, that you can use straw siltation barriers only once. This has prompted the substitution of plastic filter fabric staked down at the perimeter of the work area.

However, although you can reuse plastic siltation barriers, they do require more maintenance during construction. For example, they tend to move around and collapse and you must continuously monitor and restore them to their original positions. Both materials require good installation practices that firmly attach the barrier into the ground.

Sites containing steep slopes, or with steep slopes immediately offsite, may need to berm or dike the slope by building a

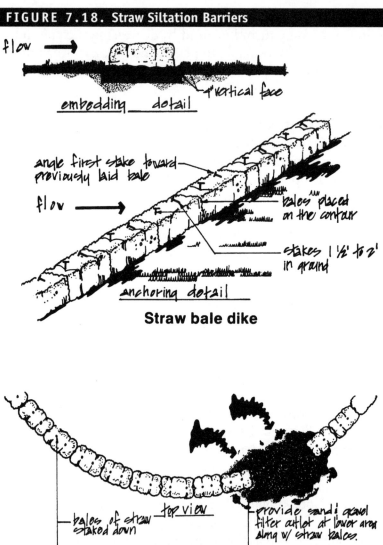

FIGURE 7.18. Straw Siltation Barriers

flow →

embedding detail — 4" vertical face

angle first stake toward previously laid bale

flow →

bales placed on the contour

stakes 1½' to 2' in ground

anchoring detail

Straw bale dike

bales of straw staked down

top view

provide sand & gravel filter outlet at lower area along w/ straw bales.

front view

Barrier with gravel outlet

barrier of earth that acts as a wall to downward flowing sediment. Depending on the length of the slope, you may have to construct several dikes to slow or trap the flow of sediment.

Finally, in areas where silt and sediment tend to collect and stormwater discharge is especially turbid, construct sediment traps to prevent eroding soil from entering into stormwater discharge systems.

Steps Used During Construction. Once you have selected the type of siltation barrier for the site, use the following steps for erosion and sediment control during construction:

1. Phase work to minimize the time each area is exposed to the wind and rain.
2. Where necessary, use temporary channels and berms to divert runoff from other areas into the work area.
3. Avoid creating steep slopes (over 3 to 1). If these are required in your master plan, cover them with plastic film or netting until they properly stabilize.
4. Use sediment traps (a screen or metal grid) at sensitive areas such as property boundaries and adjacent to streams and streets. While siltation barriers are often used for areas of 2 to 3 acres, sediment traps may be used for areas of 6 acres or more.
5. Use regular inspections to maintain siltation barriers.
6. Stabilize piles of imported fill by periodic wetting.
7. Identify and mark limits of disturbance on the site to prevent construction vehicles from traversing areas that should not be disturbed.
8. Install tracking pads at the site's entrances and exits to help remove mud before it leaves the site on the wheels of construction vehicles.

Again, it's more cost-effective to use effective management practices to prevent erosion and sediment control than to try to correct a problem that occurs later. As the amount of change in slope required for your project increases, it poses increasing challenges for erosion and sediment control. The less you disturb slope and vegetation, the lower your costs for stabilizing the new grades will be.

Permanent Control Measures

You must also secure your project from the adverse effects of erosion and subsequent sediment deposit after construction is completed. Once again, the less you disturb the natural grade of the land, the easier and less costly your long-term erosion and sediment control will be. Some of the measures you can take to control erosion and sedimentation after construction include the following:

1. Limit cut and fill. Where necessary, balance cut and fill to avoid importing excessive amounts of fill to the site.
2. Stabilize steep slopes and areas of compacted fill with proper plant cover. This includes plants that grow and bind quickly with the soil.
3. Use plastic filter fabric to stabilize steep slopes before planting.
4. Install stormwater management systems before constructing buildings.
5. Build dikes and berms to divert stormwater away from sensitive areas like floodplains and wetlands.

Dikes and Berms. Just as dikes and berms are used for temporary sedimentation control during construction, they may be used as permanent measures on your site. Figure 7.19 Diversion Dikes and Berms shows the difference between a dike and a berm along with their standard dimensions. A diversion dike acts as a dam, stopping water at a certain point and diverting it elsewhere. A berm slows down the flow of water, although some water can still flow over and through the berm. Berms generally are also shallower and more easily stabilized with geotextiles and plant cover when these engineered structures are used as part of stormwater management systems. State or local statutes and codes specify allowable slopes and dimensions.

FIGURE 7.19. Diversion Dikes and Berms

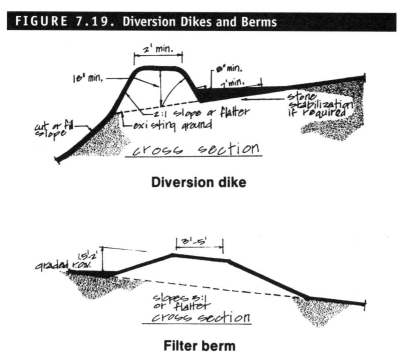

Diversion dike

Filter berm

Site Engineering and Your Project

A proficiently engineered site uses cost-effective measures to ensure functional and aesthetically pleasing placement of utilities, sewers, stormwater systems, roads, and buildings. Sound engineering also determines the best approach to long-term maintenance for all these systems. Although the cost of site engineering can become one of the highest in land development, cutting corners early on can mean excessive costs later to correct mistakes. Invest your money wisely in sound engineering practices up front. The return on your investment in proper site engineering will be high; with it you create a more attractive community that better serves the needs of the target market group.

8

Residential Streets

The pattern of streets in a residential development directly influences both the beauty and function of the neighborhood. The design of the street system acts as a framework within which everything in the development is organized. Street design dictates lot distribution, building placement, amount and location of open space, and pedestrian and vehicular traffic.

The primary elements of street design are length, width, geometry, intersections, drainage, construction methods, and materials. How each of the primary design elements is handled influences how people, cars, and other vehicles use the street. When you have a clear understanding of how the street pattern contributes to the overall goals of the master plan, you can more easily develop the most functional street layout for your project.

Street Design

Street design determines many other aspects of the master plan. The orientation of streets fixes the orientation of lots and houses. For instance, streets with north and south alignment produce lots with houses aligned east and west. The direction in which the houses face in turn affects their solar orientation and energy efficiency.

Street design also influences the size and shape of lots. A curving street pattern tends to produce irregularly shaped lots while a grid pattern produces more rectangular shapes. This could become important with smaller lots; meeting the subdivision ordinance's dimension requirements can be difficult if lots deviate too much from a regular shape. Street pattern also dictates the length and placement of utility lines, as these are usually located along the street. Remember that longer streets and utility lines contribute to higher development costs.

Street geometry and intersection design influence both vehicular and pedestrian safety by controlling how fast automobiles can travel. The overall street pattern, its geometry, and intersection design form the basis of the community's identity by producing particular arrangements of lots and houses. Street design can also encourage or discourage pedestrian activity.

New Directions in Street Design

Historically, moving cars at efficient speeds with maximum safety was a primary goal of street design. In the past, highway design goals were applied to streets of all kinds because most street design continued to emphasize the automobile. This approach resulted in the overdesign of many residential streets and increased the efficiency of automobile traffic at the expense of the pedestrian. Overdesign refers to the use of excessive street widths, overly large intersections, and curves with radii that are too large. With overdesigned streets, drivers tend to drive at the maximum speed that appears safe and comfortable to them, regardless of posted speed limits.

Many streets have overly large intersections because the corners have generous turning radii, allowing automobiles to turn more safely at faster speeds. When the street has more than two lanes, the intersection becomes even larger. Large intersections also make pedestrian crossings more dangerous. The larger turning radius increases the distance pedestrians have to walk to cross the street and requires them to fight speeding cars when crossing streets without traffic lights.

Scaled-Down Streets. Although streets are designed for the automobile, they can contribute much more than simply moving cars quickly between homes, work, and services. Street design affects pedestrian and automobile safety, level of noise, bicycle use of the street, and the overall appearance of the neighborhood.

Many developers are realizing that streets should be a more integral part of neighborhood life. To do that, some developments are designing with scaled-down street sizes, which enhances pedestrian use and decreases development costs. Figure 8.1 Pedestrian-Scaled Street shows houses pulled toward a street of smaller-than-usual width. The low pedestrian-scaled fence and sidewalk enhance the people-friendly aspects of the street.

Street design plays a large role in the character of a neighborhood. A proper, scaled-down design brings houses on opposite sides of the street closer together, contributing to a sense of enclosure that makes a space feel comfortable. Overdesigned streets eliminate this sense of intimacy and comfort.

Local Street Standards

Generally, the local subdivision or development ordinance governs public street design in residential developments. The streets in your development can be classified as either private or public. If private, they belong to the development and are installed and maintained by you the developer. Streets deemed public by the local government are subject to different regulations for installation and maintenance.

Public Streets. Standards for public streets constitute legal codes, so as a developer you must either follow them or get the standards changed or waived. If you decide to attempt the latter, remember that these codes are primarily intended to promote traffic safety and give large service and emergency vehicles easy access to every home in a development.

Convincing local authorities to adopt more sensible standards for public streets may be possible if you can show that typical standards actually encourage fast-moving traffic—the

FIGURE 8.1. Pedestrian-Scaled Street

opposite of their intended result. In those cases, you may obtain a waiver to change street dimensions and geometries if you can prove they still maintain the safety and welfare of the community's inhabitants.

Some places have adopted different design codes for streets in developments where an attempt has been made to go back to more traditional neighborhoods. These local governments actually have two separate codes for street design: one for conventional developments and another for neo-traditional developments. Among others, Bedford, New Hampshire; Sacramento County, California; and Dade County, Florida, have adopted these types of ordinances.

Private Streets. If the streets within your development are deemed private, you have more design flexibility since rules and regulations for public streets don't apply. For example, private streets can be narrower with no required right-of-way lines, allowing buildings to be placed closer to pavements. Private streets may also be exempt from local landscape and signage codes. All of this can potentially save you money on development costs. Remember, however, that the homeowners' association must maintain private streets within the development; depending on the target market, this may or may not be considered desirable. Additionally, private streets must still receive approval from the local fire department and other emergency services.

Applying Local Standards to the Master Plan

The elements of street design typically governed by local codes are the same ones that affect the important design decisions concerning your master plan. You can derive street pattern and design from the following considerations: street function, hierarchy, geometry, dimensions, traffic speed, and intersection design. View each aspect in terms of what the code allows, how it affects the neighborhood's identity, the cost of installation and maintenance, and the target market's preferences. Figure 8.2 Design Standards for Streets provides a list of various aspects of street design governed by the local subdivision ordinance or other codes.

If the minimum dimensions required by the ordinance still appear unnecessarily large, work with your design team to come up with alternatives. Any alternative dimensions must comply with access requirements for service and emergency

---

FIGURE 8.2. Design Standards for Streets

- Dimensions, including widths of pavements, rights-of-way, easements, widths and number of lanes, lengths of cul-de-sacs, distances between intersections, and shapes and dimensions of cul-de-sacs and turnarounds
- Intersection angles and grades
- Horizontal and vertical alignment of streets
- Curbs and gutter standards, including construction standards and distance between catch basins
- Provision for off- and on-street parking
- Road construction standards, including types of materials and methods of construction
- Utility placement

---

vehicles. Once you have determined these, meet with code officials to discuss possible waivers or variances in widths and geometries.

Street Hierarchy

Street hierarchy describes the classification of streets by function. For example, highways carry traffic at high speeds with limited off-road access. Arterial streets carry through traffic from one destination to another within cities. The local code sets the design standards of dimensions, geometry, and number of automobiles designed for the street classification. As Figure 8.3 Street Classification Map shows, streets essentially fall into four major classifications: arterial, collector, subcollector, and access. Residential developments may contain streets in each of those classifications except arterial.

Average Daily Traffic. Streets are classified according to the number of trips or the amount of average daily traffic (ADT) that they accommodate. The ADT is the average number of

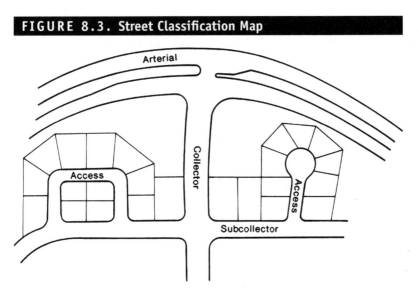

FIGURE 8.3. Street Classification Map

Source: American Society of Civil Engineers (ASCE), National Association of Home Builders (NAHB), and ULI–the Urban Land Institute, *Residential Streets, 2d ed.* (Washington, DC, 1990), p. 26.

automobiles counted at a given location on the street per day. As you design the streets in your development, have your project engineer estimate the ADT for each street and assign it to an appropriate classification. See Figure 8.4 Street Classes Based on Traffic Volume for some general guidelines to use in classifying street hierarchy. These are probably similar to the ones found in the local code for your area.

Street Width

Street width ranks among the most important design considerations. It greatly affects vehicle speed, on-street parking availability, pedestrian safety, and the design characteristics of the neighborhood.

Residential streets, unlike arterials, have several important roles to play. Collector streets, for example, serve an important traffic function, making it necessary to maintain one free lane in each direction. However, homes may also face collector streets, so providing too much room for cars would unnecessarily encourage faster driving. Space for parking on a collector may or may not be necessary, depending on the number of homes on the street and the availability of off-street parking. Many times collector streets are designed solely for automobiles. Houses are located on the smaller arterials and cul-de-sacs, which removes them from the collector.

Lower level streets (subcollectors and access or arterial streets) do not always require two free-flowing traffic lanes. At most suburban densities, parking is in driveways or garages, leaving on-street parking sporadic and scattered. Since travel

---

FIGURE 8.4. Street Classes Based on Traffic Volume

Street Class	Usual ADT Range
Access	0–250
Subcollector	250–1,000
Collector	1,000–3,000

Source: ASCE, NAHB, and ULI, *Residential Streets, 2d ed.,* p. 28.

distances on these narrow streets are short and traffic speeds should be low, encountering an occasional parked car may require a traveling vehicle to pull over and wait while an approaching vehicle passes. Although this may not occur often, the possibility of it happening tends to keep vehicle speeds low.

When planning subcollector and arterial streets, you can design the width to slow vehicle speed and create a safer environment. Figure 8.5 Recommended Pavement Widths shows street widths recommended by the American Society of Civil Engineers, the National Association of Home Builders, and the Urban Land Institute.

Cul-de-Sac Turnarounds

Cul-de-sac turnarounds are another important consideration in street design. The end of a cul-de-sac has a larger area to make it easier for vehicles to turn around; usually it's circular, although for low-volume streets a T- or Y-shape may be sufficient. (See Figure 8.6 Designs for Turnarounds.)

A turnaround does not necessarily need to be large enough for any vehicle to turn effortlessly. A properly sized turnaround does not dominate the landscape; instead, it need only be large enough for the average automobile to turn. This means the occasional moving van or other large vehicle may have to make a few maneuvers in order to turn. But creating a turnaround large enough for effortless turning by any vehicle would result

FIGURE 8.5. Recommended Pavement Widths

Street	Pavement Width (feet)
Alley	12
Access street	22–24
Subcollector	26
Collector	36 if residences face street
	28 if no residences present

Source: ASCE, NAHB, and ULI, *Residential Streets*, 2d ed., p. 38.

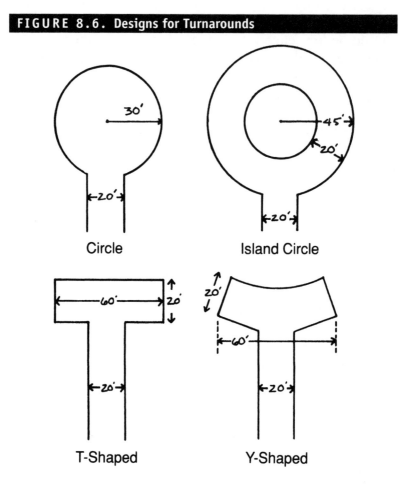

FIGURE 8.6. Designs for Turnarounds

Circle

Island Circle

T-Shaped

Y-Shaped

in excessive costs, an unsightly expanse of asphalt, and increased stormwater runoff.

Most cul-de-sacs should have a radius of 30 feet (see Figure 8.6). Some designs use center islands, which can be landscaped. These turnarounds should have a carway width of 20 feet and an outside radius of 45 feet. Center-island cul-de-sacs add substantially more to your building costs than standard circle cul-de-sacs. The former requires a much larger paved area and a curb around the center island.

For very low-volume streets, a T- or Y- shaped turnaround requires every vehicle to make a reversing movement in order to turn around. The advantage here: Only a limited area needs to be paved, saving costs, improving the landscape, and reducing stormwater runoff.

Street Geometry

Street geometry refers to overall street alignment and turning radii for curves and intersections. The sharpness of a curve is one element of the street geometry's alignment. Local or state requirements for geometry are based on protecting motorist safety, but often they ignore other community needs such as pedestrian safety and the desire for a quiet neighborhood. Also, geometry requirements for streets often make unnecessary assumptions about the need for speed of travel.

Street geometry not only affects traffic safety, it also affects your project's appearance, efficient land use, automobile speed, pedestrian safety, and residents' comfort level in their homes and front yards. Street geometry designed for greater ease of vehicular travel results in greater speeds, which creates more traffic noise and a greater danger of accidents and pedestrian injuries or deaths.

Overdesigned streets are not conducive to a residential environment. As with street width, proper geometry depends on speed limits and the amount of traffic where in the hierarchy of streets it falls. Streets intended for fast travel need different geometry than neighborhood streets intended for slower travel.

Intersections

An important part of street geometry, intersections are points in a street network that allow vehicles to change directions and enter different paths. The safety of both pedestrians and automobiles is of utmost importance here. Intersection safety depends on spacing, geometry, lines of sight, and traffic control devices such as stop signs. Local codes usually govern these considerations within developments if the streets are considered public. Codes also govern the design and location of a development entrance and its connection to an arterial road.

Intersection Spacing. If you want to use intersections to slow down traffic in your development, avoid spacing them too closely together because this can cause traffic to pile up, creating dangerous traffic conditions. Effective spacing depends on the volume of traffic on each street and the number of turning lanes. Most residential streets require turning lanes only on collector roads having a high volume of traffic.

The intent is to space intersections far enough apart so traffic waiting to turn keeps moving and does not back up to the previous intersection. Generally, for low-volume residential streets, a good guideline is a space of between 100 and 150 feet. Spacing intersections at this distance can prevent an automobile from cutting diagonally across the through streets from intersection to intersection. Figure 8.7 Intersection Spacing illustrates this concept.

Intersection Types. The safest geometry for intersection design is the T-shaped intersection. If a T-shaped intersection occurs on a curved road, the road should be straightened out at the location of the intersection for a short distance to allow for a 90-degree angle and thus easier turning. Four-way intersections work best on a grid model because you can minimize street widths and maximize lines of sight, a safer approach for both

FIGURE 8.7. Intersection Spacing

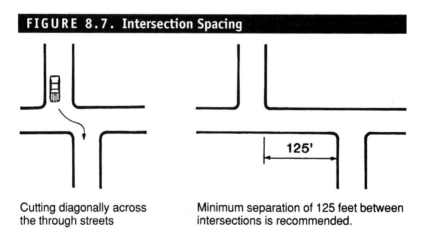

Cutting diagonally across the through streets

Minimum separation of 125 feet between intersections is recommended.

Source: ASCE, NAHB, and ULI, *Residential Streets, 2d ed.,* p. 71.

pedestrians and automobiles. Make sure that corner landscaping and signage do not obstruct the line of sight. Also, avoid four-way intersections on curving collector roads. Figure 8.8 Intersection Geometry shows examples of T-shaped and four-way intersections.

Intersection Angles. Roads should intersect at right angles where possible to maximize lines of sight and provide adequate turning radii. The local ordinance frequently stipulates minimum intersection angles, generally no less than 60 to 75 degrees. However, the more closely the intersection approaches 90 degrees, the safer it will be. If one street does angle into another, straightening out the angled road for a short distance before it intersects the other road can provide the desired 90-degree angle illustrated in Figure 8.9 Intersection Angles.

Curb or Corner Radius

Another important aspect of street geometry is the curb or corner radius. Even when two streets intersect at a 90-degree angle, you need to design the sharpness of the corner itself. This design element, which can be measured by the radius of the circle formed by the curve of the corner, is called the curb or corner radius. (See Figure 8.10 Curb Radius.)

FIGURE 8.8. Intersection Geometry

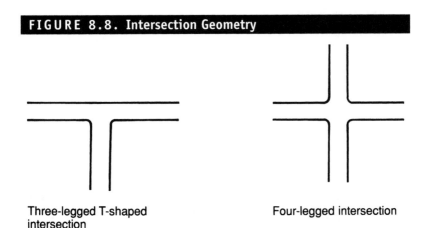

Three-legged T-shaped intersection

Four-legged intersection

Source: ASCE, NAHB, and ULI, *Residential Streets, 2d ed.,* p. 68.

FIGURE 8.9. Intersection Angles

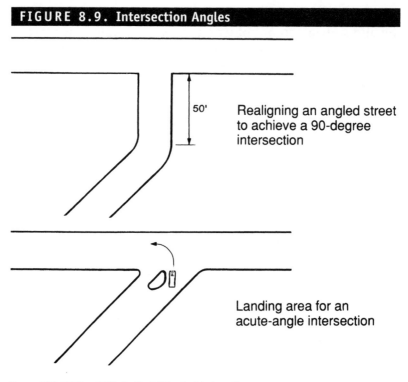

50'
Realigning an angled street
to achieve a 90-degree
intersection

Landing area for an
acute-angle intersection

Source: ASCE, NAHB, and ULI, *Residential Streets, 2d ed.,* p. 69.

The curb radius should be generous enough to allow vehicles to make the turn without driving over the curb but small enough to discourage high turning speeds and rolling stops. A proper curb radius is important for pedestrian safety. Properly scaled, it reduces the speeds of turning vehicles and the distance a pedestrian must cross; a larger curb radius means a wider crosswalk area.

Vertical and Horizontal Alignment

Vertical alignment refers to the amount of crest and sag or rise and fall as the street moves through changes in elevation. The horizontal alignment of a street refers to the sharpness of its curve and is measured by the radius of a circle having an arc that is the same as the curve.

Standards in the local code govern the amount of vertical and horizontal alignment permitted for streets to ensure public safety. Vertical and horizontal alignment affects the driver's line of sight, which is one factor that determines how safely a driver can negotiate a turn at certain speeds. In other words, the sharper the vertical or horizontal curve, the shorter the line of sight, and the more dangerous the turn. This is one reason why the use of curves tends to slow down traffic. Figures 8.11 Vertical Alignment and 8.12 Horizontal Alignment illustrate these concepts for determining the vertical and horizontal alignment of streets.

Overly steep hills (vertical curves) can be hazardous, especially in adverse weather. On the other hand, the sharpness of turns on horizontal curves is a less critical safety factor for residential streets than for streets intended for higher speeds.

Street Patterns

Although local codes usually govern street hierarchy, geometry, and dimensions, you and your project team members make the critical design decisions concerning the overall pattern of the streets. Choose a street pattern based on the way it supports the intended identity for your new development. As one example, a grid pattern can be formal and rely on the use of axial designs that celebrate the perspective view.

FIGURE 8.10. Curb Radius

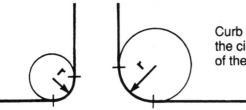

Curb radius is the radius of the circle formed by the curve of the curb at the corner.

Source: ASCE, NAHB, and ULI, *Residential Streets, 2d ed.,* p. 72.

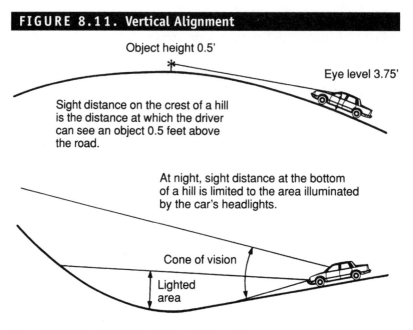

FIGURE 8.11. Vertical Alignment

Object height 0.5'

Eye level 3.75'

Sight distance on the crest of a hill
is the distance at which the driver
can see an object 0.5 feet above
the road.

At night, sight distance at the bottom
of a hill is limited to the area illuminated
by the car's headlights.

Cone of vision

Lighted
area

Source: ASCE, NAHB, and ULI, *Residential Streets, 2d ed.,* p. 46.

Besides relying on the use of axial designs, a modified grid pattern can also form the basis for a traditional small-town layout. In this model, the grid becomes less formal through use of smaller scales for streets and buildings and the strategic placement of intersections to ensure safety and social interaction. Landscaping can soften the edge of the street, bringing a friendlier, more informal atmosphere to the streetscape.

The curvilinear streets of the conventional cul-de-sac model are intended to promote a more natural or organic atmosphere compared to the grid. These can be advantageously used to create an ever-changing vista for the driver. Separating the collector road from the cul-de-sacs acknowledges the street system's two primary functions: The collector road funnels automobiles in and out of the development, while the cul-de-sac eliminates through traffic on streets where houses are located. This pattern creates small pockets of social opportunities on the cul-de-sacs, although the street pattern in this model does not encourage pedestrian activity.

What pattern of streets and public spaces will best provide a desirable environment for your target market? Using the idea of minimizing the length of all street, stormwater, and utility infrastructure as an underlying goal, evaluate the fit of the various street patterns with the physical characteristics of the site and the desired neighborhood identity. Keep in mind your most important consideration: how the pattern of streets enhances your new development's identity.

Density and Scale

Several factors influence the type of street pattern you select (grid or neo-traditional neighborhood, conventional cul-de-sac

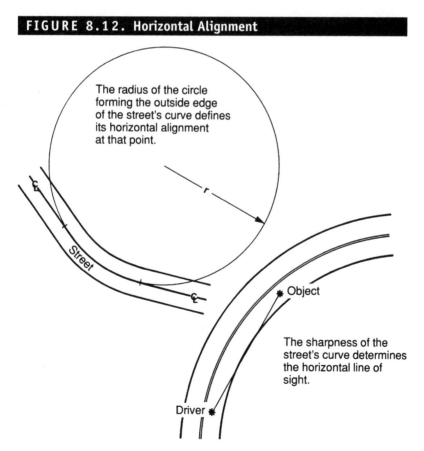

FIGURE 8.12. Horizontal Alignment

The radius of the circle forming the outside edge of the street's curve defines its horizontal alignment at that point.

r

Street

₵

Object

The sharpness of the street's curve determines the horizontal line of sight.

Driver

Source: ASCE, NAHB, and ULI, *Residential Streets*, 2d ed., p. 47.

with collector or a hybrid of the two). One is the desired density necessary for project profitability. For developments with higher densities, the grid pattern works effectively if you handle scale sensitively, satisfy the target market's demands, and include opportunities for social interaction among the neighborhood's residents. Handling scale sensitively includes using downsized streets and buildings that are compatible in size.

Neo-Traditional Grid. The neo-traditional grid has a street pattern that accommodates a higher density of housing units and can be modified for other uses as well. If you scale the buildings proportionally with this approach, you can place a variety of housing types and uses together. The network of streets can then provide access to all destinations for both pedestrians and automobiles. Figure 8.13 Modified Grid Pattern shows a development based on a grid whose geometry has been modified to accommodate a series of smaller open spaces and natural features.

Cul-de-Sac Pattern. You can sometimes achieve higher densities as well as open space by densely grouping units in areas created by cul-de-sacs. The cul-de-sacs then become the location of the housing units formed into clusters or pods, while the collector road conveys traffic to each pod. This approach works well with multifamily projects. If you include recreational, retail, or service facilities in this type of development, find a way to connect the pods with both pedestrian and automobile routes. Figure 8.14 Cul-de-Sac Pattern illustrates this concept.

Conversely, cul-de-sacs and collector roads can be used for low-density, large-lot development. With this approach, you can locate houses on the cul-de-sacs only or on both the cul-de-sacs and collector roads. The winding collector road with houses on short cul-de-sacs then provides an atmosphere of seclusion for the neighborhood. With this approach, large lots can also have more irregular shapes and use leftover pieces of land.

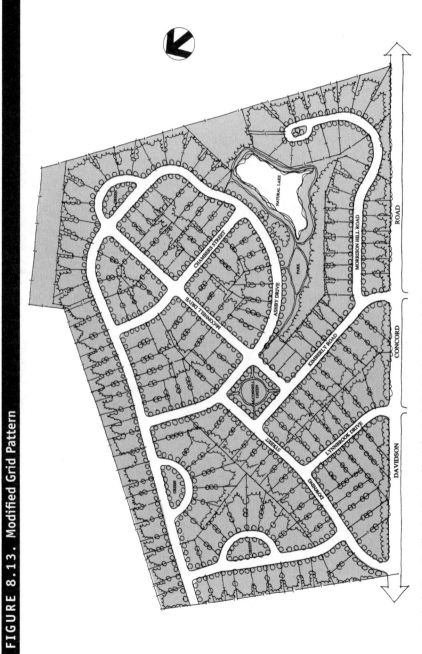

FIGURE 8.13. Modified Grid Pattern

Source: Drawing by James Wentling/Architects and land planning by Land Design. Reprinted with permission.

FIGURE 8.14. Cul-de-Sac Pattern

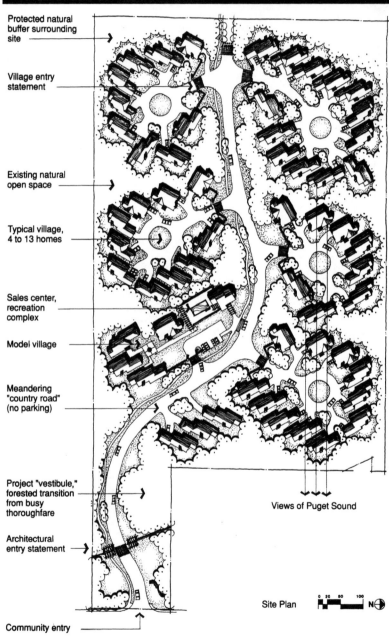

Protected natural buffer surrounding site

Village entry statement

Existing natural open space

Typical village, 4 to 13 homes

Sales center, recreation complex

Model village

Meandering "country road" (no parking)

Project "vestibule," forested transition from busy thoroughfare

Architectural entry statement

Community entry

Views of Puget Sound

Site Plan

Source: Reprinted with permission from Mithun Partners, Inc., Architecture/Planning, and Nu-Dawn Homes, Developer.

Choosing a Pattern

When choosing a model for the street pattern in your neighborhood, consider its location, project density, the target market's preferences, and the type of development concept you choose. A high-density development of smaller lots may work better with straight streets while larger estate homes may warrant a more curving pattern. Physical site constraints may prevent use of the standard grid. For example, it's more difficult and costly to use a grid on a site with significant changes in slope than on a flatter site. Certain site features such as specimen trees and water amenities may cause streets to curve.

Review the topography of your site to understand the cost and practicality of choosing the grid or a system of curving streets. Or, consider a combination of the two. The context of the site may also be a factor to consider. In building a small addition to an older town, for example, you may want to create a street pattern similar to that of the existing town.

Landscaping. Consider using landscaping along the streets to help you define your new development. You can visually punctuate the route through the development with carefully planned glimpses of scenic views, large trees, parks or open spaces, and strategic landscaping. Planting trees along the street gives it a human scale by providing a sense of enclosure. Concentrating colorful imported landscaping at corners and entrances helps to announce destinations. For optimal integration, try to have your project team create the landscape plan and the engineered street design together. Your landscaping will be more effective when you consider it in the early planning stages rather than treat it as after-the-fact decoration.

Security and Safety. The design and layout of the streets in your development directly affect safety and security issues. Street design dictates how fast a car can travel. Intersection designs affect car speeds by placing mandatory stopping points, thereby reducing speed on a long collector or sub-collector. Entrance design and location affects neighborhood security issues.

Reducing Speeds. If you plan to use sidewalks for pedestrian traffic with the grid or curvilinear streets, you can easily use street geometry to reduce automobile speed. Simply limiting the widths of streets and providing intersections at shorter intervals prevents automobiles from reaching excessive speeds on particular streets. Using traffic circles at low-volume intersections also can effectively slow traffic. Other options to decrease speeds: change center alignment and widths at strategic points or change pavement materials at intersections. For example, in the latter approach, placing brick pavers at intersections can signal automobiles to slow down. It also helps define the corner as a focal point of the neighborhood.

Figure 8.15 Greymarsh Crossing shows a development based on the concept of the Carolinas' low-country villages. The master plan uses narrow streets to reduce traffic speed and promote a village atmosphere through reduced scale. Street trees further add to this reduced sense of scale. Mask density by using access lanes between houses to cut down on the number of driveways connecting to the street.

The Safety of Entrances and Intersections

Local codes specify the distance that intersections should be placed along streets and away from the entrance to your development. In the same manner, the entrances to your development must be placed according to the local code's requirements for traffic safety along the public steet leading to your project. The local building code will specify the distance required from the nearest stop on the public street to your entrance. Intersections should provide clear sight lines for both cars and pedestrians; pedestrian walking areas should be clearly delineated.

Focal Points and Pedestrian Routes

Whether you use a grid, a curvilinear conventional plan, or a hybrid of the two, street corners both control traffic and offer increased visual interest for your development. Street corners are great opportunities to install attractive landscaping, benches, and small pedestrian shelters. These in turn can become places where neighbors meet each other for walks and conversation.

FIGURE 8.15. Greymarsh Crossing

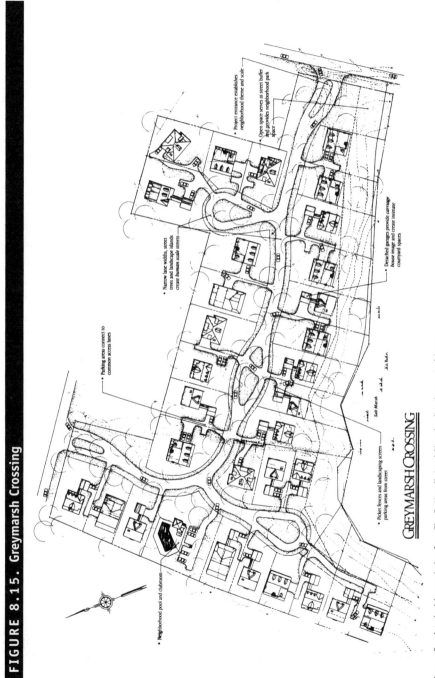

• Parking areas connect to common access lanes

• Neighborhood pool and clubroom

• Narrow lane widths, street trees and landscape islands create *human scale* streets

• Project entrance establishes neighborhood theme and scale

• Open space serves as street buffer and provides neighborhood park space

• Detached garages provide *carriage house* image and create intimate courtyard spaces

• Picket fences and landscaping screen parking areas from street

Salt Marsh

GREYMARSH CROSSING

Source: Reprinted with permission from Tim R. Newell, Land Planning/Landscape Architecture.

Also use pedestrian routes to link street corners. Clearly designate these routes as paths or sidewalks and provide buffers between pedestrians and moving automobiles. Buffers can include simple setbacks, landscaping, a line of trees defining the edge of the street, a row of parked cars, or a combination of several of these. These measures decrease the overwhelming effect of cars traveling past, increase safety, and make the entire streetscape more pleasing to the eye.

The Alley

In recent times the idea of the alley, a neighborhood design element of the past, has made somewhat of a comeback. Originally alleys provided secluded access for services, garbage collecting, and garages. Now they've become part of the menu for neo-traditional design. While serving these same functions, the alley has also become a place to take walks, work on cars or other messy household projects, and provide a more private space for play. To accomplish this, alleys must be both functional and attractive. Alleys that are sterile where backyards are designed to be completely blocked by fencing tend to be unattractive and unsafe.

If you choose to use the alley as part of your neighborhood concept, design it with low or see-through fences (such as a picket fence), and make sure the access and the alley street can accommodate service vehicles. Allow landscaping to enhance the overall appearance. Downsize front yards to make room for a reasonably sized backyard and an alley right of way.

Alleys can be charming additions to neighborhoods if designed with beauty, function, and safety in mind. Local flavor can play a big role and hilly or mountainous terrain can make this design difficult. Alleys should be short and straight to minimize infrastructure costs. Local regional preferences and the target market's tolerances should also be considered.

Basic Design Considerations

Regardless of the street pattern you choose, following a few general rules of thumb can produce safer, more attractive, and more cost-effective streets. Figure 8.16 Basic Concepts of Street Design outlines several principles of street design to consider.

Street engineering seeks to limit the lengths and widths of streets to provide the least amount of pavement necessary to service the community efficiently. This approach also cuts down on the cost of utility installation, stormwater infrastructure, and road building, since utility and stormwater systems frequently follow the street pattern. The diminished scale of the street has another benefit: It creates a more pleasant streetscape and decreases the amount of heat generated by pavement.

As with all design decisions, consider the cost-benefit ratio. While limiting the length of streets in a residential development is almost always desirable, the way in which streets are finished and utilities installed depends in part on the target market's tolerance. Streets with curbs and gutters, buried pipes for stormwater runoff, and sidewalks are more expensive than streets without them. You must make your design decisions based on what the market will bear. Weigh the costs of all design decisions in terms of their financial feasibility and the target market's tolerances and preferences.

FIGURE 8.16. Basic Concepts of Street Design

- Limit street lengths.
- Limit excessive street widths and turning radii.
- Use minimum turning radii on cul-de-sacs and corners.
- Avoid shortcut streets that may add traffic volume to other streets in the development.
- Design streets for minimum generation of stormwater runoff.
- Avoid curb and gutter design where possible to minimize the use of closed stormwater systems.
- Use intersections to reduce automobile speed and define places that create focal points for pedestrians.
- Use safety-oriented design standards for intersections, including limiting the length of pedestrian crossings, clearly marking those crossings, and maintaining a clear line of sight for cars and pedestrians.

Cross Sections and Stormwater Runoff Systems

The way streets are designed in cross section determines the direction stormwater runoff flows and the type of system used to carry it away. Streets may have center crowns where the high point falls along the center line or inverted crowns where the low point falls along that same line. You may also design streets to slope to one side.

Runoff Systems for Center Crowns. When streets have center crowns, stormwater runs off to each side and requires a closed or open system on either side. A closed system accompanied by curbs and gutters is the most costly type of stormwater runoff system to build because it requires more expensive labor and materials. However, this type of system more effectively protects pavement edges from wear. It also keeps automobiles from running onto setbacks where pedestrians may walk. In neighborhoods that use on-street parking, curbs are especially useful for keeping automobiles on the street.

With a closed system, stormwater usually enters a buried storm main through inlets in the gutter connected to catch basins. You may choose this type of system depending on the amount of stormwater your development generates and the target market's preferences. In areas that experience heavy snowfalls, curbs also aid snowplows in snow removal.

Locating open swales on each side of a center-crowned street offers the least expensive means of handling stormwater. If you use this type of open system, street edges must have no curb and gutter. You also need to properly grade the setback toward the open system for positive drainage. Once again, consider the amount of stormwater generated and the target market's tolerance for this type of system. The amount of on-street parking may influence the use of open systems as well.

Runoff Systems for Inverted Crowns. Streets with inverted crowns use a closed system running along the center line of the street. The most prevalent use of centerline drainage is in alleys. Unlike closed systems placed along both sides of streets with center crowns, you need to construct only one line of closed infrastructure for streets with inverted crowns. Stormwater enters this system through inlets placed in the center of the street. These inlets are connected to catch basins, which are in turn connected to the storm main. Having one line of closed infrastructure cuts down significantly on initial construction costs. However, when maintenance or repair is required, this type of system can become costly to fix because you must tear up and rebuild the street.

Street Design Process

Whether you select the modified grid, neo-traditional grid, conventional cul-de-sac, or hybrid models, several decisions affecting street layout apply to all three. Early in the design process, you need to acknowledge the topography and physical features of the site. Streets should generally follow contours on sites with significant slopes instead of traveling perpendicular to those contours; that increases the cost of installing roads as well as the amount of stormwater runoff. It also makes proper grading at intersections difficult where the grade should be as flat as possible.

Once you have located the buildable and unbuildable areas of your site, you need to choose a basic street pattern that fits the identity of the new development and understand how that pattern fits with site topography. Once you have done that, begin to test several patterns of street layout. Start at points of entry and create the shortest loop that passes by the designated buildable areas. You can curve the loop, place it on a grid, or even combine the two approaches. Test each concept for efficiency of service, cost, and density of units achieved. Make maximum use of the site's buildable areas and avoid leftover, irregular areas that serve no purpose in the development. Also make the streets comply with all codes and standards.

Entrances

Regardless what pattern you choose for street layout, be especially mindful of the access to your development. The location of the entrance and its treatment heavily influence the way people perceive the development. If your intention is to make a grand statement, choose good materials such as brick, stone, and metal with the appearance of permanence. Spend extra money on good landscaping. Make sure your entrance conveys a sense of arriving at a special place. In some cases, such as large estate homes in the country, your target market may not want to announce the project, opting for seclusion instead.

Multiple Entrances. Depending on its size, a development can have one, two, or multiple entrances. Multiple entrances help with traffic volume and help eliminate dead-end streets by creating loop systems for service and emergency vehicles. For larger developments, multiple entrances reduce the distance from the entrance to the home, making access time shorter for service and emergency vehicles.

Single Entrance. Although multiple entrances have several advantages, many developers prefer single entrances, especially for smaller developments, because they are perceived to promote security. With gated communities, the development frequently has only one point of access. If you choose a single entrance, however, take care that the development has no dead-end streets over a certain length. They would impede the turnaround capabilities of service and emergency vehicles. Again, local codes govern these lengths. Figures 8.17 Single-Entrance Development and 8.18 Multiple-Entrance Development depict conventional cul-de-sac patterns for each of these choices.

Developers sometimes choose single entrances to prevent individuals from cutting through a development on their way to another destination. A single entrance can also project an image of exclusivity and privacy, especially if gated, and can make it easier to market a new development to visitors. Base your decision about single versus multiple entrances on the size of the development, the nature of the contiguous development, and the preferences of the target market.

FIGURE 8.17. Single-Entrance Development

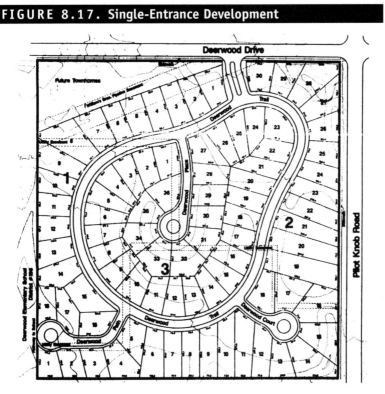

Source: ASCE, NAHB, and ULI, *Residential Streets, 2d ed.*, p. 31. Deerwood, Eagan, Minnesota. Developer: Robert Engstrom Companies. Planner: Architectural Forum, Inc. Reprinted with permission.

Enhancing Your Project's Identity

The street pattern you choose for your development helps give the project its special identify. Have the design professionals on your project team plan the street pattern to create this identity in the most cost-effective and efficient manner. This means they should have a clear understanding of the development you want to provide for your target group. They should also know all mandatory code requirements because this critical stage of your project influences many subsequent decisions. Professional ability, effective communication among team members, and proficient team management provided by your leadership can make street design the cornerstone of a successful project.

FIGURE 8.18. Multiple-Entrance Development

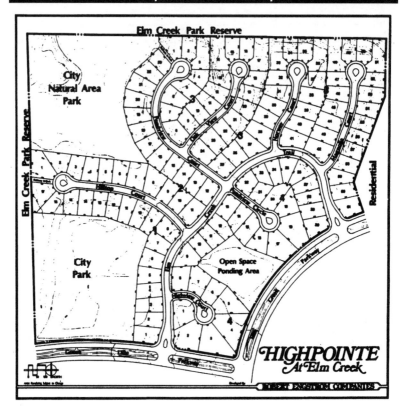

Source: ASCE, NAHB, and ULI, *Residential Streets, 2d ed.,* p. 31. HIGHPOINTE at Elm Creek, Champlin, Minnesota. Developer: Robert Engstrom Companies. Planner: Architectural Forum, Inc. Reprinted with permission.

9

Selecting Housing Types

The type of housing you choose for your new development should serve the needs of your target market, fit the site's characteristics, and strengthen the overall image you have chosen. Besides these primary considerations, a knowledge of regional styles, materials, and building methods can be useful in producing designs compatible with local traditions. Finally, you need to acknowledge the effect climate will have on your chosen housing type so you can produce an energy-efficient home with strong appeal for buyers.

What the Buyer Wants

When new ideas are incorporated into housing design, some are short-lived while others end up having long-term appeal to the market. For example, when the split plan (master bedroom separated from other bedrooms by the main living area) was first introduced in the late 1950s and early 1960s, it was a radical departure from the convention of locating all the bedrooms on one side of the house. But soon the target market of married couples with children began to demand this item. In this way, desirable new ideas in housing quickly become assimilated into the market as developers and builders copy and then improve on previous successes.

However, merely copying previously successful ideas is not by itself an effective marketing strategy. This worked better in the past when change came more slowly than it does today. Now marketable ideas have a shorter life span than ever. Society changes rapidly in response to shifts in the economy, growing needs for safety and security, and increased job pressures and other demands on people's time. When buying a home today, people make conscious and unconscious choices about their lifestyles, self-images, financial security, and leisure time. Changes in society's attitudes toward work, the family, and the environment tend to redefine what a home is all about for every segment of the population.

Recent advances in technology add a challenge to the task of selecting the most appealing styles and features for homes in your development. However, maintaining your market appeal means keeping up with your target market's changing demands for styles, types of interior spaces, and features. As you evaluate how far to go with new technologies and materials for your target market, your selection of housing types should be driven by affordability, climate-driven features that save energy, efficient land use, and current market acceptance.

General Design Issues

The target group profile generated by your market analysis outlines demands and desires you must consider when selecting housing for your development. A thorough understanding of the group's characteristics can help you make sound judgments about their preferences for certain housing types and details. Figure 9.1 Characteristics of Housing Types lists some of the design issues you should consider when choosing housing types. Review this list and match the characteristics up with your target market's demands. Ideally you should select and conceptualize the housing types for your project while you are doing site planning; for a project to succeed, the home and site designs need to work well together.

FIGURE 9.1. Characteristics of Housing Types

When selecting housing types, you need to make design decisions about the following issues:

- Density of units
- Attached or detached
- Form of ownership
- Square footage
- Single or multiple stories
- Architectural style
- Number and type of interior spaces
- Amount of outdoor private space
- Maintenance requirements for outdoor space

Density and Pattern

The first choice you must make about residential units concerns density and the way you position the unit on the lot. Housing types fall into the following broad categories:

- single-family detached, large or small lot
- single-family attached: duplex, triplex, or fourplex
- multifamily attached: townhouse, midrise, or highrise

In different parts of the country, housing types have different names. In some areas, multifamily refers to apartments. In other areas duplexes, triplexes, fourplexes, and townhouses are all considered multifamily. Regardless what people call a particular housing type, a key distinction is whether the units are detached or attached.

Single-Family Detached, Large Lot

In the United States, owning a small piece of land and a single-family detached house still remains the goal for most target market groups. However, the features in a single-family detached house and the amount of land these groups want have changed. In the past developers positioned this type of house in the middle of the lot, surrounded by front, side, and rear yards.

Front setbacks were typically a generous 25 to 40 feet from the street and side setbacks at least 10 to 20 feet. The intent was to provide as much space as possible between each home.

This additional space increased the amount of personal territory and allowed room for creating vegetative areas that acted as visual barriers and provided privacy. In fact, the most desirable feature of large-lot ownership has always been the privacy it offers. Today, this generous amount of land is referred to as an estate lot, thereby marking its rarity among the lot sizes for single-family homes. While some target groups both desire and can afford this additional space, others are less attracted to the demands of large-lot ownership or find the initial purchase price and subsequent cost of upkeep combine to price large lots out of their budget.

In addition, lawn maintenance proves time-consuming— and many target groups would rather spend their spare time doing other things. Unless a person considers yard work a hobby, taking care of a large lot means either a significant time commitment or the increased expense of a lawn-care service.

In addition, although large lots can offer more privacy, certain target groups prefer the feeling of security that comes with smaller lot sizes. They want less distance between neighbors and home entrances that are more visible and well lit rather than secluded. At the same time, most people still want the sense of private territory that the single-family detached house affords. This desire has led to a variety of housing placements and designs on downsized lots.

Single-Family Detached, Small Lot

The detached single-family house on a small lot should be designed to give the individual a sense of private territory. The trick is to design the layout of the lots and the siting of the houses to provide both private outdoor space and protected views from the interior of each house. You should strive to create the best of both worlds by offering the buyer a sense of private territory with the advantage of decreased purchase price and maintenance.

Modified Grid Pattern. Smaller lots generally result in higher densities, which can be achieved in several ways. The modified grid pattern of the traditional small town accommodates smaller lots without compromising privacy by pulling the house toward the street and decreasing the size of the front yard. With this approach, houses are usually still sited at the center point of the lot's width. Decreasing the size of the front yard increases the total number of lots within the development. If side and rear setbacks are handled properly, they can furnish the required privacy.

Garden or Patio Homes. Decreasing the size of the lot by decreasing all setbacks offers another method for achieving higher density with detached single-family homes. These are sometimes marketed as garden or patio homes because the yards are very small. Generally, it's easier to accommodate higher density detached housing of any kind on more regularly shaped lots. A variety of street patterns can be used, but the modified grid especially suits this type of housing. Care must be taken, though, to provide privacy when houses are placed close together. You'll find that many buyers prefer this to attached housing because of the stronger sense of private territory and the elimination of some of the pitfalls of attached housing such as walls with no windows, sound transmission between units, and little individuality. Value becomes apparent when houses are sited with backs facing open spaces, golf courses, greenbelts, or water views.

Zero Lot Line Plan. The zero lot line plan provides another method of siting detached single-family housing. A zero lot line plan consists of a series of narrow-width lots with houses placed to one side or as close to the adjacent property line as possible. This creates a usable yard on one side of each house. You can then distribute the primary rooms, such as living and dining rooms, kitchen, and master bedroom, along the side of the house facing the side yard. The other side of the house contains the dead spaces, such as closets, garages, and bathrooms that require no windows or can function with clerestory windows.

Figure 9.2 Zero Lot Line Plan shows a typical treatment for this type of layout.

A zero lot line plan also calls for a small backyard that, when combined with the side yard, forms an L-shaped outdoor space for each house. One approach to a zero lot line plan gives all houses the same front setback dimension. Since this approach results in a linear plan, you need to locate the garages in the front of the house. Once you do, this layout provides a dead wall for an additional side yard. In the plan shown in Figure 9.2 all living areas have a view to the outside. Furthermore, the line of sight from each interior space prevents a view into another house's private outdoor or interior spaces.

As another approach to the zero lot line plan, you can also place the houses at different distances from the street. This approach produces a staggered effect. The houses can also be angled on the lots and the lots themselves angled to the street. Angling lots in this manner produces the so-called angled zero lot line plan shown in Figure 9.3.

By placing the lots diagonally instead of perpendicular to the street, you create a plan in which the garages no longer

FIGURE 9.2. Zero Lot Line Plan

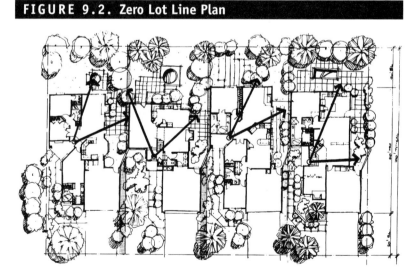

Source: Reprinted with permission from EDI Architecture.

FIGURE 9.3. Angled Zero Lot Line Plan

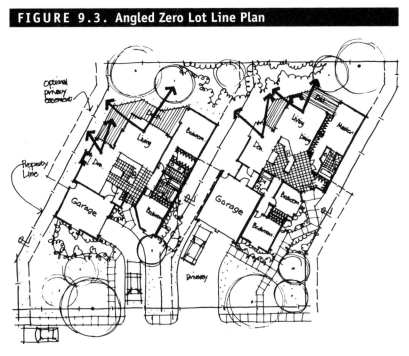

Source: Reprinted with permission from the Martin Architectural Group.

face the street. This approach helps diminish the appearance of a high-density, multifamily development caused by having the garages placed close together in front of the house. In addition, the angle of the lines of sight from the primary living spaces includes more adjacent, private outdoor space. At the same time, this approach has the advantage of decreasing views onto the dead walls (windowless walls) of other houses. You can provide some privacy for adjacent outdoor spaces in this type of plan by planting vegetative buffers at strategic points along the lot lines.

Also, rather than placing the house squarely on the property line, an angled zero lot line plan leaves a small easement at the side of each house even though each side is a dead wall. (See Figure 9.3.) This can facilitate drainage design for all houses and ensure that eaves and overhangs do not encroach into another property's space. Before deciding on a zero lot line plan, consider how you'll manage stormwater runoff; these plans eliminate or reduce side-yard setbacks and easements needed to provide swales and underground pipes for stormwater drainage.

Zero lot line plans offer a viable solution to providing single-family houses in higher-density neighborhoods. However, as with all solutions, you must consider the advantages and disadvantages. This approach provides garages, storage, and the privacy of a single-family house without extensive maintenance. In addition, land development costs are generally lower due to the higher density, and you can pass these savings on to the home buyer.

In evaluating zero lot line plans, you need to review several aspects of the site's physical characteristics, local zoning regulations, and basic design parameters. Figure 9.4 Design Considerations for Zero Lot Line Housing lists issues you must address in making this a favorable choice for project profitability.

FIGURE 9.4. Design Considerations for Zero Lot Line Housing

- Because lots are smaller and houses are located on the lot line, stormwater runoff design is difficult to achieve with open systems such as swales, thereby increasing the potential for higher engineering costs.
- The local zoning code must support the intended use of easements and rights-of-way for building and utility placement. Otherwise a variance is needed.
- Fire-rated walls involving special construction are often required by local fire codes when you place dead walls too close together.
- To avoid monotony, carefully plan streetscapes to include sidewalks, landscaping, and varied driveway placement.
- Stagger the position of 2-story houses to avoid blocking sunlight and eliminating privacy for adjacent outdoor spaces.
- The long, narrow form of this housing unit can create awkward outdoor spaces unless units are staggered and varied.
- To avoid creating dark interior spaces, place features requiring less natural light like closets, bathrooms, and garages adjacent to the dead wall.

Clustering. Consider using a cluster pattern for the units when you're attempting to reposition density or achieve higher density for single-family housing. Clustering houses around a courtyard in circular or U-shaped patterns can concentrate single-family houses on a smaller area of land, leaving other areas in the development in their natural state. With these patterns, houses frequently share a single driveway that leads to an automobile court. When two to four houses share one driveway, this reduces the number of driveways connected to the street. With appropriate landscaping, a cluster plan can produce a neighborhood that appears composed of lower-density, single-family houses. Figure 9.5 Courtyard Cluster Plan demonstrates this concept.

In any method of siting single-family detached houses on small lots, you can concentrate public exposure at the entrances and parking areas. Then, as you leave the public areas for the primary living areas, the privacy of each unit increases through the use of protected views and private outdoor spaces.

Attached Housing

Attached housing offers another solution for affordable, higher-density neighborhoods. However, attached housing proves more acceptable in some parts of the country than in others. Home buyers in cities that have experienced most of their growth since World War II generally have favored single-family detached houses. These cities have few established traditions for attached housing like the townhomes or row housing of the Northeast. Now, urban revitalization plans have made parts of the older commercial areas of a city desirable for renovation into multifamily housing. As downtown areas are redesigned for shopping, entertainment, and restaurants, nearby older office buildings take on new life as desirable locations to renovate as housing.

The advantages of attached housing are its affordability, lower maintenance, and location. Infill development near urban work centers or recreational areas frequently takes the form of attached, higher-density housing since land prices there make the cost of detached single-family homes prohibitive. The

FIGURE 9.5. Courtyard Cluster Plan

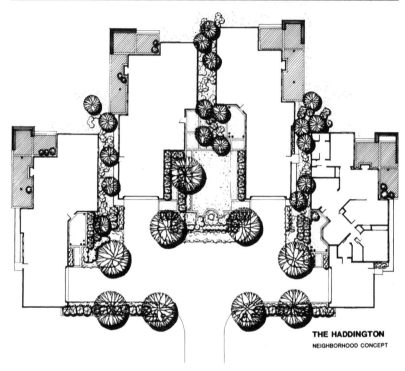

THE HADDINGTON
NEIGHBORHOOD CONCEPT

Source: Reprinted with permission from Mithun Partners, Inc., Architecture/Planning, and Pope Resources, Developer.

advantages of attached housing also hold true in older cities with established urban areas. But in these cities, attached housing has the additional advantage of being traditional and highly accepted.

Duplex, Triplex, and Fourplex. Attached housing conventionally takes the form of a duplex, triplex, or fourplex. The duplex consists of two units sharing a common wall in one building. You generally place these units side by side, but you can also place them back to back or on two separate floors. The triplex and fourplex contain three and four units respectively. Traditionally developers placed the doors for this type of housing side by side, making it apparent that the building contained more than one unit. Today new designs use scattered entrances and architectural details such as porches, courtyards, and patios to make the buildings appear as large single-family homes. Figure 9.6 Facade of Triplex Unit shows a building that appears to be a large single-family residence with a generous porch. As Figure 9.6 shows, carefully placing the entrances has successfully camouflaged the three units of this triplex.

Historically, developers also placed these types of units in neighborhoods with single-family houses. Although their function as multifamily units was clear, developers generally made the size and scale of these buildings compatible with those of the surrounding houses. This technique produced a mixture of housing types in one location without it being noticeable. In designing neo-traditional neighborhoods, developers are once again revisiting this concept because it provides an

FIGURE 9.6. Facade of Triplex Unit

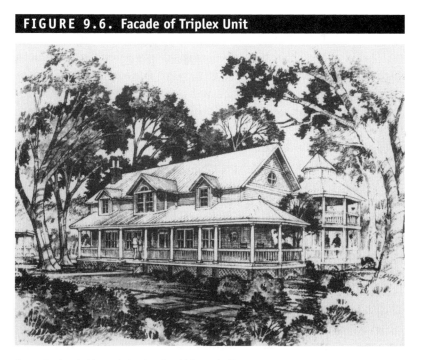

Source: Reprinted with permission from Ronald Haase, Architect.

aesthetically pleasing way to intersperse different densities in one place.

In fact, with careful handling of design details that disguise the duplex, triplex, and fourplex as single-family houses, you can achieve a compatible mix of housing densities in one location. Figure 9.7 Triplex Floorplan shows the floorplan for the triplex depicted in Figure 9.6. As you can see, this floorplan incorporates several design details to minimize some of the features associated with higher density housing, including separate entrances and porches to provide an additional feeling of privacy and open living rooms and dining areas to provide a sense of space.

The basic unit, a duplex, is marketed to empty nesters and young professional couples. These two target markets have shown a preference for attached and zero lot line houses due to their affordability and low-maintenance requirements. One of the challenges with this design—how to handle automobiles—requires some careful thought.

Distributing the units around an automobile courtyard offers one solution. With this approach—as you can see in Figure 9.8 Courtyard Fourplex—garage doors open onto a courtyard and not the street. The courtyard option has two major advantages: It provides an added measure of safety for automobiles and people, and it eliminates the impact of the automobile on the street. By placing the garages behind the courtyard walls, you also eliminate the monotony of closely spaced garages and driveways.

Using the duplex, triplex, or fourplex as your choice of housing gives you the advantage of higher density with smaller buildings. Unlike with other types of large-scaled, multifamily housing, you can successfully integrate these units on streets that also contain single-family houses. Architecturally, you should try to design the facades and massing of these units to resemble a single-family residence as shown in Figures 9.6 and 9.7.

Additionally, on sites where the topography has significant slopes, you can more successfully position these types of smaller buildings than larger multifamily buildings. Figure 9.9 Evalu-

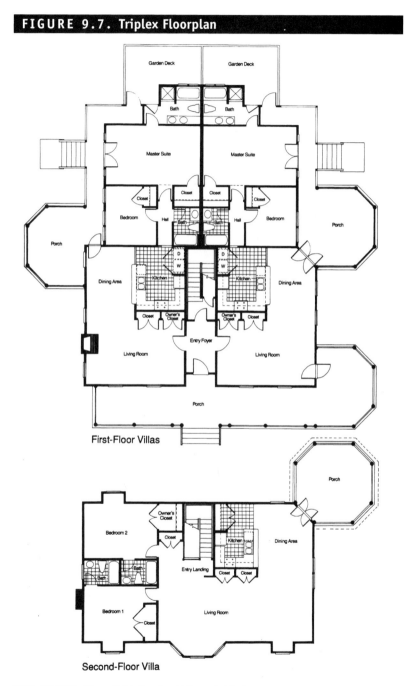

FIGURE 9.7. Triplex Floorplan

First-Floor Villas

Second-Floor Villa

Source: Reprinted with permission from Ronald Haase, Architect.

FIGURE 9.8. Courtyard Fourplex

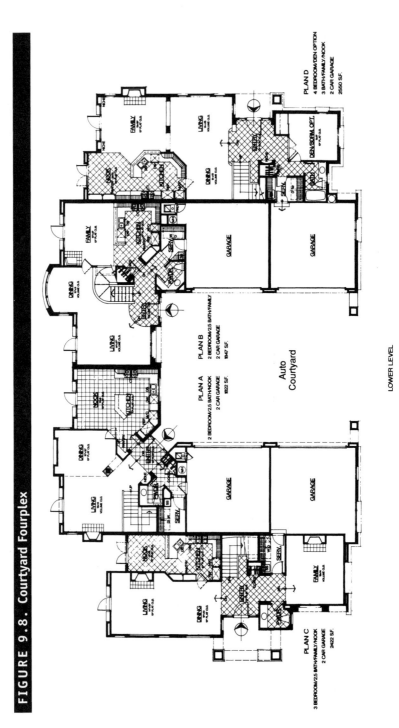

Source: Reprinted with permission from William Hezmalhalch Architects, Inc. (architecture and planning) and California Pacific Homes (builder).

ating a Duplex, Triplex, or Fourplex Design lists concepts to evaluate when choosing these options for your project.

Townhouses. As attached, single-family units sharing at least one common wall, townhouses are modeled after the English rowhouse. As such, they can be owned individually or as condominiums. Developers usually choose to have townhouses designed in a linear fashion, but they can also come staggered or clustered. With this type of housing, building heights rarely exceed 3 stories. Figure 9.10 Townhouse Plan shows a project combining the rowhouse model with the cluster. This plan distributes the buildings around a central courtyard, which creates a village atmosphere. Owners can access townhouse garages directly from the street.

Townhouses have the same appeal to buyers as other types of attached housing. Affordability and low maintenance are the chief attraction for target groups whose busy lifestyles allow little time for home maintenance. In choosing this housing type for your target market, evaluate the considerations shown in Figure 9.11 Evaluating Townhouse Designs.

Midrises and Highrises. Midrise and highrise residential buildings are common in larger cities where land is scarce within the urban core. Although the definition for each depends on

---

FIGURE 9.9. Evaluating a Duplex, Triplex, or Fourplex Design

When evaluating a duplex, triplex, or fourplex design, consider the following:

- **Zoning Code Requirements:** Local codes may prohibit attached housing in single-family residential areas.
- **Size of Project:** Townhouse designs are less costly for the same number of units and thus are especially appropriate for larger projects.
- **Form of Ownership:** The target market may prefer individual ownership over condominium or collective ownership.
- **Building Orientation:** Where building orientation is critical for views or energy conservation, you can more easily manipulate these forms than townhouses.

FIGURE 9.10. Townhouse Plan

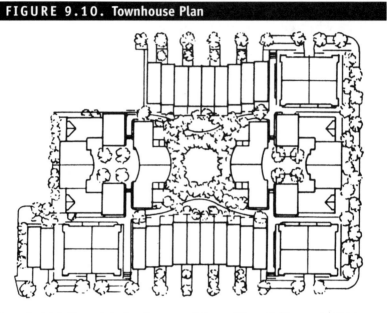

Source: Reprinted with permission from Pappageorge & Haymes, Ltd., and *Builder* magazine (October 1990), p. 176.

the local area, midrise buildings usually have a minimum of 3 to 8 stories, while highrise buildings have more than 8. Units in these buildings can be either purchased or rented. When buyers purchase units, they own them as condominiums. With this form of ownership, the buyer owns the unit individually

FIGURE 9.11. Evaluating Townhouse Designs

When evaluating townhouse designs, consider the following:

- Target market's acceptance of attached housing and collective ownership of land
- Regional tolerances for attached housing
- Zoning code regulations, which may prevent high-density land use unless a variance is obtained
- Slope of site, which if significant is not well suited to long, linear buildings
- Cost-effective site engineering for drainage, since this housing type covers more site area and thus causes more stormwater runoff

and the land the building sits on collectively with other condominium owners.

Choosing between midrise and highrise buildings depends on the building heights and density of units permitted in the zoning for your site. Other considerations include the target market's acceptance of this type of housing, the location, regional preferences, and cost. More costly to construct than single-story buildings, they require higher rents and sales prices for project profitability.

Matching the Target Market's Demands To Housing Types

After you have determined a viable target group, match its lifestyle characteristics to the design features in the homes you will offer. Suppose, for example, you are marketing to empty nesters as a target group. Members of this group are frequently in a move-down category due to lifestyle changes. Their most significant lifestyle change involves the sudden absence of children who are old enough to leave home for college or work. Empty nesters are generally young enough that retirement is still years away. As a result, they have busy lifestyles involving work and leisure time. They often want to move from a home oriented toward the needs of a larger family with children to one designed primarily for a couple.

Using the categories found in Figure 9.1, you can make choices about housing types based on this group's lifestyle characteristics. For example, for the first time this group may consider attached housing as a viable option. They no longer need big backyards for children, and unless they garden as a hobby, they want lower household maintenance demands on their leisure time.

Having owned their single-family home for many years, members of this group may not prefer an apartment or condominium. The type of ownership may be more critical to this group than to younger buyers who foresee making perhaps several more home purchases in the future as they move up.

You should test this consideration through surveys or reviewing comparable projects in the area. Depending on what is acceptable in the area, empty nesters may also show more tolerance for an increased density of residential units but at the same time require a lot of privacy.

Generally, as members of this group approach retirement, they prefer one-story homes to two stories. They have less need now to separate the functions of interior spaces such as distancing children's bedrooms from adults'. Because they can live in smaller spaces and are concerned with ease of maintenance, one-story homes fit their needs well. In addition, if they decide to stay in place once they retire, one-story homes without staircases may become more convenient.

The kinds of interior spaces empty nesters desire have changed as well. They are often willing to trade square footage for a higher quality of materials, features, and interior finishes. Although they need less space because of the smaller family size, they still want the best they can afford in a home. They also frequently require fewer bedrooms. The auxiliary bedrooms should serve several functions, including guestroom, study, or home office. Entertaining at home usually remains important to this group. If they gear entertainment primarily toward friends and family, you need to emphasize the space and quality of the informal dining areas through better finishes, expanded views, and downsized formal dining rooms.

Many design questions can be answered by a clear understanding of lifestyle characteristics. In the sample target market just discussed, even basic lifestyle characteristics such as marital status revealed fairly specific design features. The more focused the characteristics become, the more specific the design features will be.

Style Preferences

Once you have decided upon the basic features of the homes in your development, evaluate additional factors that contribute to the overall style of the homes. Regional attitudes and demographic characteristics such as age and educational level influence preferences in housing styles. For instance, move-up buyers tend to have more established style preferences. Often they have more furniture purchased as lifetime choices and seek a housing style that accommodates their choices. Generally, the more established home buyer may have more traditional tastes, while extreme contemporary styles may fit young, single professionals.

Regional Preferences

When selecting housing types, you should take regional style preferences into consideration. In some areas, the regional style has become symbolic of the character of the place. These styles often evolve from such practical considerations as the availability of materials and response to climate. Over time, the materials and methods once used out of necessity begin to make up a style associated with the region itself and become part of local tradition and culture.

Buyers tend to prefer styles with a strong regional identity, so recognizing them in your housing choices is not only practical but good marketing sense. Many people have strong associations with the materials and styles of certain regions. Consider the simple shape of the saltbox with steep roofs and wood siding—the hallmark of many parts of New England. Large timber-and-beam construction with stone facades and oversized hearths calls to mind the Rocky Mountain region. Inner courtyards, flat roofs, and adobe facades characterize many Southwestern styles. Figure 9.6 shows the elegant, porch-wrapped style of a traditional southeastern home.

In most cases, you will be able to incorporate regional color, material, or detail as part of your design concept without directly copying a regional housing type in its entirety. These styles and many others hold a great attraction for home buyers who wish to participate in the regional culture and traditions of the place where they live. Therefore, adapting styles and materials in your choice of housing types is preferable to ignoring them. You should also recognize that regional preferences could be a difficult force to challenge if you are introducing a new housing style.

Site Characteristics

The regulatory constraints and physical characteristics of your site also play an important role in determining housing types. The zoning for your site influences the density of units per acre, the ability to construct highrise and midrise buildings, and whether units are attached or detached. Since zoning governs setbacks and easements, it also affects building placement on the lots.

While zoning determines unit types, setbacks, and easements, topography influences the ease with which you can place certain types of units on the site. Sites with flat topography can support larger and longer buildings such as highrise, midrise, and other attached housing much more easily at a lower cost than sites with significant slopes. Sites with flat areas and significant slopes are more suited to the clustering of units in those flat areas than to the use of the traditional grid. Duplexes, triplexes, and fourplexes are also better for this type of site than long rows of attached housing.

Outstanding physical features such as lake and ocean frontage or hilltop sites influence the amount and type of window treatment for the facades, building orientation, and use of outdoor porches and decks. Where possible, try to maximize exposure to desirable views throughout the entire development. Use facades with large window areas to capture desirable views or minimal window areas to hide undesirable ones.

Figure 9.12, Single-Family House and Site, shows a 3,300-square-foot single-family house uniquely adapted to special site characteristics. Not only are materials and form related to the heavily wooded region, but the house itself

FIGURE 9.12.
Single-Family House and Site

Source: Greg G. Hall, AIA, NCARB, PhD, Architect.

is sited midway up the slope so it fits within its wooded context instead of dominating it. By placing the main level above a half-basement, the house design acknowledges the sloping site and minimizes the cut and fill needed for its placement and location. The entrance is on the second level, which contains the main living spaces. Window sizes and placement maximize views and minimize solar exposure. A large, two-story window wall faces east and provides views of the mountains and pond. Windows on the south side are protected from direct sun by generous eaves.

The pathway leading down to the pergola at the edge of the pond ties the house to its site. Because the house nestles into its environment, direct views from other properties are not disturbed. In this way, all homesites can maintain the character of the region while still commanding valuable natural views prized by homeowners.

For developments with a variety of housing choices, the physical characteristics of the site and the location of the entrances determine the most appropriate places to put single-family and multifamily units. Lots with better views or adjacent to more desirable features command higher purchase prices. Therefore, you might capitalize on this fact by placing higher-priced single-family rather than multifamily units in these locations.

Climate

The choice of housing units should acknowledge the special requirements of climate. Again, many regional styles are directly associated with certain climates. For instance, traditionally people built steep roof pitches in northern climates to handle heavy seasonal snow loads. They also built flat roofs in the Southwest because it was a more efficient and less expensive technique and because heavy rain and snow are infrequent there. The use of a steep or flat roof helps to define a regional style based on climate. Even when advances in technology make the use of certain details obsolete, the image created by the original response to climate remains desirable because it has become part of the regional style.

Buildings in your development should respond appropriately to extreme temperatures, heavy rainfall and snow, and solar orientation. The more extreme the climate conditions, the more critical are the design requirements. Even though technology can handle many of these extreme weather conditions, your building design affects the cost of the heating, ventilation, and air conditioning systems necessary to make the home livable. The most important considerations in building design as a response to climate are window treatments, architectural features such as porches and overhangs, and proper solar orientation of buildings.

Solar Orientation. Road layout determines lot and thus building orientation. If you orient the street layout primarily north and south as shown in Figure 9.13 North-South Street Orientation, the lots and the houses on them will have an east-west orientation. This means that the longest facades of the homes (the front and back) will face east and west. Since the facades of the houses in Figure 9.13 face west, the heat gain in the main interior spaces will be high, causing those rooms to be difficult to cool.

To take advantage of proper solar orientation, have the facades containing the greatest amount of window area face a southeast direction. This approach gives the building on the lot proper solar orientation. In other words, it establishes the proper relation of a building to the angle and direction of the sun in order to conserve energy. Avoid western exposures for the same facades to reduce severe heat gain within interior spaces during the summer. Avoid northern exposures for these facades to reduce the effect of sunless rooms receiving the brunt of winter winds. Using these techniques can improve energy efficiency for all the units on your site.

Try to position as many homes as possible to take advantage of proper solar orientation. If some buildings do not have optimum solar orientation, use architectural features such as porches and large overhangs. In the winter, the angle of the sun is lower than during the summer. As a result, you need to design overhangs in such a way as to allow the winter sun to

FIGURE 9.13. North-South Street Orientation

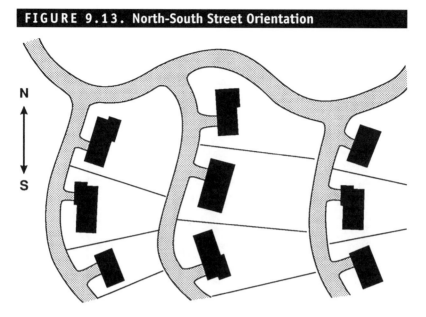

Source: Adapted from Donald H. Brandes, Jr., and J. Michael Luzier, *Developing Difficult Sites: Solutions for Developers and Builders* (Washington, DC: Home Builder Press, National Association of Home Builders, 1991), Figure 25, p. 49.

penetrate the interior spaces of the house from those lower angles. At the same time, you need to make the overhangs broad enough to block the summer sun that streams into the interior spaces from higher angles. Figure 9.14 Sun Angles shows how you can design overhangs to properly control the entry of the sun into the interior of the home.

Other Climate Factors. In hot, humid climates, try to take advantage of the prevailing winds to cool outdoor spaces such as decks and patios. This factor can also influence the layout of the streets and houses in the master plan. (For an example of this, see Figure 9.15 Site Planning for Prevailing Winds.) Using passive cooling techniques such as capturing prevailing summer winds and providing proper shading through screening, landscaping, and architectural details makes the outdoor spaces more usable and helps cool the house itself.

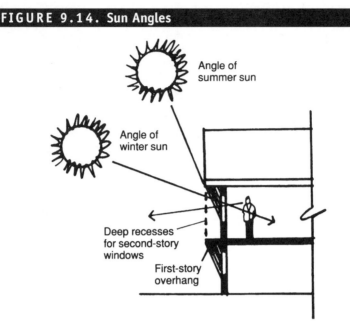

FIGURE 9.14. Sun Angles

Angle of summer sun

Angle of winter sun

Deep recesses for second-story windows

First-story overhang

In colder climates, the idea is to protect entrances and windows from the effects of harsh winter winds. By using architectural devices such as porches, screens, and walls, you can block winds from these sensitive areas. Proper landscaping can also provide protective barriers against winter winds. Coniferous trees, for example, can be located to the northwest of each lot to buffer cool prevailing winds. However, avoid relying solely on landscaping for protection from wind, cold, or solar heat gain. Trees and plants can fall prey to diseases, drought, and other stresses. In most cases, it's difficult to replace mature vegetation such as full-grown trees with equally mature vegetation. Therefore, try to use a combination of landscaping and architectural details to respond to climate conditions. For an example of this combined approach, see Figure 9.16 Landscaping and Architectural Response to Climate.

Once you have determined the preference of the target market for particular housing types, regional preferences, and site characteristics, including climate, evaluate each of the factors both separately and as they affect one another. For example, the site's physical characteristics may require extensive and costly engineering to support a certain type of housing. However, if the target market prefers this type of housing and you have priced the units competitively, then this housing type is right for the project.

Home Buyer's Identity

Choose housing types for your new development based on practical considerations such as affordability, proper fit with site characteristics, and adequate response to the climate. However, remember that a person's home expresses his or her identity and status in life. Therefore, the lifestyle characteristics and attitudes of the target market should also play a critical role in your choice of housing types. In fact, understanding the needs, demands, and desires of the target group should drive many of your decisions concerning housing types, styles, and features. This understanding coupled with an awareness of new trends, materials, and methods can help you make the right

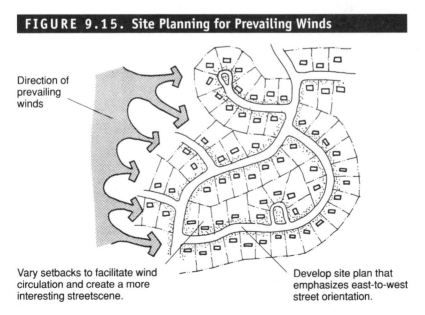

FIGURE 9.15. Site Planning for Prevailing Winds

Direction of prevailing winds

Vary setbacks to facilitate wind circulation and create a more interesting streetscene.

Develop site plan that emphasizes east-to-west street orientation.

Source: Brandes and Luzier, *Developing Difficult Sites,* p. 72.

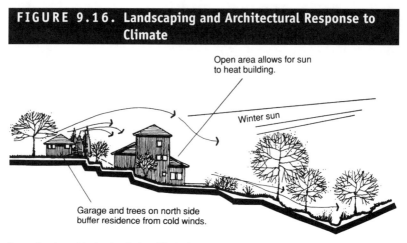

FIGURE 9.16. Landscaping and Architectural Response to Climate

Open area allows for sun to heat building.

Winter sun

Garage and trees on north side buffer residence from cold winds.

Source: Brandes and Luzier, *Developing Difficult Sites,* p. 77

choices as you integrate your choice of housing types with your site plan.

Planning as the Key to Success

In summary, successful land development requires more than reliance on past successes, sound intuition, or good timing. You also need to engage in careful planning and a realistic assessment of your own business capabilities as a developer. In other words, you need to identify early on the critical financial, marketing, and site-related factors that can help or hinder the success of your project. For example, you should know ahead of time how much time and money you can spend on preproject planning without damaging your profit margins. This information will influence your choice of sites by eliminating difficult ones early on or encouraging you to hold on to a particular site because the potential profit will be worth the expense.

Each project that you develop involves different circumstances and thus requires unique strategies. Careful planning allows you to select the appropriate strategies that can lead to optimal success for each particular project. Increasingly you will face difficult sites or projects with development limitations that require careful assessment of project parameters in the early stages of development. However, remember that careful planning from the beginning can turn any site, especially a challenging one, into a unique and attractive community with high market appeal.

A

Sources of Marketing Data

Demographic Data
U.S. Bureau of the Census: Census Reports

Census reports may be found in public libraries but the best sources for these reports are college and university libraries. The basic census publications are as follows:

1. *Census of Population, 1990.* C3.223 / 7: 1990 cp - 2.
This publication includes the following:
Chapter A = Number of Inhabitants
Chapter B = General Population Characteristics
Chapter C = General Social and Economic Characteristics
Chapter D = Detailed Characteristics (does not include many smaller towns)

2. *Census of Housing, 1990.* C3.224 / 3: 1990 ch - 2.
This publication includes the following:
Chapter A = General Housing Characteristics
Chapter B = Detailed Housing Characteristics
Metropolitan Housing Characteristics
Block Statistics

3. *Census of Population and Housing, 1980.* Census Tract Reports. C3. 223 / 21 - 2 : 80.

U.S. Bureau of the Census: Other Publications

1. *Statistical Abstract of the United States*. HA 202.U5. Published annually.

This compilation of U.S. statistics on demographic characteristics of the country includes population statistics; vital statistics, including age, race, gender, marital status, and number of children; socioeconomic (lifestyle) characteristics; business, industry, and trade data; and other types of statistics. Sources are cited and in some cases historical data are provided for comparison. This source emphasizes national statistics but includes regional and state data.

2. *The County and City Data Book*. HA 202 .A36. Published annually. Companion volume to the *Statistical Abstract.*

3. *The State and Metropolitan Area Data Book*. HA 202 .S84. Published annually. Companion volume to the *Statistical Abstract.*

4. *Current Population Reports*. Call numbers vary. Published annually.

This collection contains a series of reports based on surveys and provides social, demographic, and economic information about the population. Most reports provide data on the national and regional level. However, some also provide information on the state, county, or metropolitan level. None provide data on small geographic areas such as small cities or census tracts of metropolitan areas. The following are some of the current reports presenting data for state, county, and metropolitan areas:

a. *Patterns of Metropolitan Areas and County Population Growth: 1980 to 1987. 1989 and upward.* One volume. Series P 25, No. 1039. C3.186:P 25/1039. (This reference shows patterns of change in births, deaths, and net migration.)

b. *County Population Estimates: July 1, 1988, 1987, and 1986. 1989.* One volume. Series P 26, No. 88 A. C3.186/20 2:986 88.

c. *State Population and Household Estimates, with Age, Sex, and Components of Change. 1981-88. 1989 and upward.* Series P 25, No. 1044. C3.186/21:981 88.

d. *State Population and Household Estimates: July 1, 1989. 1990.* Series P 25, No. 1058. C3.186/21.989.

The references in b, c, and d show patterns of change in births, deaths, and net migration. Data in these publications have only been collected through 1989.

e. *State and Local Agencies Preparing Population and Housing Estimates. 1990.* Series P 25, No. 1063. C3.186.P 25/1063.

This is a list of state and local agencies that collect statistics on population and housing along with the types of estimates made by the agencies and the methods used.

Congressional Information Service

1. *ASI: American Statistics Index.* Z 7554. U5 A 46. Published monthly with annual cumulations.

This publication gives index tables that provide access to the extensive statistics found in U.S. government publications. Part One is an index arranged by specific subjects, which references abstracts in Part Two arranged by publishing agency. The abstracts are detailed summaries of the statistical information found in the source documents.

2. *SRI: Statistical Reference Index.* 7554 .U5 S79. Published monthly with annual cumulations.

This publication is a companion to the *American Statistics Index* and has the same format. Its index tables provide access to statistics found in publications of trade, professional, and other nonprofit associations; business organizations; commercial publishers, including trade journals; independent and university research centers; and state government agencies.

Private Sources of Demographic Data

1. *Statistic Sources.* Two Volumes. Z 7551 .S84. Detroit: Gale Research Co., 1989.

Gale Research produces guides to sources of statistics on thousands of subjects. The primary subjects include products and industries, as well as demographic, social, economic, and financial topics.

2. *Predicasts Forecasts.* HC 101 .P7. *Predicasts Basebook.* HA 214. p73A. *Predicasts F&S Index United States.* Z7165. 5 F23. *Promt.* HD9650.1. Cleveland: Predicast, Inc. Published quarterly.

These publications contain a great amount of historical and forecast data arranged by product group. In addition, they cite sources for all data.

3. *Survey of Buying Power.* 658.805 S163. Chicago: Dartnell Corp. Published 21 times each year.

This publication is a good source of consumer market data. It contains population, income, disposable income, and retail sales data for states, counties, Metropolitan Statistical Areas, and major cities.

4. *Commercial Atlas and Marketing Guide.* G 1019 .R22. Chicago: Rand McNally. Published annually.

This publication contains detailed maps of each state along with estimates of population, households, total effective buying income (EBI), median household income, and total retail sales.

5. *Market Guide.* 659.1 E23. New York: Market Guide. Published annually.

This publication provides statistics including employment and demographic statistics for U.S. and Canadian cities that have a daily newspaper. It also provides consumer market data for cities, counties, and metropolitan areas.

6. *Study of Media and Markets*. HF 5415.2 .S554. New York: Simmons Market Research Bureau. Published annually.

This multivolume publication contains surveys of consumers' use of media and products. It reports data by sex, age, race, marital status, education, and income.

7. *Mediamark Reports*. HF 5412.3 .M43. New York: Media-mark Research. Published annually.

This publication is similar to the preceding publication with multivolume surveys of consumers' use of media and products. Data are reported by sex, age, race, marital status, education, and income.

8. *Sourcebook of Demographics and Buying Power for Every Zip Code in the USA*. HA 203. 566. Arlington, Va.: C.A.C.I. Published annually.

This publication is arranged by business categories. The residential section contains a demographic profile (1987 age distribution, median age, and race); a population and housing profile (population, number of households, and 1990 housing profile); a socioeconomic profile (median household income, education, and employment profile); and an income and buying-power profile (distribution of households by income and a purchasing potential index for goods). The business statistics section gives estimated employment data.

Psychographic Data

The Lifestyle Market Analyst. HF 5415.3 .L5. New York: Standard Rate and Data Service. Published annually.

This publication provides demographic and lifestyle information for 212 Area of Dominant Influence (ADI) markets in the United States and is divided into three sections: market, lifestyle, and consumer segment profiles.

Land Development Checklist

Market Analysis

Target Market Identification

1. Viable target market identified?
2. If not, data required to identify market? (household incomes in local area, local population characteristics, national demographic trends, previously successful target market)
3. Marketing consultant required to perform market study?
4. In-house capabilities available to perform market study?
5. Pertinent demographic characteristics of chosen target market? (age, marital status, gender, age and number of children, double or single household income, amount of household income, profession, education level)
6. Pertinent psychographic characteristics of chosen target market? (amount of leisure time available; preferred leisure time activities; type of preferred home entertainment; use of home for work activities; type of work activities done at home; requirements related to parent and child spaces; special spatial and architectural requirements related to age, work status, and entertainment)
7. Any previous market studies produced by city or county?

Relating Product to Target Market

1. Demographic and psychographic characteristics translated into housing types, styles, interior spaces, and amenities?
2. Type of resulting product (home) offered to target market?
3. Neighborhood characteristics in terms of size, street layout, number of units, appearance, services, and amenities producing greatest appeal to target market and highest profit?
4. Company's experience in providing type of home planned for target market?
5. Target market's location requirements for school districts, police and fire protection, shopping districts, hospitals and medical care, and employment?
6. Target market's location requirements for recreational activities such as golf, parks, and water recreation?
7. Any contiguous or nearby land uses not tolerated by target market?
8. Any contiguous or nearby land uses not preferred by target market?
9. Any contiguous or nearby land uses attractive to target market?
10. Target market's location requirements for commuting distances to work, services, and amenities?
11. Maximum affordable sales price for target market?
12. Amount of equity target market likely to bring to home purchase?
13. Current interest rates? Interest rates projected for time of sales?
14. Amount of interest rate increase at which chosen type of home no longer affordable for target market?

Determining Capture Ratio

1. Impact of competition for target market on number of units offered?
2. Impact of company's financial status and past success on number of units offered?

3. Sufficient personnel to build and manage construction of planned number of units?

Financial Analysis

Land Acquisition

1. Amount of equity available for land purchase?
2. Method of financing remainder?
3. Possible to option part of land?
4. Seeking both land acquisition and development loan?
5. Comparison of estimated land, development, and construction costs with estimated sales rates, prices, and profit to determine if land is fairly priced?
6. If relevant, adequate cash flow to cover balloon payment when due?
7. Any financing offered by land owners?
8. Land as equity in project from other land owners?

Loan Structure and Disbursement

1. Type of personal and company documents required by lender for loan approval?
2. Type of documents, tests, studies, and reports required by lender to support project feasibility?
3. Cost and payment method for providing lender-requested documentation?
4. Best loan-to-value ratio available? Based on most accurate appraisal?
5. Effect of company's creditworthiness on loan-to-value ratio?
6. Method for financing required equity? (personal or company funds, partnerships, joint ventures, investors)
7. Eligibility for line of credit?
8. Commitment for permanent financing?
9. Loan disbursements based on? (progress inspections, completion of specified work items)
10. Draw request verified by whom?

Pro Forma Analysis and Cash Flow

1. Effect of hard and soft costs and schedule on cash flow requirements?
2. Effect of changes in labor and material costs over project's life?
3. Effect of changes in pro forma variables on cash flow requirements for all reasonable scenarios?
4. Pro forma analysis based on reasonable sales rates under varied conditions?
5. Changes in interest rates considered throughout life of loan? Effect on cost of borrowing money?
6. Methods for measuring profit?
7. Required rate of return on investment?

Site Analysis

Physical Factors

Geotechnical Factors

A. Geology
1. Type and depth of bedrock?
2. Effect of bedrock on excavation? Placement of utilities and other structures? Roadbeds? Foundations?
3. Effect of engineering costs on project feasibility?
4. Any sinkholes on site?
5. Effect of sinkhole location on number of units? Placement of buildings, roads, stormwater management systems, and utilities?

B. Soils
1. Soil types and locations?
2. Any poor percolation rates? Any soils with collapse potential when under excavation? Any shrinking and swelling characteristics when soils are wet and dry?
3. Effect of soils on potential number of units, engineering costs, and project feasibility?
4. Special construction methods required to install building foundations, roads, and utilities? Effect on project costs and feasibility?

C. Topographic Factors
   1. Site too flat or steep to be cost-effectively engineered?
   2. Effect of slopes on installation and function of proposed stormwater management systems, utilities, roads, and buildings?
   3. Cut-and-fill requirements balanced?
   4. If not, amount of excavation and imported fill required?
   5. Methods for stabilizing cut-and-filled areas?
   6. Effect of engineering costs for cut and fill on project feasibility?
   7. Methods for limiting erosion and sedimentation before and after site development?
   8. Effect of design and cost of these methods on required number of units and placement of stormwater management systems, roads, utilities, and buildings?
   9. Any low-lying areas suitable for stormwater runoff deposit?
   10. Areas adequate for stormwater disposal and containment?
   11. Slope of site conducive to installing open stormwater management systems?

Site Features

A. Location
   1. Location of site in relation to target market's demand for services, amenities, and commuting distances to work?
   2. Location where property values may increase or remain stable?
   3. Location within a recognizable territory such as downtown, uptown, or waterfront area?
   4. Territory generally regarded as favorable or unfavorable to local residents?

B. Natural Features
   1. Any existing water bodies that can be used for recreation?

2. Costs of installing improvements, such as marinas, boat ramps, or piers, on water bodies?

3. Can lots with views of existing water bodies command higher sales prices?

4. Any existing water bodies that must be protected from development by controlling or cleaning stormwater runoff into those water bodies?

5. Any designated floodplains or frequently flooded areas on site?

6. If so, discharge of stormwater runoff into these areas permitted? Measures required, if any, to clean runoff?

7. Effect of engineering costs for diverting or cleaning stormwater runoff on project feasibility?

8. Effect of existing water bodies or floodplains on required number of units or placement of roads, utilities, and buildings?

9. Location in sensitive watershed area that supplies local drinking water?

10. If so, special measures required to clean stormwater runoff or limit number of units?

11. Any federally designated wetlands on site?

12. Any areas appearing to be wetlands on site?

13. Any portion of wetlands requiring dredge or fill or accepting stormwater discharge?

14. Effect of wetlands on required number of units?

15. Type of existing vegetation on site?

16. Sufficient trees and vegetation to avoid importing significant amounts of landscape materials?

17. Effect of costs for clearing vegetation on project feasibility?

18. Any special features such as large specimen trees, hills, rock outcroppings, or other special landforms that are visually appealing and might increase project marketability?

19. Effect of special features on required number of units or placement of roads, utilities, and buildings?

20. Effect of special features on project costs and feasibility?

21. Any special plant or animal habitats requiring protection or permits for disturbing?
22. Any areas with important views to a water body, mountains or hills, or other special natural features?
23. If so, can lots with views to these areas command higher sales prices?

Hazards

1. Any former uses on site that could have caused deposit of hazardous materials?
2. Type of inquiry used to prove due diligence in discovery of possible contamination?
3. Costs of cleaning up hazardous materials if found on site? Effect of cleanup costs on project feasibility?
4. Effect of awareness of hazardous materials on target market in spite of adequate cleanup?
5. Electric and magnetic fields caused by power lines either on or adjacent to site?
6. Soils on site prone to radon contamination?
7. If so, use of radon-resistant construction methods required?

Improvements

1. Any existing structures on site?
2. If so, incorporate any of these structures into project?
3. If structures unusable, cost of demolition and removal and effect on project feasibility?
4. Any existing roadways, drainageways, cleared roadbeds, or cleared rights-of-way?
5. If so, incorporate any existing improvements into master plan? Effect on project costs and feasibility?
6. If improvements not incorporated, methods and costs of demolition and removal? Effect of methods and costs on project feasibility?

Site History

1. Location of site within recognized historic district?

2. Any structures or areas of site considered to have historic value?
3. Historic preservation survey of existing buildings or foundations of historic structures required?
4. Preservation or restoration of any historic structures required?
5. If so, incorporate historic structures into master plan to enhance project marketability?
6. Any archaeological significance to site?
7. Archaeological survey required?
8. Any historic or archaeologically significant structures left intact? If so, required number of units for project still met?

Legal Factors
Land Acquisition
1. Number of owners to negotiate land sales with, in order to acquire required amount of land?
2. All owners willing to sell? Strategies to ensure all owners sell at reasonable price?
3. Clear title to property?
4. Effect of land price on project feasibility?
5. Current survey of site?
6. Replatting of site required?

Regulatory Factors
A. Zoning
   1. Current zoning of site appropriate for intended use?
   2. If several parcels involved, current zoning for each parcel appropriate for intended use?
   3. If zoning inappropriate, necessary zoning reclassification obtainable?
   4. Approximate cost and time involved in obtaining zoning reclassification?
   5. Documents required to obtain zoning reclassification?
   6. Site under PUD zoning classification?
   7. Local written guidelines for project compliance with PUD design standards?

8. Required compliance with local comprehensive land use plan in requesting zoning reclassification?
9. Compliance of project with each restriction under appropriate zoning classification? (i.e., number of units per acre, setback and height restrictions)
10. Variance obtainable for zoning restrictions not met by project?
11. Permitted uses under zoning classification for site and contiguous properties?
12. Special use permit required for any part of master plan?
13. Any open space requirements in restrictions of zoning classification?
14. Effect of open space requirements on required number of units?
15. Current and future zoning of properties contiguous to the site? Effect of future contiguous land uses on project marketability?
16. Effect of any permitted uses in zoning classification for contiguous properties on project marketability?
17. Any dedication of land for special uses or rights-of-way for schools, churches, fire protection, public art, public recreation areas, or other special uses required?

B. Codes and Ordinances
1. Compliance of dimensions and design standards in master plan with local subdivision ordinances?
2. Private streets and utilities allowed?
3. Code review conducted to establish all pertinent building, life, health, and safety codes relevant to project?
4. Any special building codes relevant because of project location? (i.e., coastal or earthquake zones)
5. If so, costs of complying with special building codes? Effect of required construction methods on building design and project feasibility?
6. Compliance with local landscape and signage ordinances?
7. Types and costs of site development and building permits?

8. Any impact fees? Effect of impact fees on project feasibility?
9. Required permits for sanitary sewer, potable water, power, cable television, and telephone line installation? Effect of each on project feasibility?

C. Environmental Permits and Special Studies
1. Due diligence demonstrated by environmental review or Phase I environmental assessment?
2. Environmental impact statement required for project?
3. Local area participation in National Flood Insurance Program?
4. FEMA-designated floodplain on site?
5. Elevation of 100-year flood depicted on floodplain maps?
6. Methods used to elevate the first floor above 100-year flood level? Fill? Stilts?
7. National Pollutant Discharge Elimination System (NPDES) program administered by state? NPDES permit required from state or EPA?
8. Section 404 dredge and fill permit required?
9. Traffic impact study required from local government?
10. Types of federal, state, and local environmental permits required? Application process for each? Tests and reports required for each? Effect of obtaining various permits on project schedule and feasibility?
11. Types of special studies required? Types of professionals needed to conduct studies? Types of tests and reports required for each study?
12. Costs of tests, reports, and applications? Time requirements for studies and permits? Effects of both on project feasibility?

Political Factors

1. Any neighborhood associations or other organizations oppose project?
2. Meeting held with appropriate groups to determine concerns?

3. Amount of time and money available to work with various groups to develop alternative strategies to address concerns?

Offsite Factors

1. Capacity of public utilities to accept project's demand?
2. Tap-ins and hookups for all utilities conveniently located?
3. If not, effect of bringing in utilities in terms of infrastructure or escrow fees on project costs and feasibility?
4. If utilities not adjacent to site, ability of local government to extend utility infrastructure to project?
5. If public utilities not present or over capacity, effect of supplying utilities on project costs and feasibility?
6. Amount of impact fees associated with project's load on public utilities?
7. Discharge of stormwater runoff into available public infrastructure permitted or containment of all or portion of runoff required on site?
8. Public transportation required for project marketability?
9. Safe access to frontage arterial road?
10. Infrastructure required (traffic light, turning lane) to create safe access to project?
11. Adequate police and fire protection for project?
12. Any undesirable land uses contiguous to the property?
13. If so, effect of screening undesirable uses on project costs and feasibility?
14. Project near Superfund site?
15. Any desirable land uses contiguous or nearby that would enhance project marketability?

References

Publications

Ambrose, James, and Peter Brandow. 1991. *Simplified site design*. NY: Wiley.

American Society for Testing and Materials (ASTM). 1993. *ASTM standards on environmental site assessments for commercial real estate* (E 152793 and E 152893). Philadelphia: American Society for Testing and Materials.

American Society of Civil Engineers, National Association of Home Builders, and the Urban Land Institute (ULI). 1990. *Residential streets, 2nd ed.* Washington, DC: American Society of Civil Engineers, National Association of Home Builders, and the Urban Land Institute.

Brandes, Donald H., Jr., and J. Michael Luzier. 1991. *Developing difficult sites: Solutions for developers and builders.* Washington, DC: Home Builder Press, National Association of Home Builders.

Brown, Peter H. 1993. The economics of traditional neighborhoods. *Land Development*, 2.

Calthorpe, Peter. 1993. *The next American metropolis.* NY: Princeton Architectural Press.

City of Austin Green Builder Program. 1998, August. *Green Builder News.*

Economic and Housing Policy Department, National Association of Home Builders. 1990. *Acquisition, development, and construction financing survey.* Washington, DC: Economic and Housing Policy Department, National Association of Home Builders.

Engineering Division, Soil Conservation Service, U.S. Department of Agriculture. 1940. *Technical paper No. 40, Rainfall frequency atlas of the United States for durations from 30 minutes to 24 hours and return periods from 1 to 100 years.* Washington, DC.

Environmental Protection Agency. 1988. *Radon reduction techniques for detached houses: Technical guidance,* 2nd ed., EP88. Washington, DC.

Federal Emergency Management Agency. 1986. *Coastal construction manual.* Washington, DC.

Jarvis, Frederick D., and LDR International, Inc. 1993. *Site planning and community design for great neighborhoods.* Washington, DC: Home Builder Press, National Association of Home Builders.

Kone, D. Linda, and Daniel E. Whiteman. 1994. *The role of the lending institution in residential construction.* State of Florida, Building Industry Advisory Committee.

Leibesman, Lawrence R. 1993. *Developer's guide to federal wetlands regulation, 2nd ed.* Washington, DC: Environmental Regulation Department, National Association of Home Builders.

Moyer, Craig, and Francis Michael. 1991. *Clean air act handbook.* NY: Clark Boardman.

National Arbor Day Foundation and National Association of Home Builders. 1998. *Building with trees.* Washington DC.

National Association of Home Builders. 1999. *Smart growth: Building better places to live, work and play.* National Association of Home Builders. Washington, DC.

National Association of Home Builders. 1987. *Land development, 7th ed.* Washington, DC: Home Builder Press, National Association of Home Builders.

National Association of Home Builders Research Center. 1993. *Proposed model land development standards and accompanying model state enabling legislation.* Washington, DC: Office of Policy Development and Research, U.S. Department of Housing and Urban Development.

National Oceanic and Atmospheric Administration, U.S. Department of Commerce. 1993. *"Hurricane!" A familiarization booklet.* NOAA PA 91001. Washington, DC.

Netter, Edith M. Using mediation to solve land use disputes. 1992. *Zoning and Planning Law Report,* 15, 4.

Newell, Tim. 1993. Increase buyer confidence in your community with neighborhood design guidelines. *Land Development.* 15, 3.

Page, Robert A., David M. Boore, Robert C. Bucknam, and Wayne R. Thatcher. 1992. *Goals, opportunities, and priorities for the USGS Earthquake Hazards Reduction Program, U.S. Geological Circular 1079.* Washington, DC: U.S. Geological Survey.

Parker, Harry, John W. Macquire, and James Ambrose. 1991. *Simplified site engineering,* 2nd ed. NY: Wiley.

Rona, Donna C. 1988. *Environmental permits: A time saving guide.* NY: Van Rostrand Reinhold.

Rubenstein, Harvey M. 1987. *A guide to site and environmental planning,* 3rd ed. NY: Wiley.

Winburn, William A. 1992. The development realities of traditional town design. *Urban Land.* 51 (8):20-21.

Web Sites

American Factfinder; U.S. Census Bureau
http://factfinder.census.gov

Center for Excellence for Sustainable Development; Department of Energy
http://www.sustainable.doe.gov.

Code of Federal Regulations; National Archives and Records Administration
http://www.nara.gov/nara/efr.html

Environmental Protection Agency
http://www.epa.gov/

Government Printing Office; GPO Gate; Federal Register
http://www.gpo.ucop.edu/search/fedfld.html

Index

Other Books for Developers and Builders from Home Builder Press

Building Greener Neighborhoods: Trees as Part of the Plan

By American Forests and NAHB

Studies show that developed lots with trees sell for an average 20–30 percent more than similarly sized lots without trees. Tree planning and preservation pays off not only on upscale properties but can be economically feasible on smaller lots.

Land Buying Checklist

By Ralph Lewis

Now in its fifth edition, this comprehensive checklist helps you evaluate everything from physical inspection, purchase agreements, and financial projections to resale options, escrow and title, government requirements, and more.

Developer's Guide to Endangered Species

By NAHB

This book presents essential information all developers and builders need to know before—or after—they find an endangered species on their property.

Impact Fee Handbook

By NAHB

This book covers the basic facts and guides the reader to additional sources of information on impact fees, including legal and economic aspects, political and public relations strategies, feasible alternatives and other issues.

Building Partnerships: How to Work with Trade Contractors

By Bob Whitten

This new title shows you how to increase the professionalism and loyalty to your trade contractors by treating them as an extension of your building team.

Producing Affordable Housing: Partnerships for Profit

By NAHB

Drawing from the experience of successful affordable builders and developers, this book shares the expertise and insights of those builders with you so you can learn to build affordable housing in your market.

Basic Construction Management

By Leon Rogers

This book helps superintendents sharpen their skills in maintaining budgets, complying with schedules, and establishing quality control. The inclusion of checklists and forms makes this book an essential reference.

To order any of these books or request an up-to-date catalog of Home Builder Press titles, contact:

NAHB Home Builder Bookstore
1-800-223-2665

To order on-line, go to: http://www.BuilderBooks.com

NAHB Members Receive a 20% Discount on All Books.

Keep up-to-date
on Land Development issues with

Land Development

THE NATIONAL ASSOCIATION OF HOME BUILDERS

LAND DEVELOPMENT magazine, published by the National Association of Home Builders, focuses entirely on land development issues confronting today's developers. Its in-depth coverage includes:

- Land acquisition and development finance
- Environmental regulations and issues
- Housing affordability
- Building with trees
- Land planning
- Infrastructure
- Endangered species
- Community planning and design
- Market trends
- Smart Growth
- Impact fees
- Dealing with community and local governmental opposition

Printed three times a year, LAND DEVELOPMENT magazine includes features written by nationally recognized experts—information and insight found only in these pages.

Subscribe today to get the information you need to survive in an ever-changing industry. Call 1-800-368-5242 extension 351 for more information.